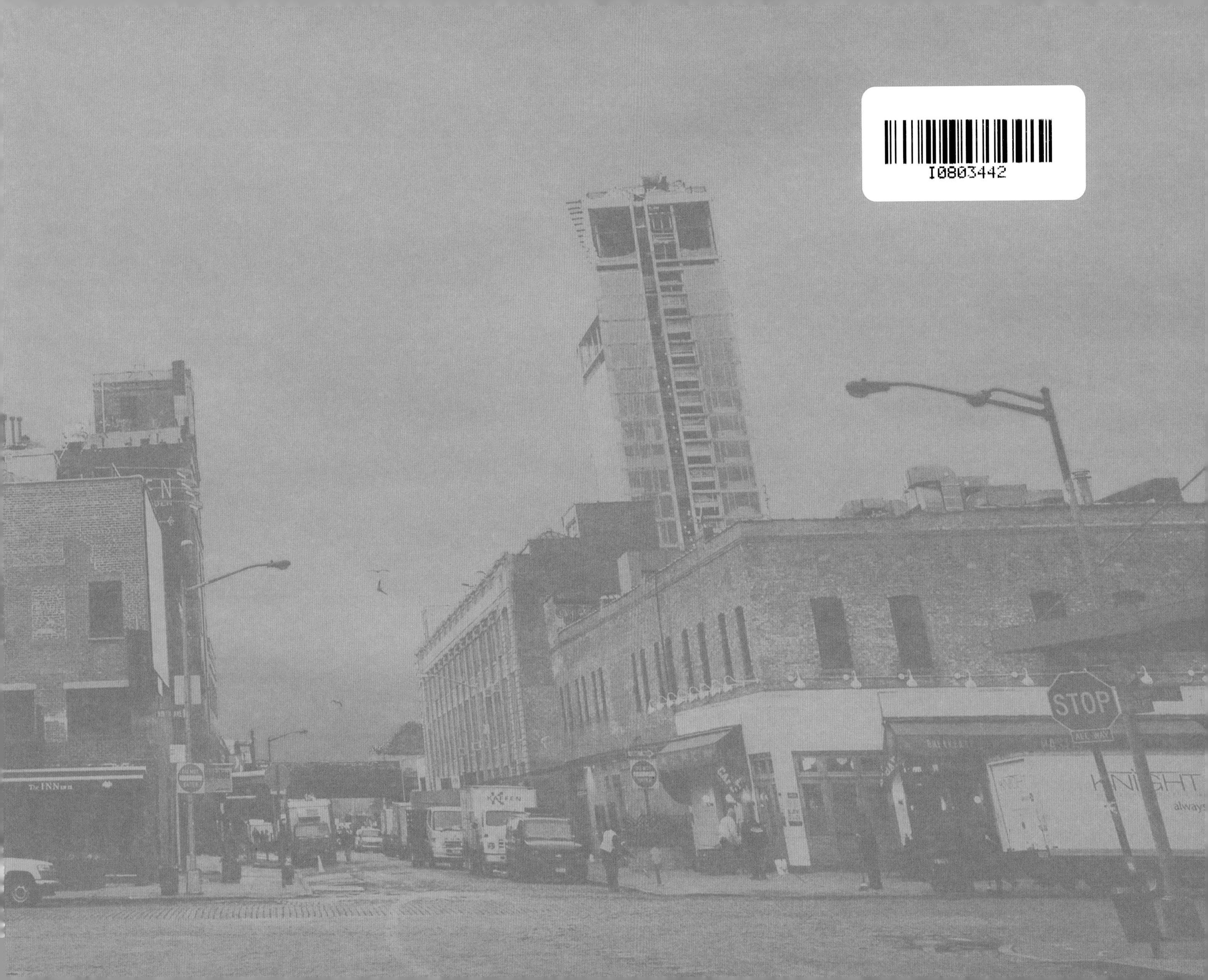
STOP
KNIGHT
always

PAMELA GREENE

BLOOD & BEAUTY

MANHATTAN'S MEATPACKING DISTRICT

Designed by Justin Watkinson
Type set in Myriad Pro / Minion Pro

ISBN: 978-0-7643-3884-7
Printed in Hong Kong

Schiffer Books are available at special discounts for bulk purchases for sales promotions or premiums. Special editions, including personalized covers, corporate imprints, and excerpts can be created in large quantities for special needs. For more information contact the publisher:

Published by Schiffer Publishing Ltd.
4880 Lower Valley Road
Atglen, PA 19310
Phone: (610) 593-1777; Fax: (610) 593-2002
E-mail: Info@schifferbooks.com

For the largest selection of fine reference books on this and related subjects, please visit our website at **www.schifferbooks.com**
We are always looking for people to write books on new and related subjects. If you have an idea for a book please contact us at the above address.

This book may be purchased from the publisher.
Include $5.00 for shipping.
Please try your bookstore first.
You may write for a free catalog.

In Europe, Schiffer books are distributed by
Bushwood Books
6 Marksbury Ave.
Kew Gardens
Surrey TW9 4JF England
Phone: 44 (0) 20 8392 8585; Fax: 44 (0) 20 8392 9876
E-mail: info@bushwoodbooks.co.uk
Website: www.bushwoodbooks.co.uk

This book is dedicated to
the people I photographed,
and to my great loves,
George and Cassandra.

PREFACE

The Meatpacking District is famous today for glitz and glamour, but it used to be known for blood, muscle, and sweat. When I first started shooting there, I found it strangely beautiful.

I remember the district around 4:00 A.M., chaotic and energetic, lit by headlights and softened by shadow. The streets were electric with action, as workmen pulled, pushed, lugged, and loaded. By dawn I was exhausted and thankful for the first touch of sunlight because, after a frigid night with my fingers freezing on the shutter, I could finally start to warm up.

Daytime was different and, sometimes, just as exciting. People walked quickly across the plaza at Gansevoort Street and Ninth Avenue on their way to the new businesses—offices, stores, and restaurants—that had been opening since the late 1990s. On the corner of Little West 12th Street, the restaurant, Pastis, attracted a stylish crowd. The sidewalks outside were a prime location for movies, TV, and fashion shoots. Once, on a chilly fall day, I was a little surprised to see a naked blonde out on the cobblestones, making a telephone commercial (talk about phoning home). Even as it changed, the Meatpacking District was irreverent, and always unpredictable.

The scene on any warm Saturday night included at least 20,000 people ready to party, and dressed to see and be seen. Spilling over the sidewalks, buoyed by the racket from the traffic, they lined up behind the red velvet ropes, hoping to be among the lucky few thousand making it into the clubs. By 2:00 A.M. things were just getting started, by 4:00 A.M. residents on Horatio Street, just south of the plaza, could only dream of sleep.

Visible for all to see behind the big plate glass window at 69 Gansevoort Street was Florent, the first bistro to open in the Meatpacking District. Beginning in August 1986, this rarified diner, named for its extroverted, French owner, Florent Morellet, functioned as the District's happy hang out and unofficial communications center. The menu board listed top events in the city suited to the taste of the regulars—celebrities, gays, straights, big names, little names, and (as time went on) tourists. On holidays like New Year's Eve or Bastille Day, Florent put on shows that were truly memorable in both a funny and a down-to-the-skin sort of a way. Entertainers danced on the counter, celebrating a life they could lead only in New York and, more specifically, at Florent.

The District has cleaned up now. Most of the meatpacking plants have closed, their space rebuilt as expensive outposts for international designers like Stella McCartney or Carlos Miele. Clubs rule the night. Inevitably, rising rents have forced out the key businesses that first started to polish up the Meatpacking District. Florent Morellet, the original urban pioneer, closed his restaurant in 2008.

The photographs in this volume are my vision of the Meatpacking District during the years of evolution, when it changed every 24 hours from grit to glamour, glamour to grit. Today the hotels are elegant, the restaurants top notch, and, above Washington Street across from the shuttered plants, there's a new elevated park, the Highline. A ribbon of plants and walkways, the Highline replaces an old railway dating from 1934 that used to transport cattle to market. Now it brings in more than a million visitors a year.

Consisting of no more than a small patchwork of streets, the Meatpacking District reflects nothing more or less than this reality—that New York is a city made by change, and made for change. Yet despite the current elegance, or because of it, I can't help missing a little what has gone for good: the rowdy toughness of the old market and the edgy frenzy of life at night. I'm glad I was there to photograph the people who passed in front of me, stopping for a moment so I could take their pictures, placing them in a panorama of a certain time.

PAMELA GREENE *2010*

ACKNOWLEDGMENTS

From the moment I began photographing in the Meatpacking District in late 2002, I have been fortunate to have the support of family and friends. There are so many people who have helped me with kind words and pointed criticism that I cannot name them all, but a special tribute goes to Harvey Stein, a remarkable photographer and a gifted teacher at the International Center of Photography, who first introduced me to street photography.

My subjects were always a joy. From the very beginning they were willing to let me become a part of their lives at work and at play, and for this I am grateful. I am indebted to Miro Rames, the owner of Walmir, a meatpacking plant on Washington Street, who made it possible for me to photograph his staff at work, and to tell me what work has meant to him; my thanks go also to Raymond De Stefano, the Walmir shop steward, whose advice and friendship became an invaluable guide to the business of the Meatpacking District.

Florent Morellet, the owner of Florent, a knowledgeable urban activist and a good friend to his community and to New York City, made his restaurant available to me so I could photograph the happenings there, and take a closer look at the night life of the Meatpacking District.

Don Polzo, photographer and technical expert, is responsible for teaching me everything I know about Photoshop, the dark hole that swallows many photographers; he saved me from that fate, and I owe him great thanks. My gratitude goes as well to Puneet Kapoor at Baboo Photo Labs, in New York City, who for years carefully scanned my shots from film to digital and produced beautiful prints, which are a testament to his skill and dedication.

My friends have looked at my work with critical finesse. Ross Wagner, who heads the Unique Vision Workshop in Watchung, New Jersey, has critiqued these images from the very beginning, encouraging me to move beyond the conventional; he was among the first to display my work. My friend, Maddi Ring, has always offered good, perceptive critiques. And great thanks go to Lanny Powers, who as the curator of the Durst Corporation's Show Walls Gallery, in New York City, mounted a comprehensive exhibition of *Blood & Beauty* in 2009.

The team at Schiffer brought this book from dream to reality, and I thank them.

My deep appreciation goes, as always, to my daughter, Cassandra Bujarski, who has blessed my life simply by her presence, and who helped choose sites and subjects, reviewed images and offered a penetrating point of view over the years of this long term project.

My greatest thanks go to a photographer with an incredible eye and discerning judgment, who has reviewed thousands of images with me during these years, who knew that I needed to shoot this project mostly alone and at all hours of the day and night, and who has offered great encouragement as I tired and picked myself up, again and again, to continue with this book. He is my husband, George T. Bujarski, my most fervent supporter.

INTRODUCTION

New York's Meatpacking District has been a vibrant, bustling neighborhood for almost 200 years. Today its streets are lined with elegant retail stores, high-end restaurants, galleries, and clubs that are visited almost daily by movie stars, the paparazzi, tourists, and New Yorkers themselves, who love its light-filled streets and 24-hour activity.

Officially designated the Gansevoort Market Historic District by the New York City Landmarks Preservation Commission in 2003, the Meatpacking District has been wearing its sophisticated new clothes for only a few years. During the late 1990s, New York's soaring, speculative economy made possible the high-end renovation of the old, huge structures that housed the meat packing plants, and turned them into glossy new homes for upscale, fashionable businesses. Only a handful of plants remain on the edges of the district, surviving representatives of a rich history as a mixed-use, industrial neighborhood that covers only a few city blocks—between 14th and Horatio Streets, to the north and south, Hudson Street and the West Side Highway from east to west.

Named after Revolutionary War General Peter Gansevoort, the area was first developed aggressively after the Civil War, as New York became the financial center of the United States. There were two official city markets in the neighborhood—an open-air produce market and a meat, poultry, and dairy market by the river, along with other industries. By 1906, underground pipes provided refrigeration to the market buildings, which were remarkable structures.

Commissioned by the owners of the land, originally the estate of John Jacob Astor, his heirs, and other prominent New York families, they were designed in the late nineteenth century by New York's leading architects. Metal awnings shaded the sidewalks; Belgian paving blocks secured the streets. The area became what many considered one of the best markets in the world.

As immigrants flooded into New York City in the nineteenth and twentieth centuries, joining the poor who were already in residence, the Gansevoort Market became a place for getting started. If you were hopeful but hungry, you could find a job in the meat market. By the later twentieth century, if you were a photographer or a painter, a designer or an architect who needed cheap studio space, you could find it in the Meatpacking District—if you didn't mind locating upstairs, above the butchers and the frenetic, smelly streets.

Old money may have commissioned the buildings of the Gansevoort Market, but it is the people who worked in it who lost their footing as change accelerated, time and again. Still, one man's loss is another man's gain. Some saw opportunity in the Meatpacking District and put down stakes in new businesses on old streets. Their voices tell a story of change as one New York City neighborhood, the Gansevoort Market Historic District, took on an entirely new persona.

REFERENCE:

Shockley, Jay. "Gansevoort Market Historic District Designation Report," (New York, NY: New York City Landmarks Preservation Commission, 2003); Part 1, pp. 1–23 [www.nyc.gov/html/lpc/downloads/pdf/reports/gansevoortpt1.pdf]; Part 2, pp. 299–302 [www.nyc.gov/html/lpc/downloads/pdf/reports/gansevoortpt2.pdf].

Miro Rames

BUSINESS OWNER

Walmir Meat, Inc.

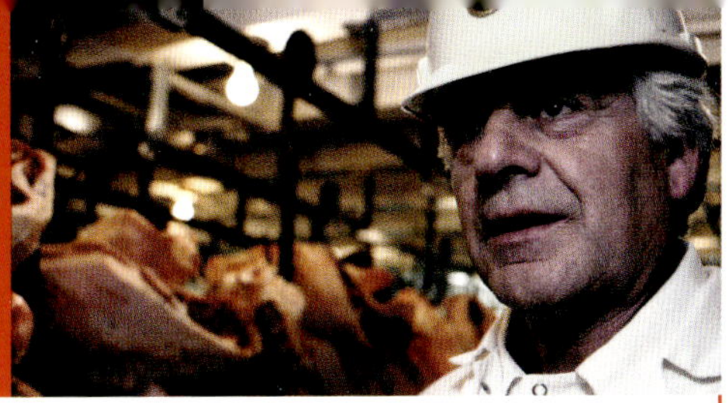

I escaped from Croatia by sailboat, with my friends, in 1962. We had waited for the right kind of wind to come and, when we caught it, we took it straight West. I was in an international refugee camp in Italy when I applied to come to the United States. I arrived on a Wednesday, in August, and I started working the next Monday. I had an uncle in the US, who got me the job. I was 17.

I found it a little hard at first. In Croatia, I had lived in a small town where I knew everybody. When I came to New York, I lost everything. I couldn't speak the language. But, somehow you manage. I met a young lady, who spoke English…and I started picking it up pretty good. We got married just after I turned twenty, on January 18, 1964. We have six children, aged 26 to 45.

There was a lot of work in the meat market when I started. No matter how much work you did, there was more coming in. Our bosses were tough: we got a break for 15—not 16—minutes. We worked hard. We competed. We gave our bosses a full day's work, and we were proud of it. And, we had a big circle of friendly guys then, a lot of Europeans—Germans, Czechs, Poles, and Italians. We spent so much time together we became family. I miss those guys, they knew the meat business.

I went to work for myself in 1973. I found a partner and we opened Walmir. (My name is Miro and his name was Wally.) Later I bought him out and the business was solely mine. Walmir was here for 35 years, and I had some very good years because everyone knew that I had quality meat, that I supplied very good restaurants, and that I took care of my customers.

About 15 years ago, I had a chance to buy the building. The landlord asked me if I wanted it for $1.5 million. I said, "$1.5 million…where am I going to get a million five?" You know, you don't think right, you don't realize that you have tenants, that they'll pay the mortgage, that you'll only need about ten percent down, and that nothing will change, except you'll own something. But I was in the meat business, not the real estate business. I worried about when the meat was going to show up, how I was going to take care of my customers, and how I was going to make ten cents a pound. That's what's built inside of me.

The building was sold in 2008 and I closed the business. Now I'm with John Jobbagy, on Washington Street. I bring in suppliers for him. He used to be one of my better customers.

If I had bought the building for a million five, I guess I would have made millions on the sale. I'd probably be in the Bahamas right now, or the Caribbean, sailing my boat—or, maybe not. Sometimes you get so much money you go crazy. You can screw up your life altogether.

I could retire, if I wanted to. I have a few hobbies. I'm pretty handy with woodworking. I made a beautiful model sailboat, 48 inches long. But a hobby isn't enough for me. I like working. I never got rich, but I made a decent living and I am happy. What else you want?

October 2010

James Rogers

WORKER

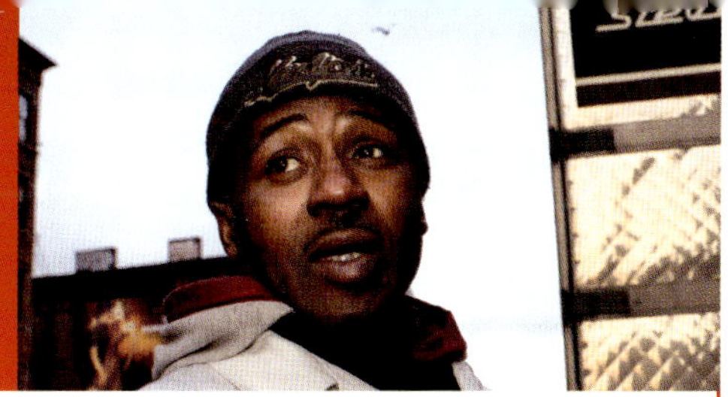

I was born in Rome, Georgia, in 1951, and I came by myself to New York in 1969, when I was 18. I was a football star on the high school team in Georgia, but after school I used to work in a slaughter house, about two hours a day. It was a great opportunity for me. I killed the cows with an air gun, and got paid good money.

When I broke both knees and found out I couldn't get no scholarship to go to college, I went into the meat business up here. I started in 1971. I was a natural, I had experience, and I fit in. It was busy, busy. There were jobs everywhere. You could quit one job and go to another one. It was just much better then.

Now you got to fight to keep a job. Mondays and Tuesdays are my busy days. I work from about 2:00 A.M. in the morning until I finish. On other days, I ain't got no work until 4: 00 A.M. I'm an independent, too; around 1987 I had my books froze with the union, but I still got almost 17 years with them, so I get about a one-quarter pension. I'm also a super, so I've got back up.

There's one change in the market that I would like to see. I'd like to see people hired because of their qualifications. Not because you save a dime or a dollar on cheap labor. I think I'm the most qualified guy down here in the market, and I'd like to see someone walk up to me and say, "James, I'll pay you money to come work." Just hire the one person who's the most qualified…

August 2003

Yigal Azrouël

FASHION DESIGNER

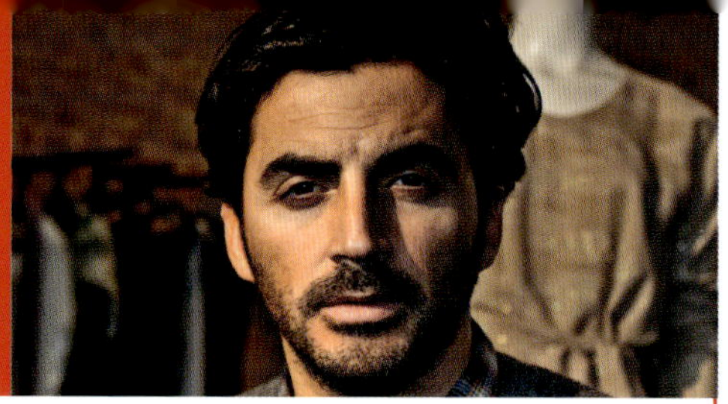

I used to go to the Meatpacking District before I opened a store here because it was a kind of underground place, with great restaurants, like Florent, and quite a few others that don't exist now. There was raw meat crowding the sidewalks, a stink in all the streets and prostitutes on the corners—but there were also touches of luxury and a few small shops. I had a feeling that something was going to happen here and that this was going to be a new, cool place.

I signed my lease in 2002. Our site, at 408 West 14th, off the corner of 9th Ave., used to be the H&H Bagel factory; there were meatpacking plants across the street, next door, and around the corner. It took me and my business partner, Donna Minelli, about a year to fix up the store. Since we were opening in an historic district, we wanted to keep some of the raw space in the new design—the beams and brick walls. The front window, a single piece of glass, is so big we had to close off 14th Street completely to get it in here.

My store opened in 2003. There was still blood and dirt everywhere, and the store actually got robbed by drag queens—they walked in and grabbed clothes off the racks. (We put in security.) But the Meatpacking District had personality and energy. The neighborhood was up and coming and it definitely helped us grow. In early 2004, we played a big part in founding the Meatpacking District Initiative, which still exists today. I like to think that I helped pioneer the neighborhood.

Actually, locating in the Meatpacking District helped brand our label. We were positioned in the right place, and new designers kept opening up from the time that I started: Stella McCartney, Alexander McQueen, and Carlos Miele. The designer who influenced me the most was McQueen—I really appreciate what he was trying to do.

Being in the neighborhood helped the evolution of my business, and theirs, too; when you have a combination of creative people you get energy. At the end of the day, every designer has contributed a unique vision to the neighborhood's character: that's what makes it exciting. And, I think our location has probably influenced the way I design. Maybe now I'm putting a little more edge in my clothes, a bit more personality, instead of finishing them perfectly.

My biggest department store accounts are Saks and Bergdorf Goodman, where clients are willing to browse and try the label. But in the Meatpacking District we attract a different sort of client, someone with a well defined, focused sense of style. Of course, when you have your own store, you also have great customer contact—I listen to what my customers say, I see what they like, and that affects the way I work, too. I always design wearable clothes.

I grew up in Israel and came to this country when I was 22. Now I am member of the Council of Fashion Designers of America (CFDA), I show menswear twice a year in Paris and women's wear during New York Fashion Week. I have a showroom in Milan, and I manufacture almost all of my clothes in Manhattan's Garment District, where I design. I also do a big package business, sending clothes out on approval in the US and around the world. We have a decent business, so I am very happy.

Something special happened here: the Meatpacking District changed faster than I ever thought it would, but the neighborhood kept a sense of history and has real character. You know, I think architecture plays a role, too—on the edge of the historic district, we have great new buildings, like the Standard Hotel and SoHo House. We have a new look.

January 2011

Florent Morellet

RESTAURATEUR, COMMUNITY ACTIVIST, & BON VIVANT

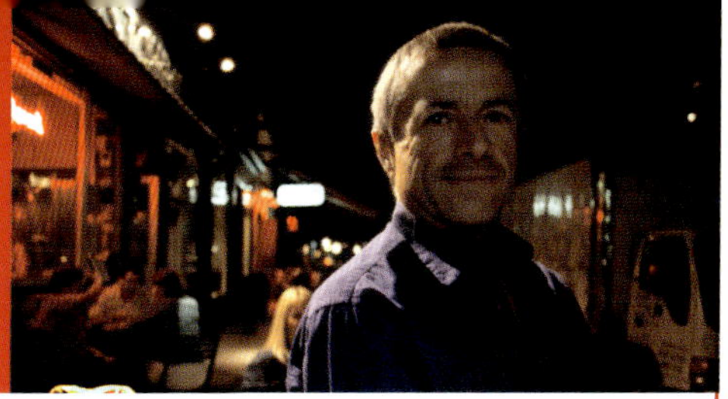

I bought the lease for my restaurant in March, 1985, so I've been here for 18 years. The district was a meat market then, period, opening around midnight and closing about noon, with some creative businesses—artists, people doing films—on the upper floors. I was familiar with the neighborhood because I used to visit the gay bars when I came to New York, and I really loved coming out of them around 4 o'clock in the morning to streets that were full of life, while the rest of the city was sleeping. It reminded me very much of Covent Garden, in London, or Les Halles, the old market in the center of Paris. I'd been to this restaurant, too, which was called the R & L. It opened around midnight or 1:00 A.M. to feed the meatpackers and truck drivers, and closed at noon.

When I was looking for a place in the second half of 1984, the R & L was available, and I knew it was perfect. I didn't want to be on Main Street, I wanted to be a little bit difficult to find, tucked away but not far away. It was a diner, unpretentious, and all my friends told me I was crazy. The neighborhood was scary, bleak at night. But I was very self confident.

I had arrived in New York in 1978. My first job was as a bicycle messenger but I'd moved on to managing a restaurant in SoHo, La Gamelle, until 1984. (I'd also had a restaurant in Paris.) And, I was organizing a major retrospective for my father, the artist François Morellet, at the Brooklyn Museum. I'd put together a mailing list of 5,000 to 6,000 people, and I knew I had a following.

We opened Florent in late August 1985. After one week, we were busy. Not too busy, because I really wanted to grow slowly, but we broke even and we were paying our bills. By the end of December, both New York Magazine and the New York Times had reviewed us, and by January 1986, we were packed. Florent was the hottest restaurant in town.

Change started slowly in the Meatpacking District, with a few milestones: the opening of Jeffrey [the first upscale boutique on 14th Street], and Pastis [a large, popular French restaurant, open for breakfast, lunch, dinner and late night dining] but that was mild compared to what's going on now. It's like a train leaving the station. First you're going ten miles an hour and before you know it, you're going 120.

The number of liquor licenses coming into the neighborhood now is incredible. Some of the new restaurants and clubs each seat more than a 1000 people per night. On Thursday, Friday, and Saturday nights the streets are still jammed at 2:00 A.M., the limousines are double parked, and cars and taxis are backed up to Jane Street, in Greenwich Village.

In 2000, I became co-chairperson with Jo Hamilton of the Taskforce for the Gansevoort Market, an offshoot of the Greenwich Village Society for Historic Preservation. There has been a very strong real estate frenzy here, and we worked for a landmarks designation to preserve the neighborhood (I was particularly worried about what was happening to the awnings in front of the meatpacking plants). We got almost everything we wanted. In September 2003, the Landmarks Preservation Commission voted to create the Gansevoort Market Historic District, excluding the three blocks west of Washington Street to the West Side Highway.

At the moment, the City is renegotiating leases for the meat market on Gansevoort and Washington Streets, for 10 or 12 years. We also want galleries, independent businesses like art production, film production, photography studios, and shopping, with no one segment overwhelming the others. Otherwise, the neighborhood will end up looking like Bourbon Street in New Orleans, or South Beach in Miami.

I don't think the neighborhood is dangerous anymore. And, I don't see much prostitution on Gansevoort Street. At the time of the crack epidemic, drugs were a really big problem. But now, the only problem we have is middle class misbehavior.

July 2004

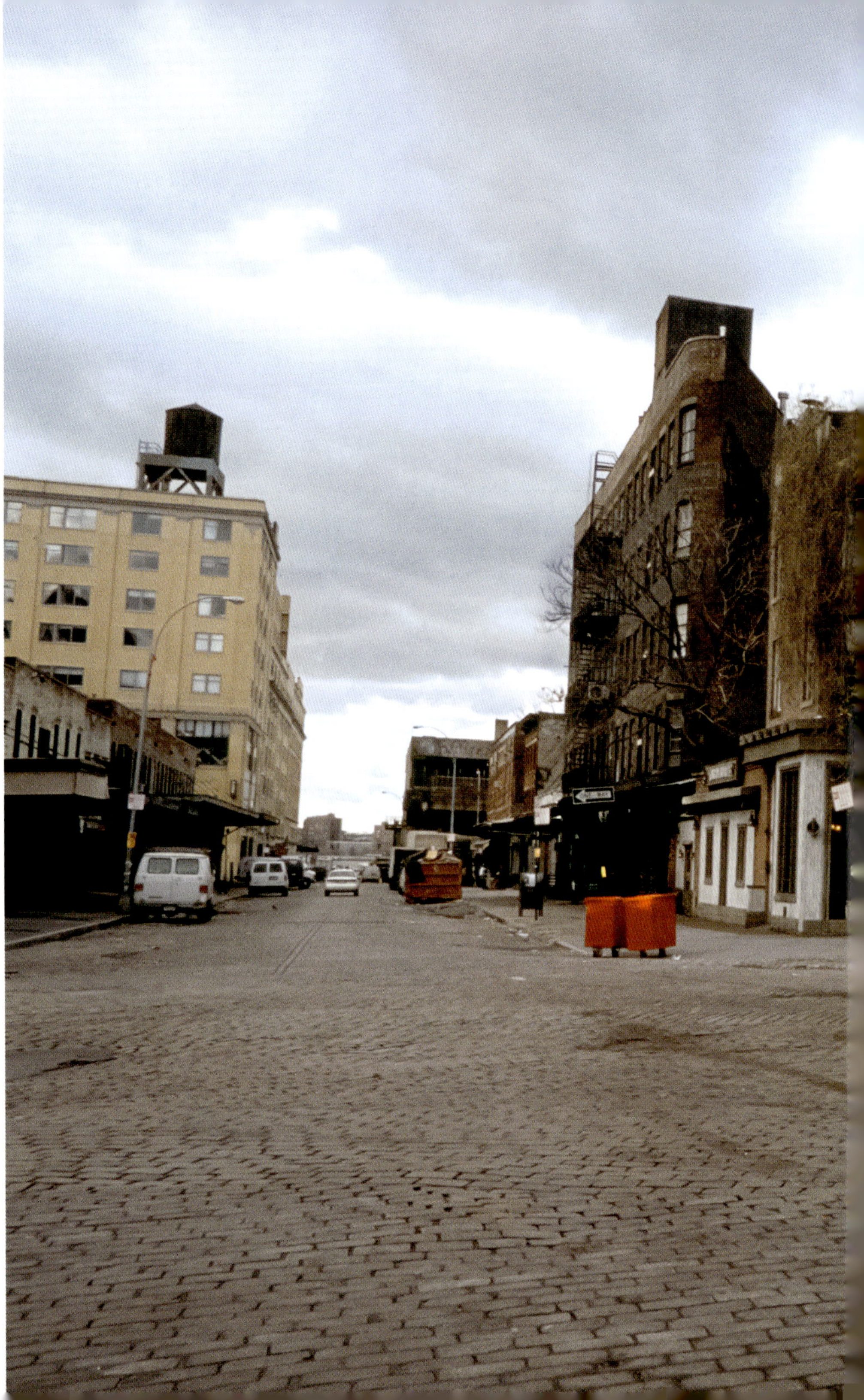

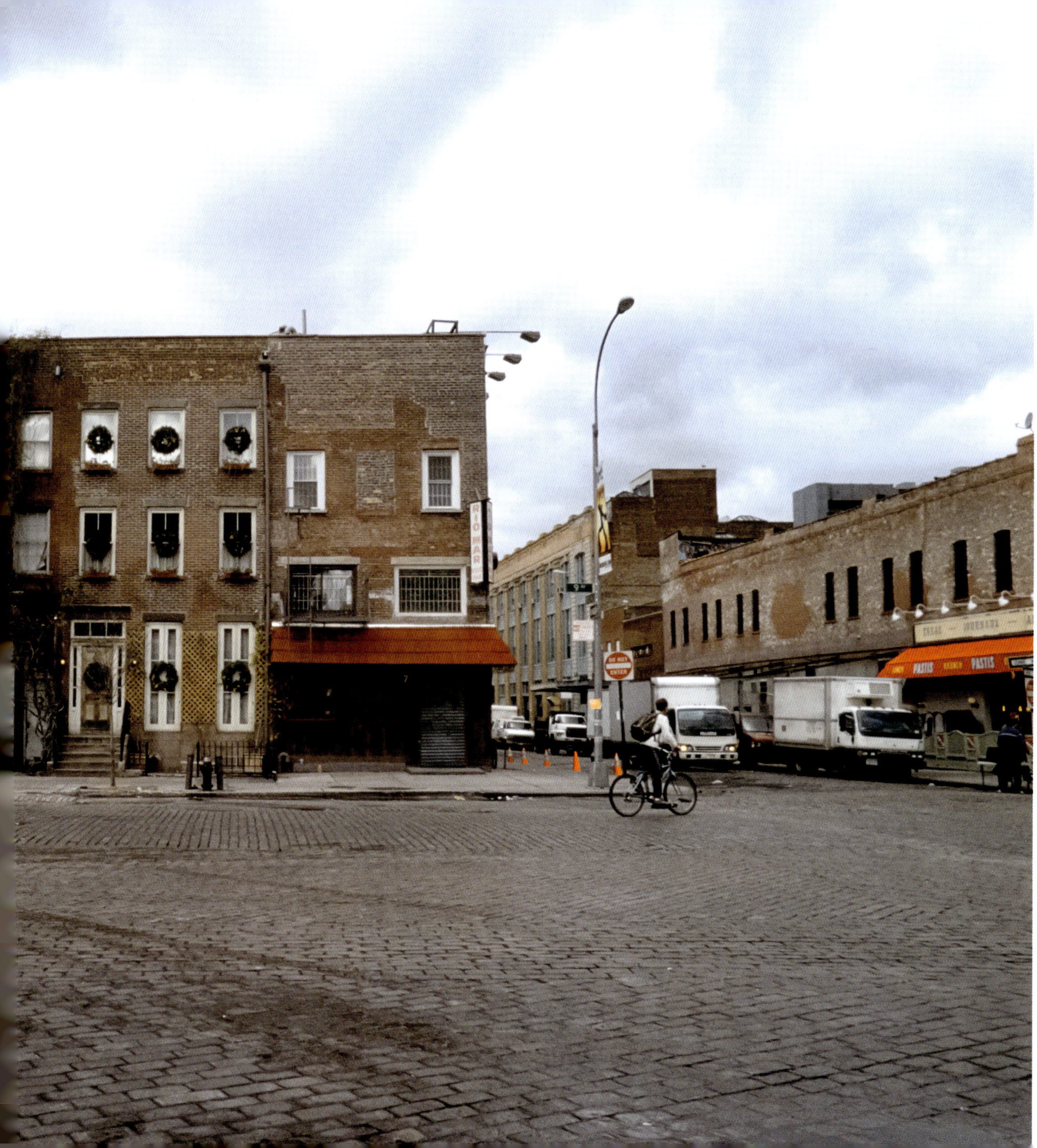
RIO MAR
DO NOT ENTER
PASTIS
PASTIS

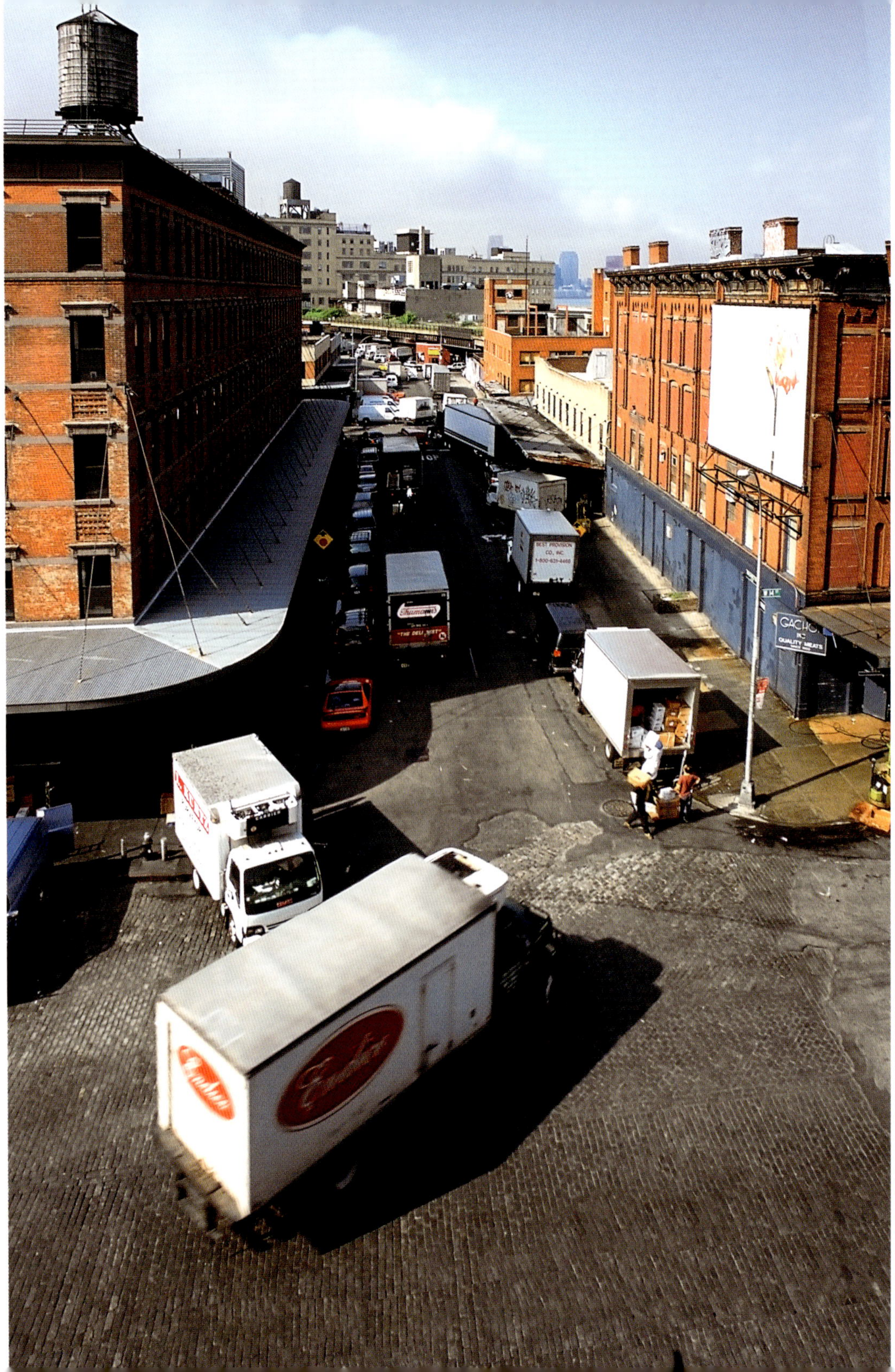
BEST PROVISION
CO., INC.
QUALITY MEATS

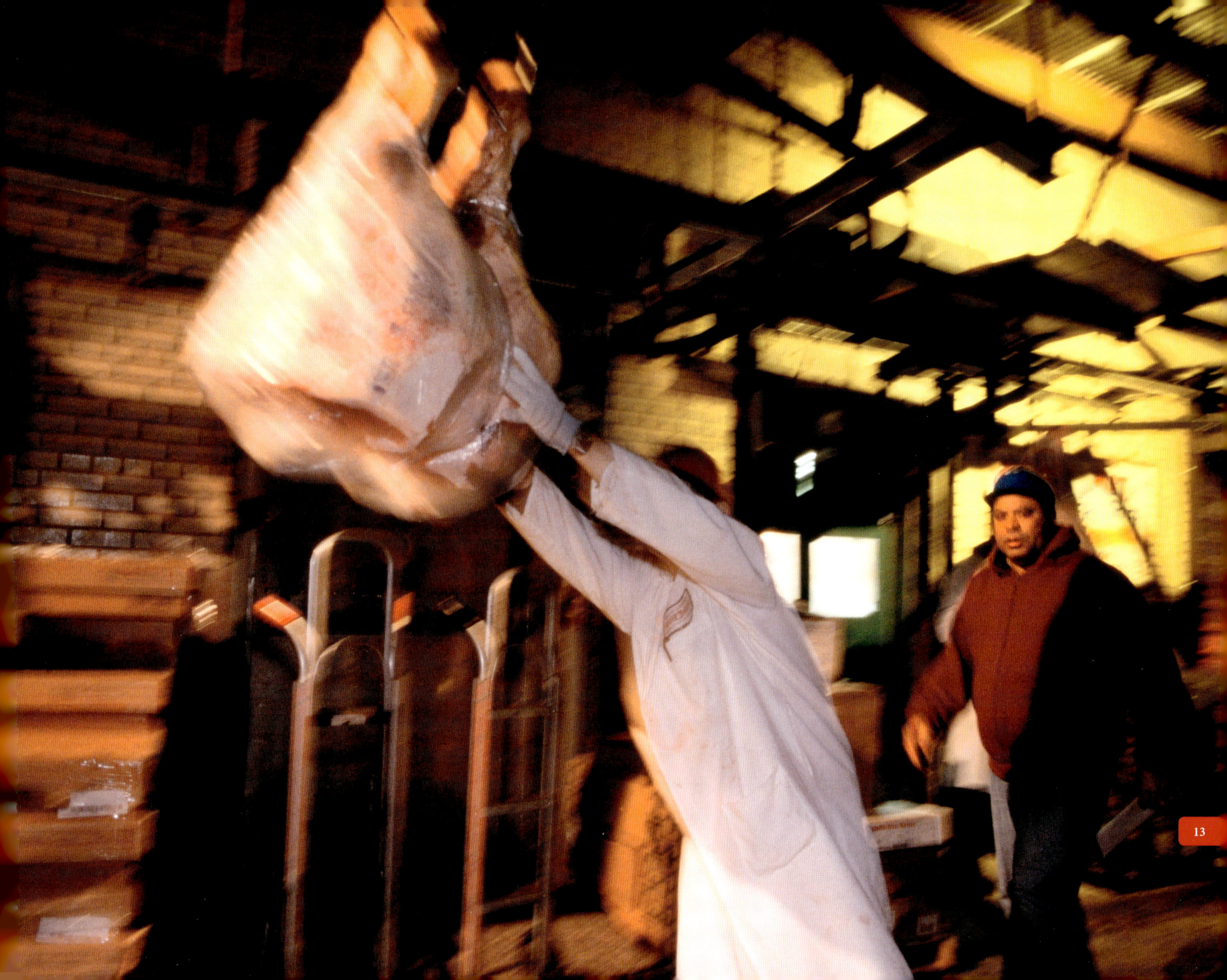

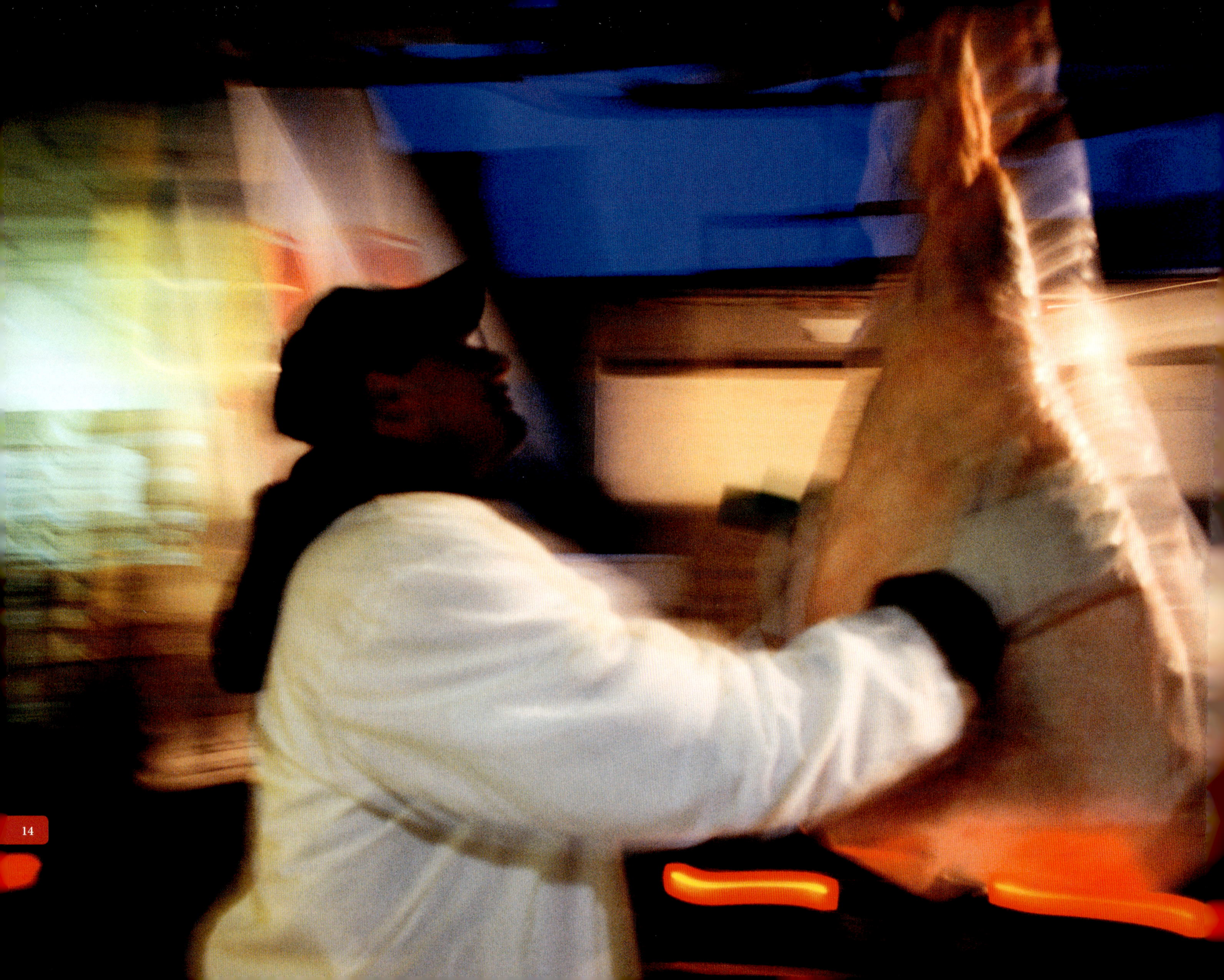

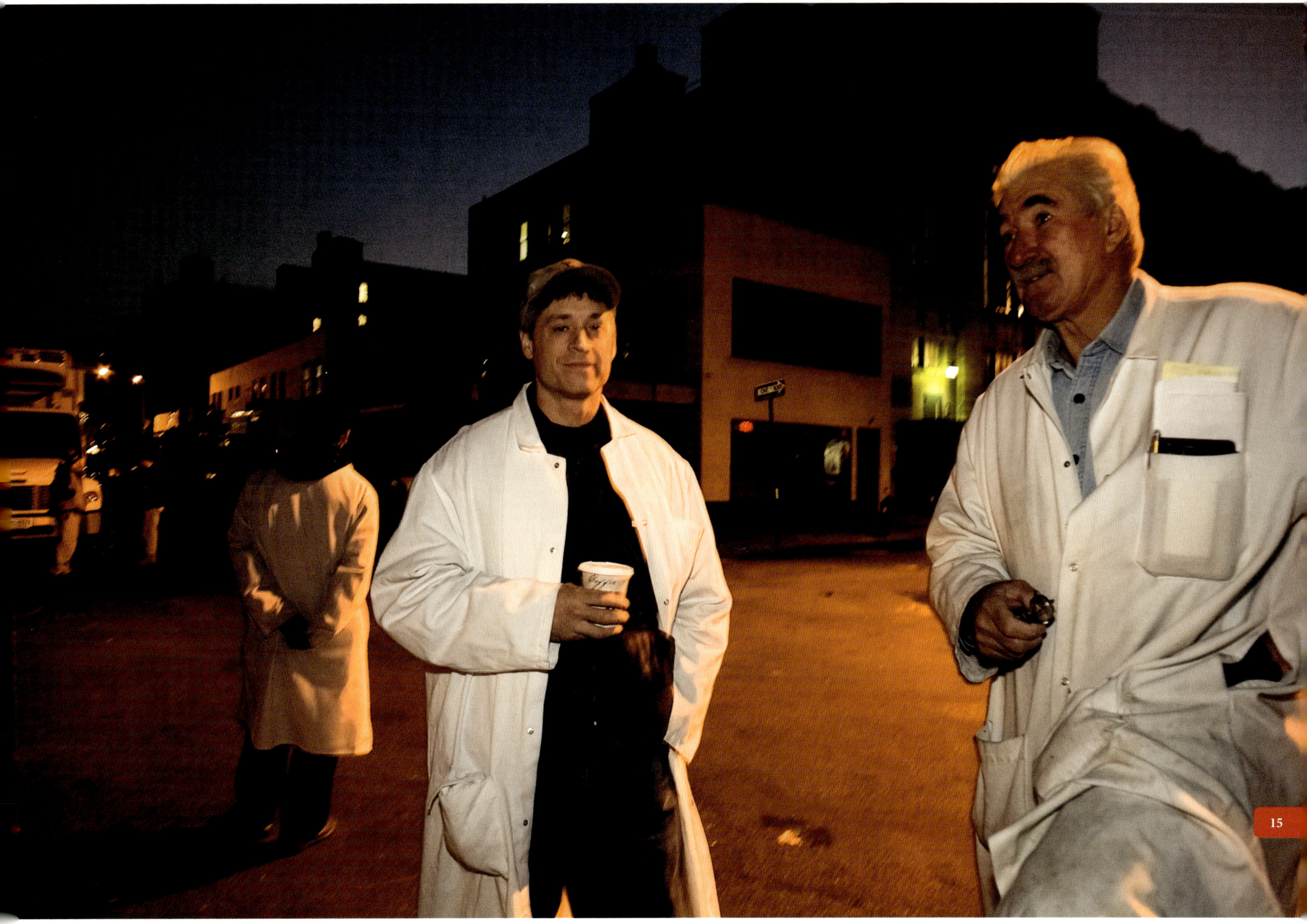

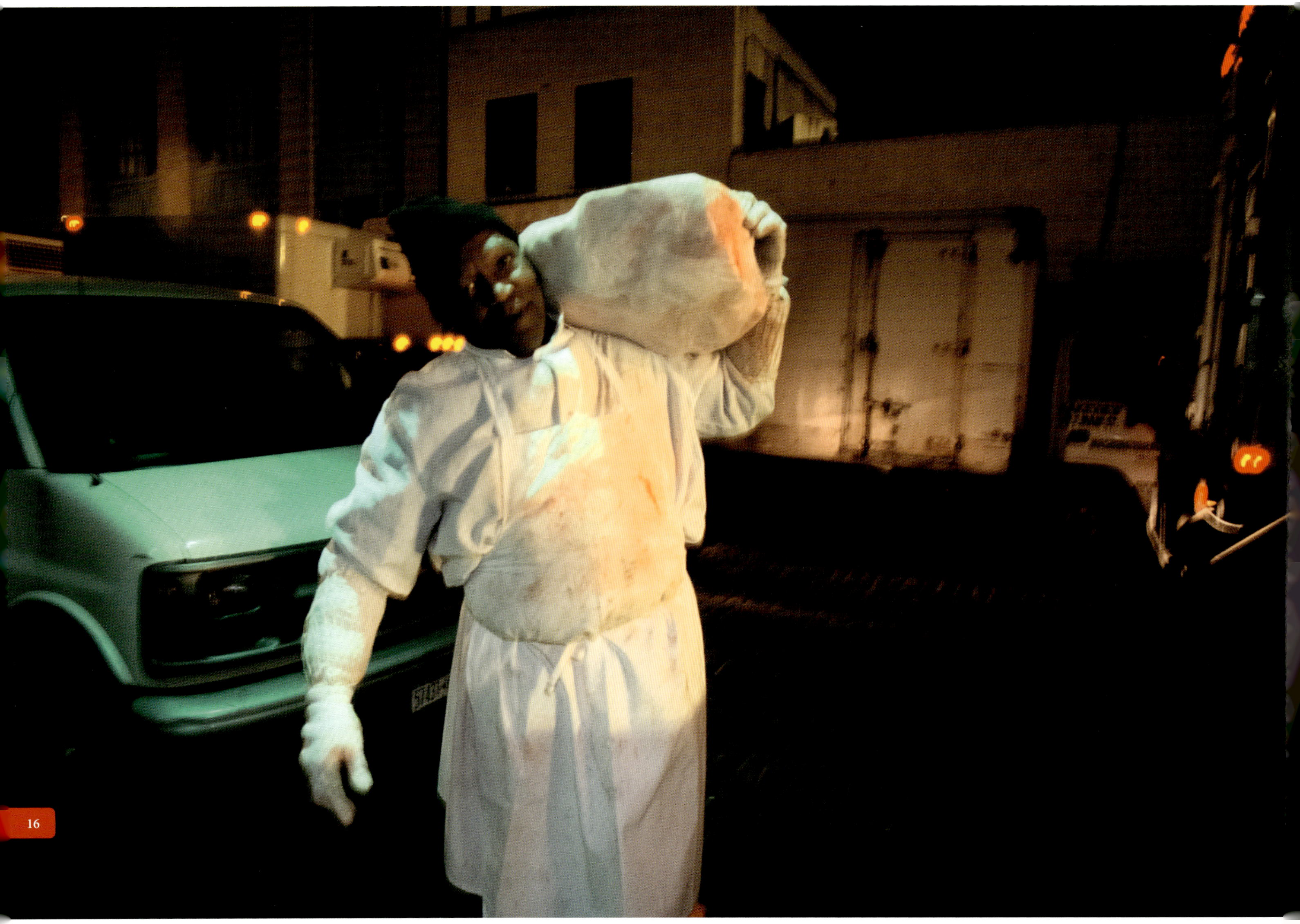

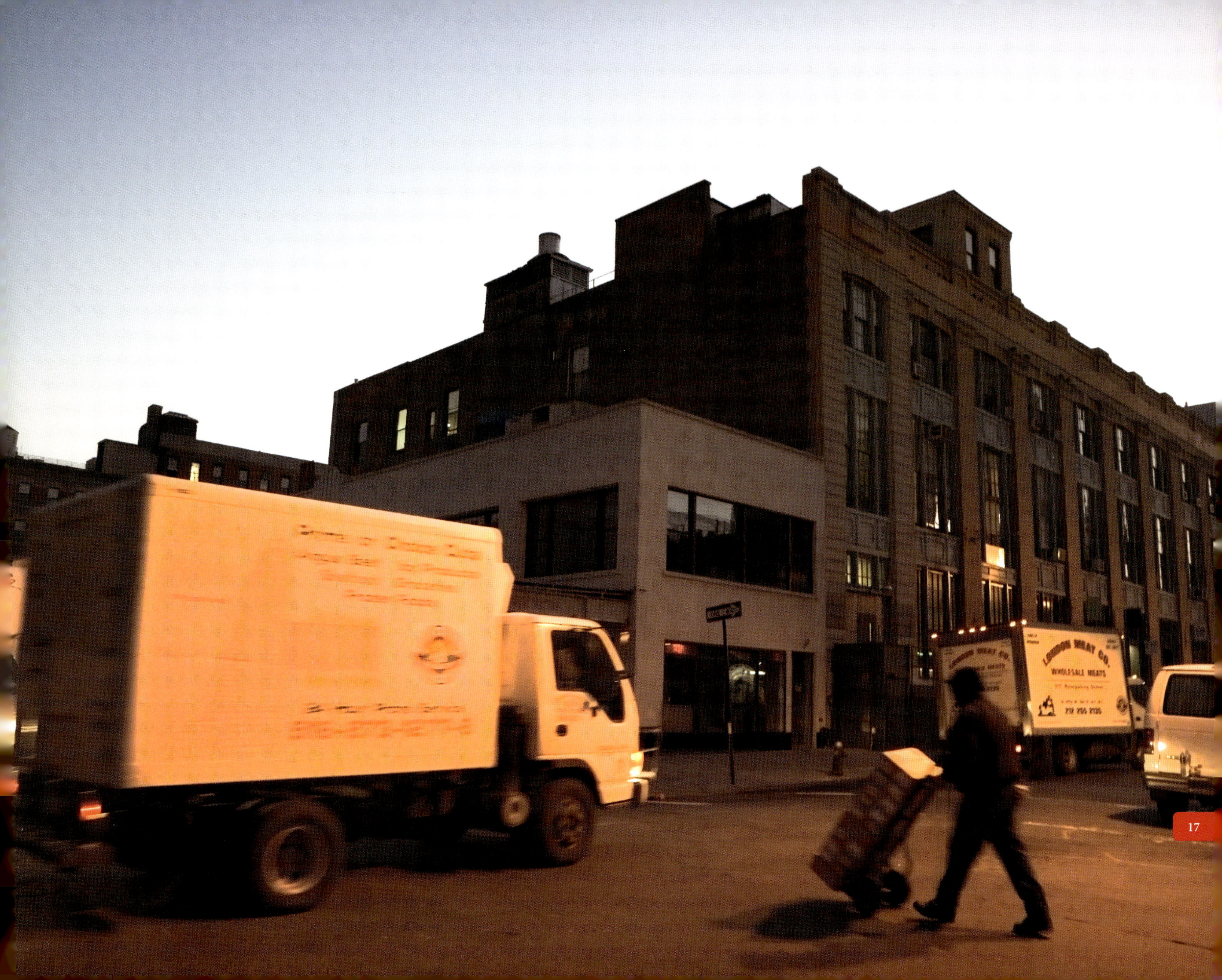
LONDON MEAT CO.
WHOLESALE MEATS

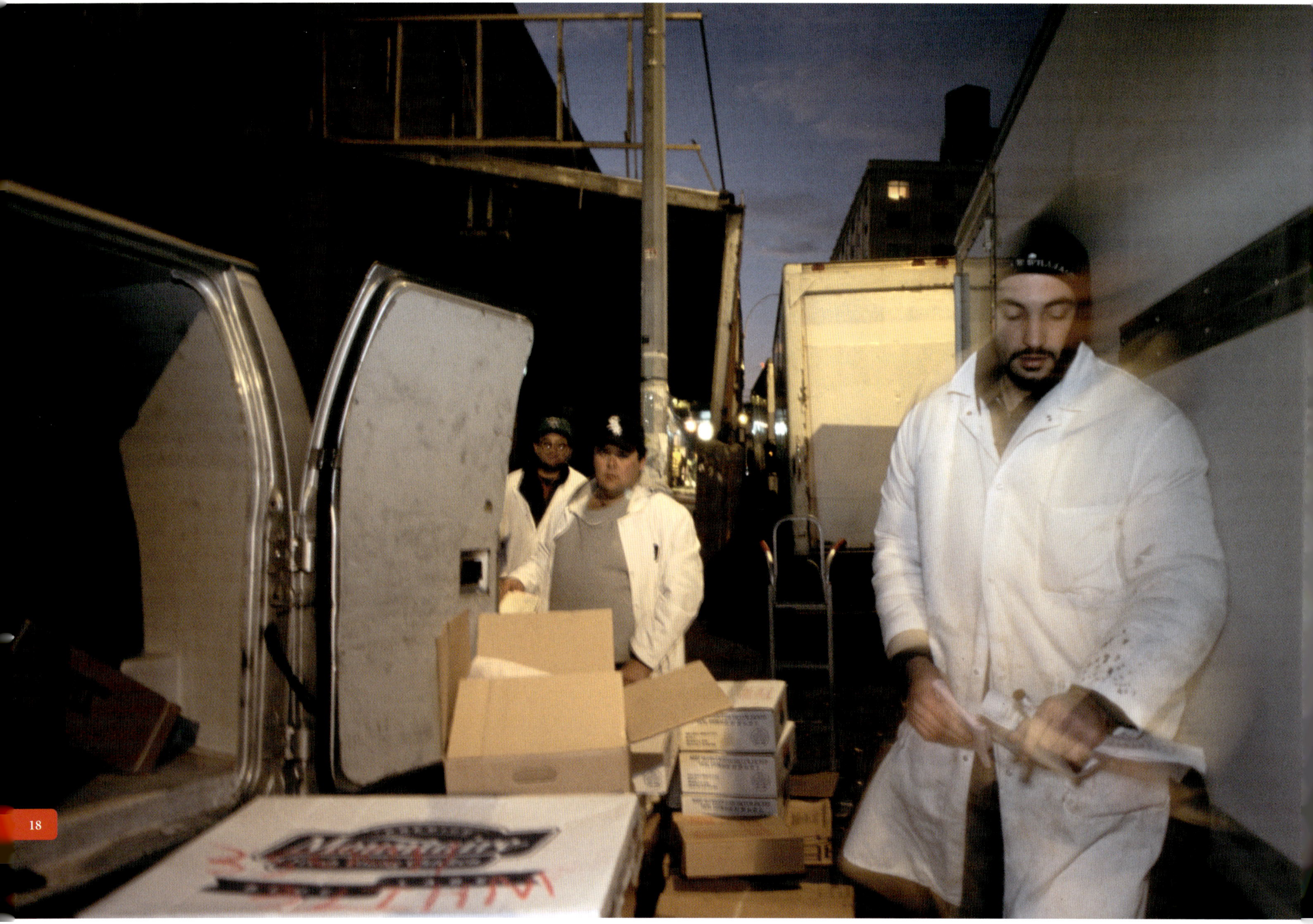

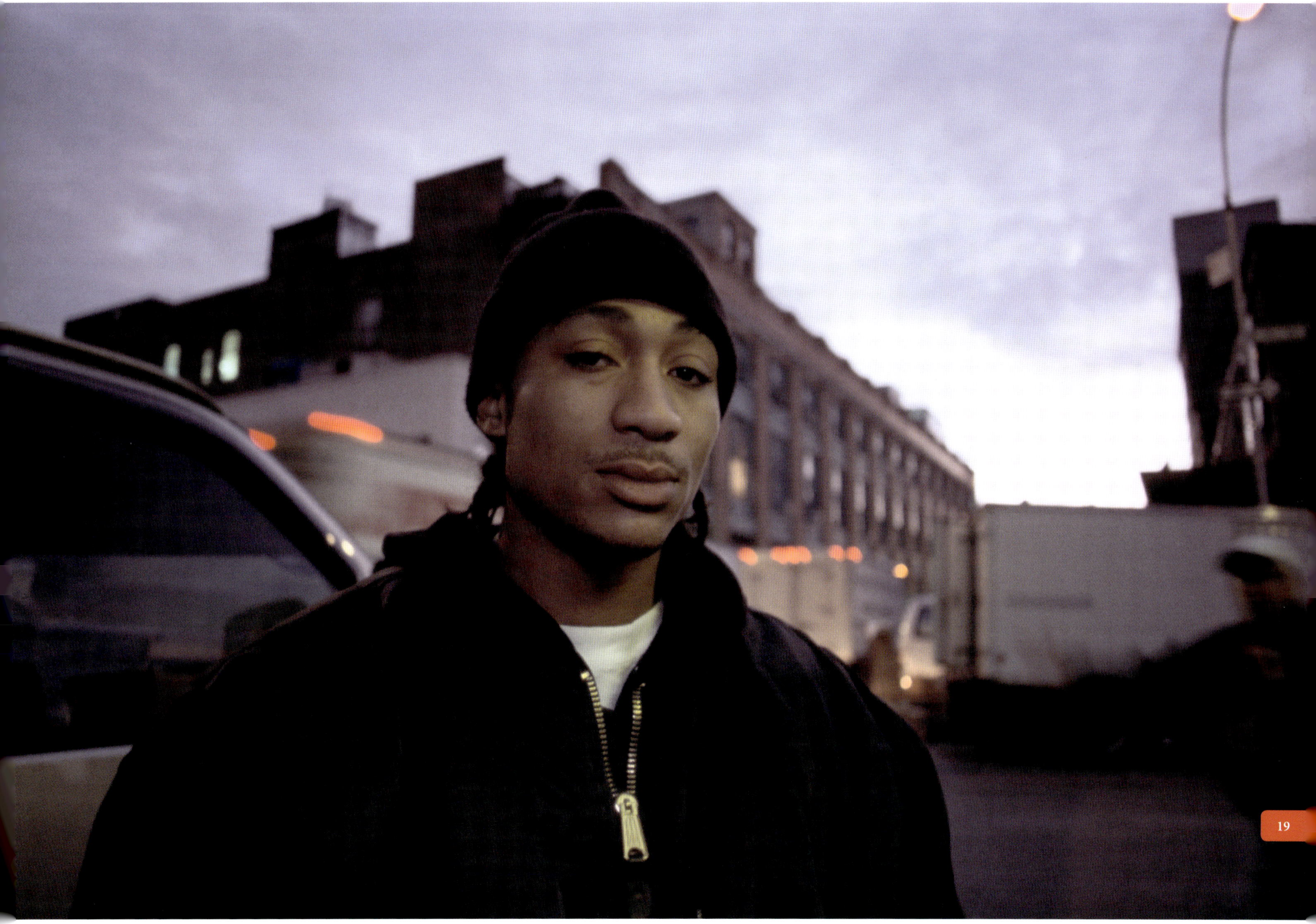

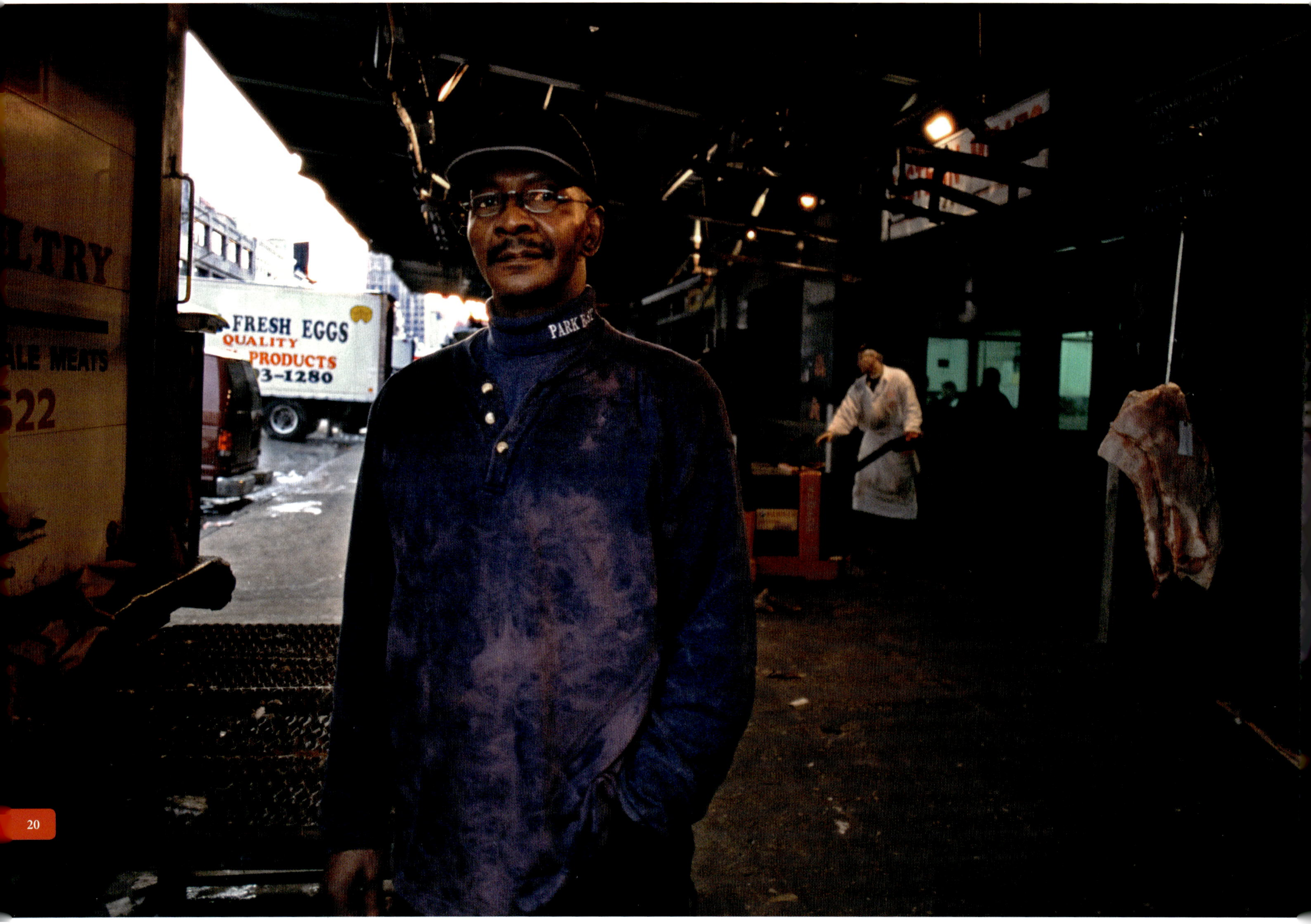
FRESH EGGS
QUALITY
PRODUCTS
PARK

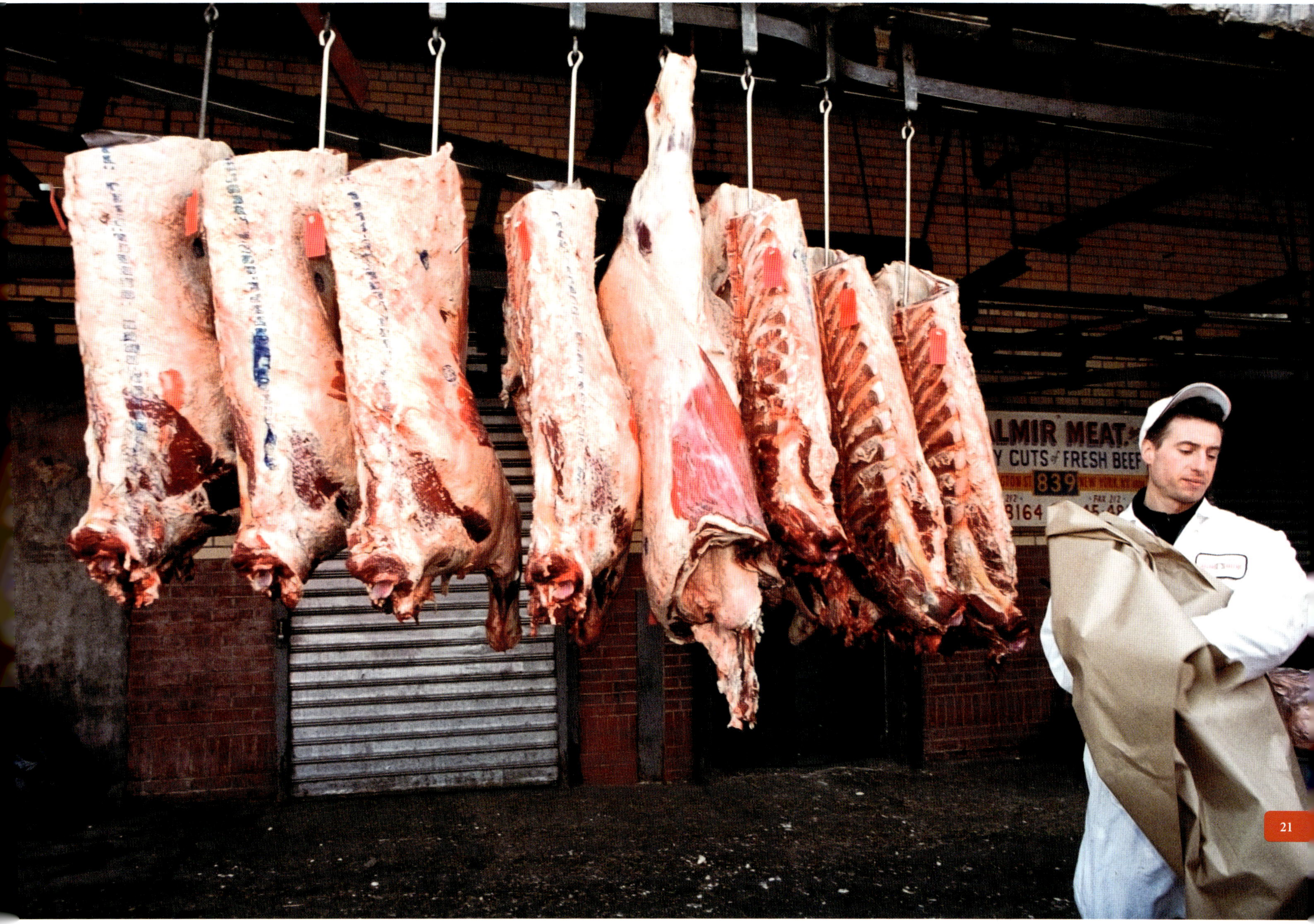
ALMIR MEAT
CUTS of FRESH BEEF
839

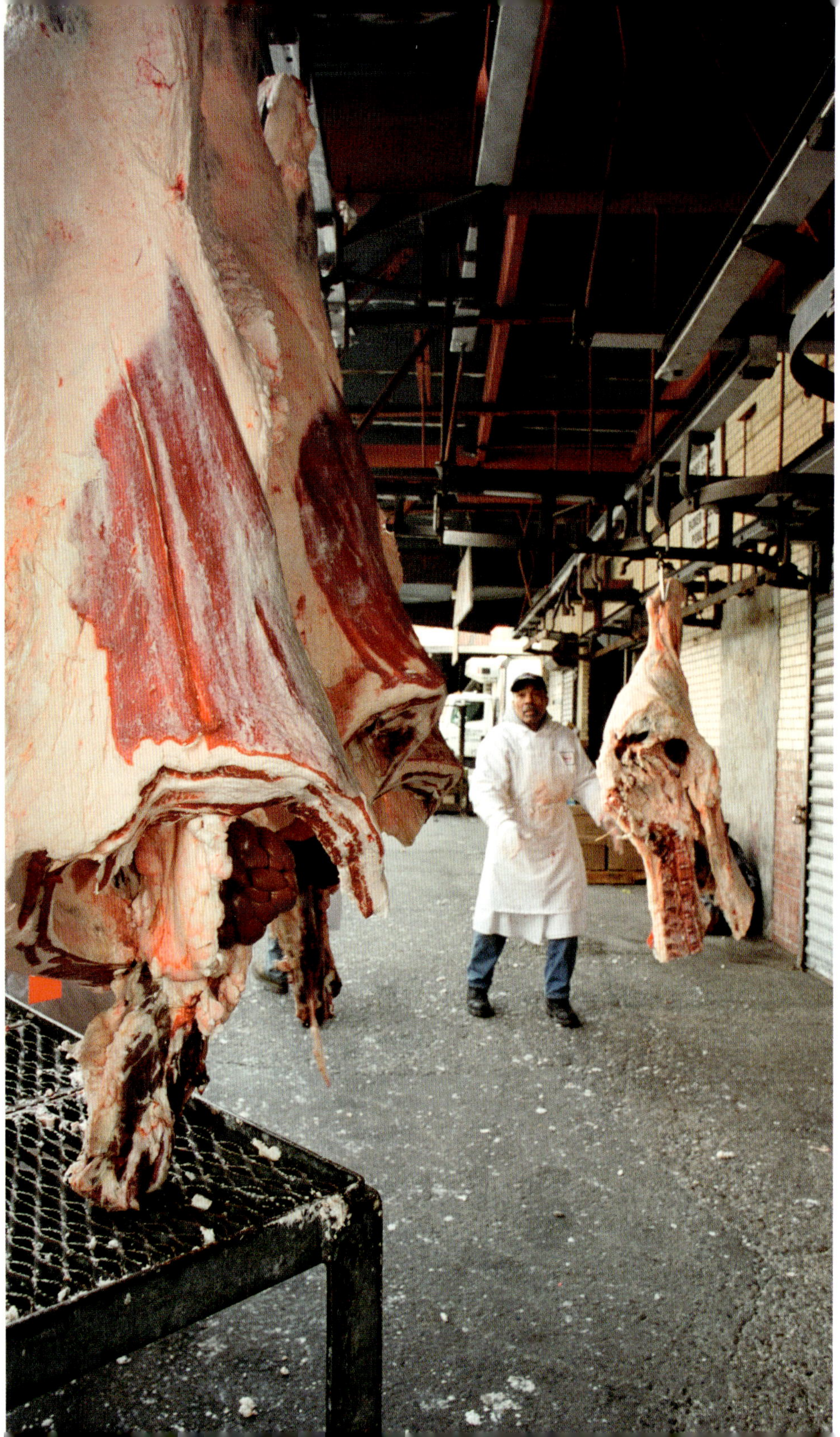

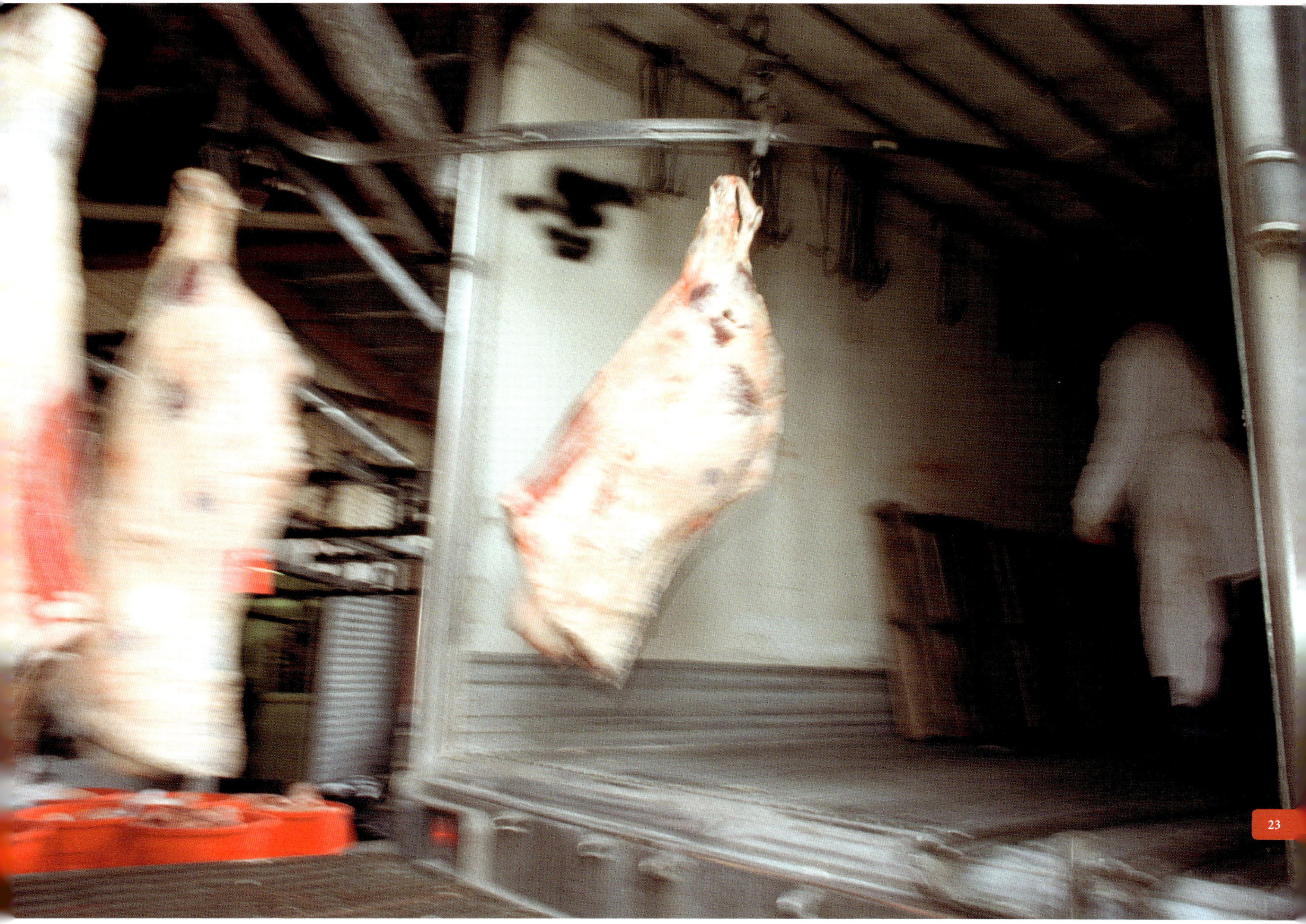

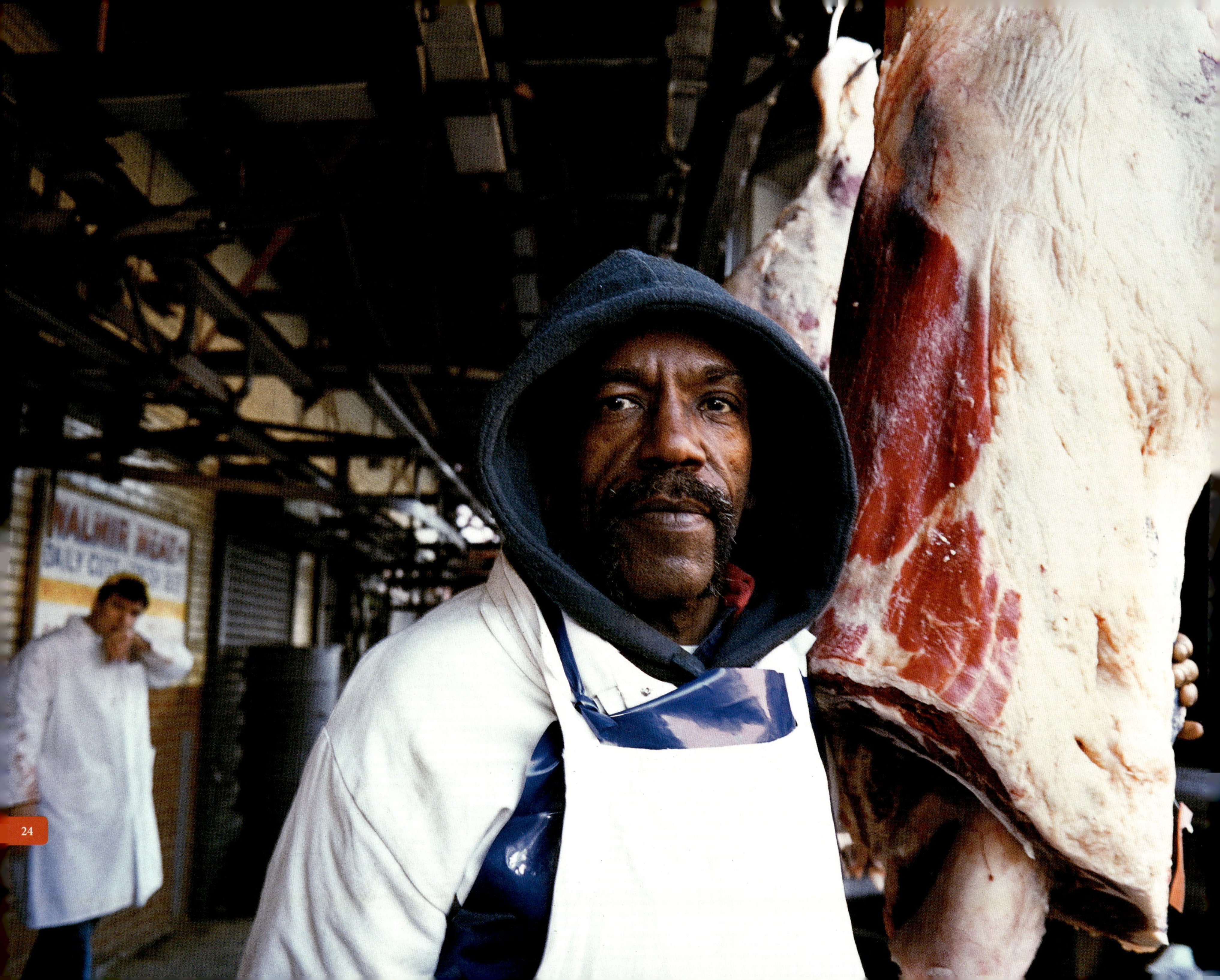

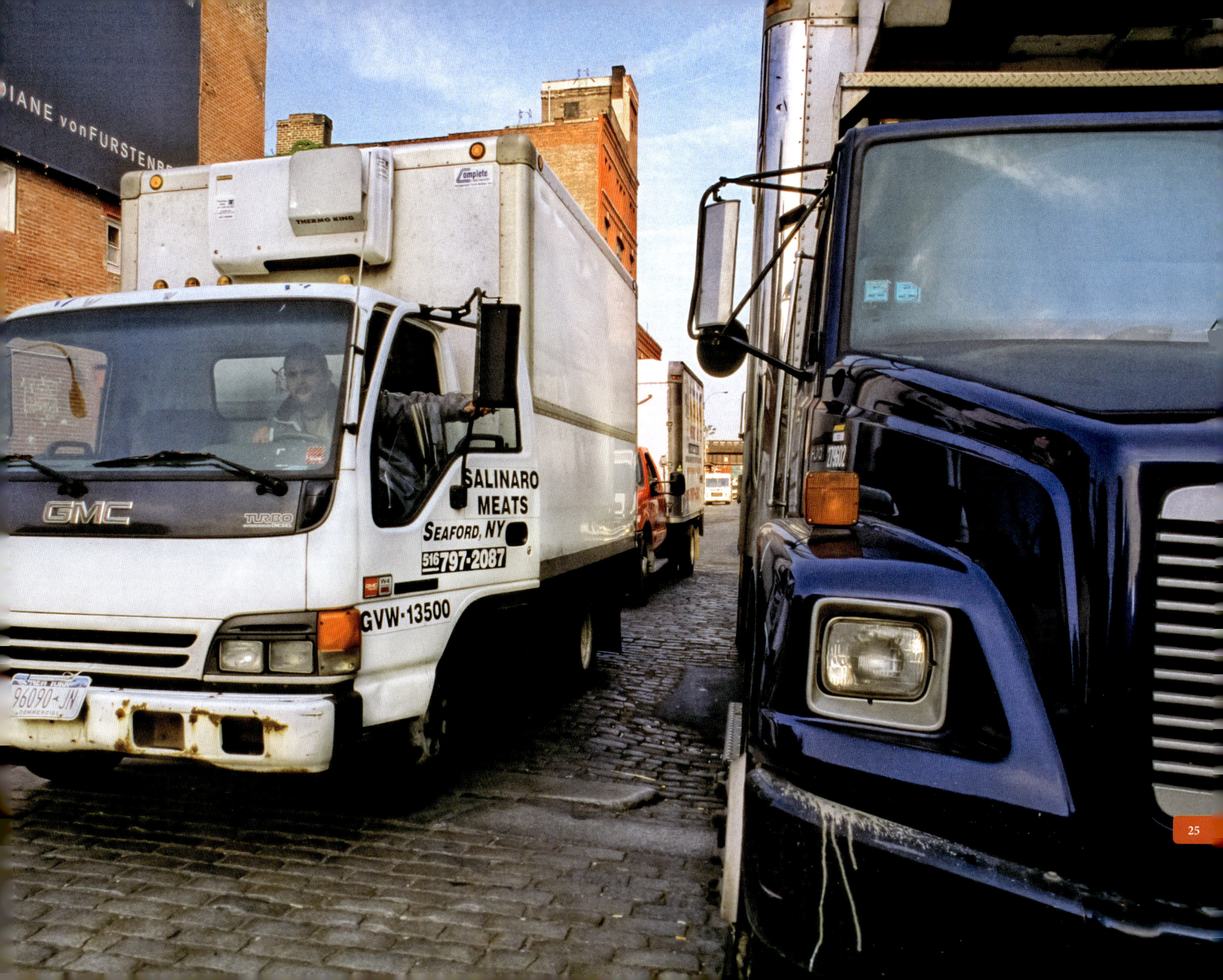
DIANE vonFURSTENB
THERMO KING
GMC
TURBO
SALINARO
MEATS
SEAFORD, NY
516 797-2087
GVW-13500

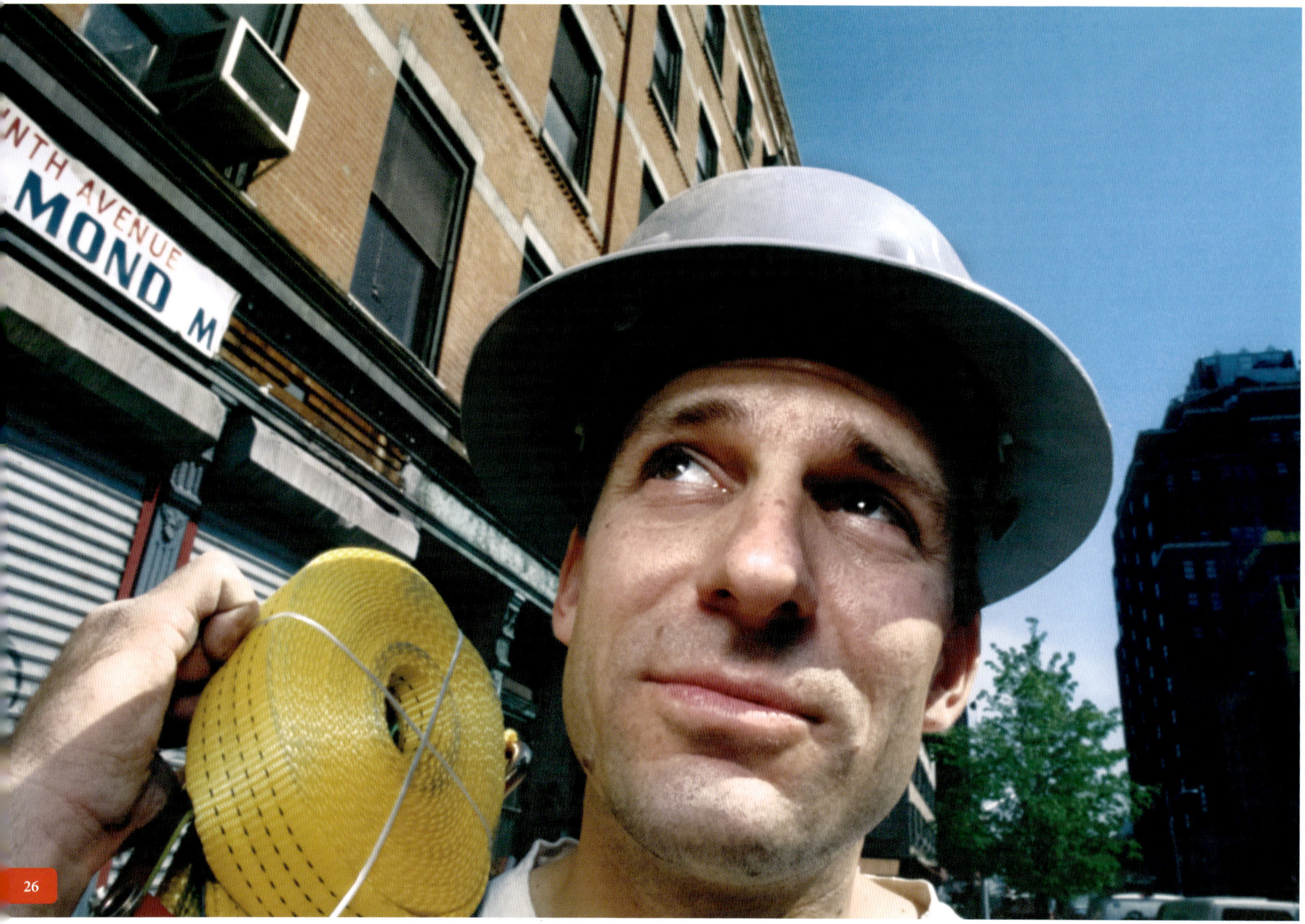
NTH AVENUE
MOND M

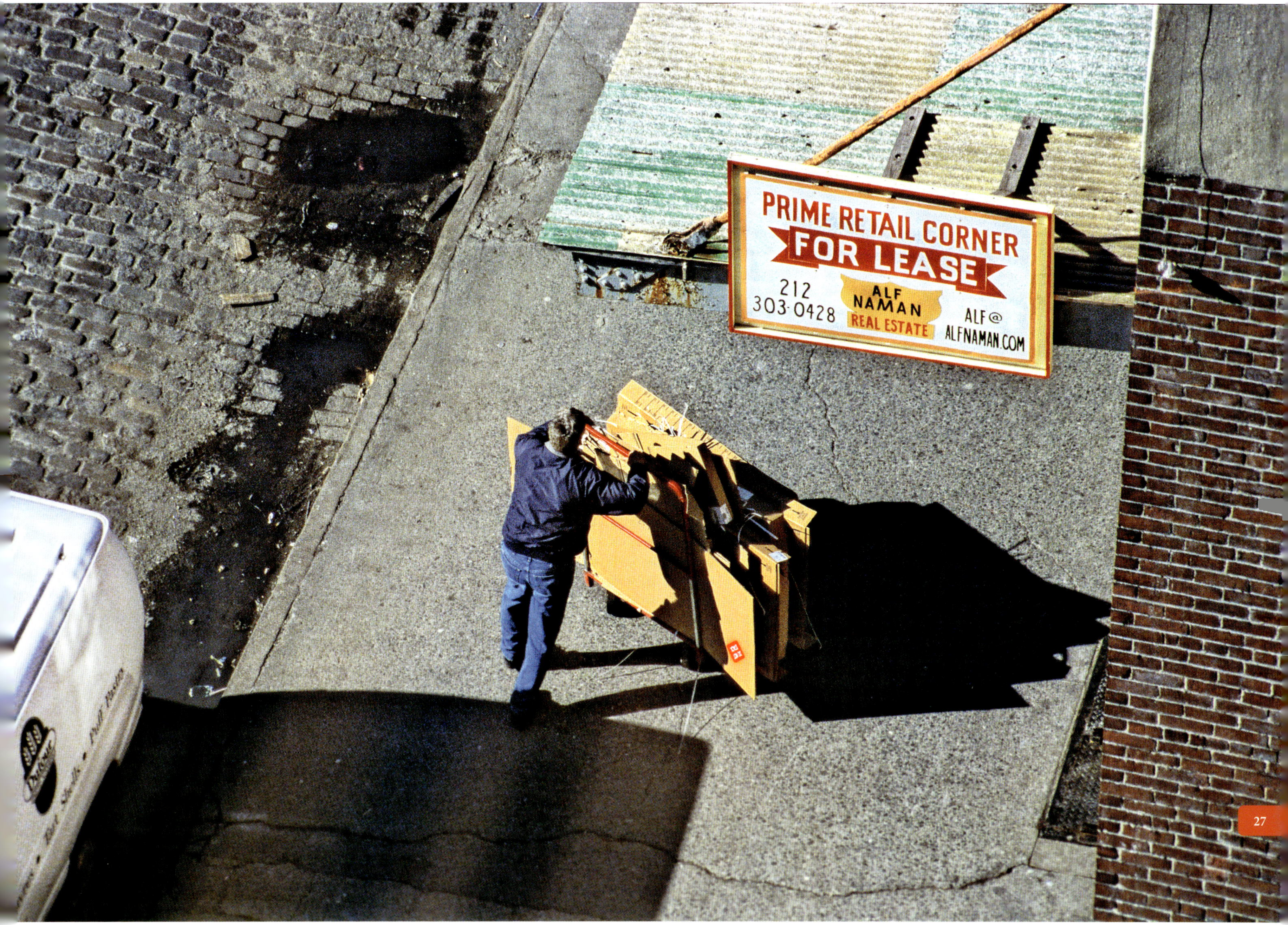
PRIME RETAIL CORNER
FOR LEASE
212
303-0428
ALF
NAMAN
REAL ESTATE
ALF@
ALFNAMAN.COM

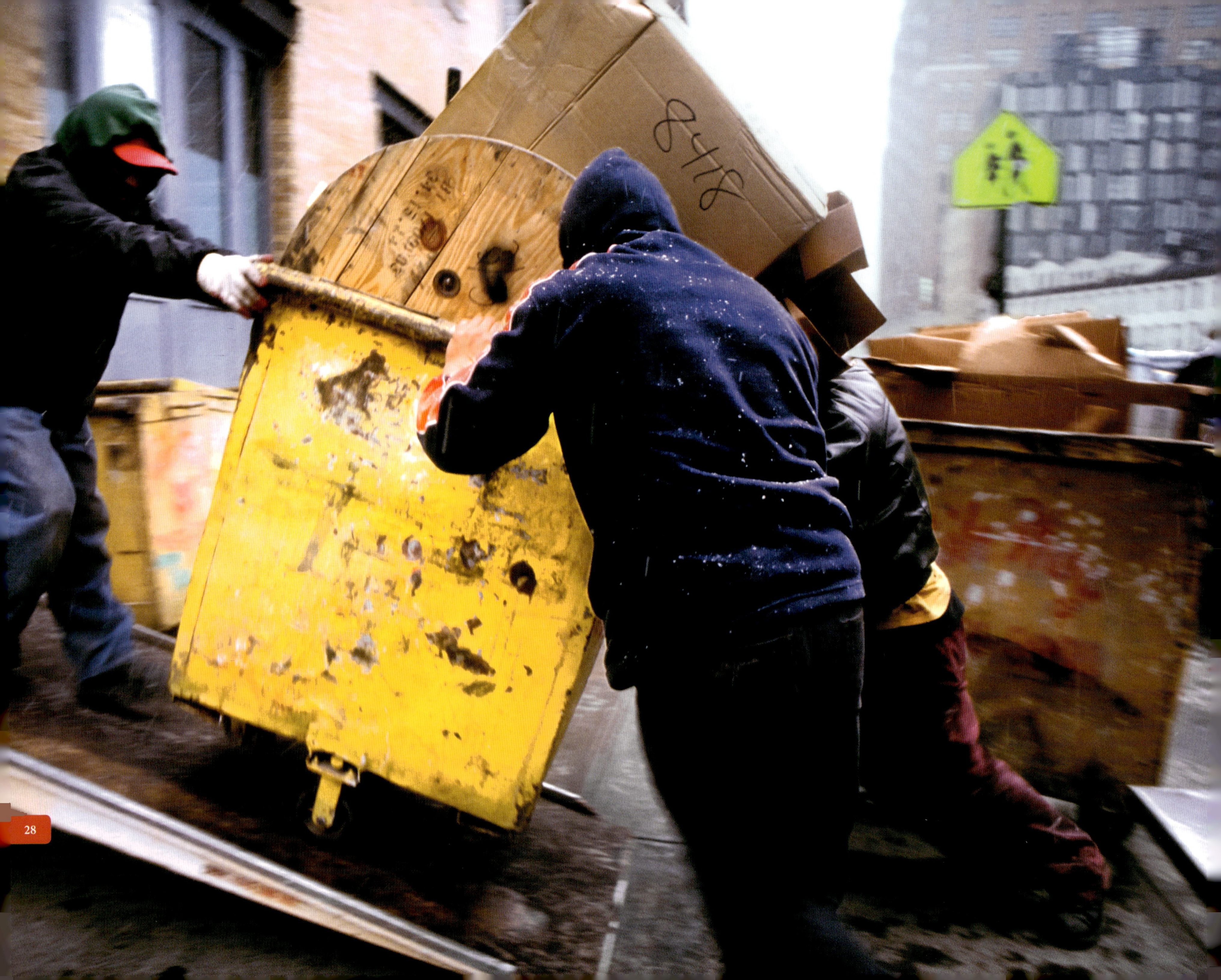

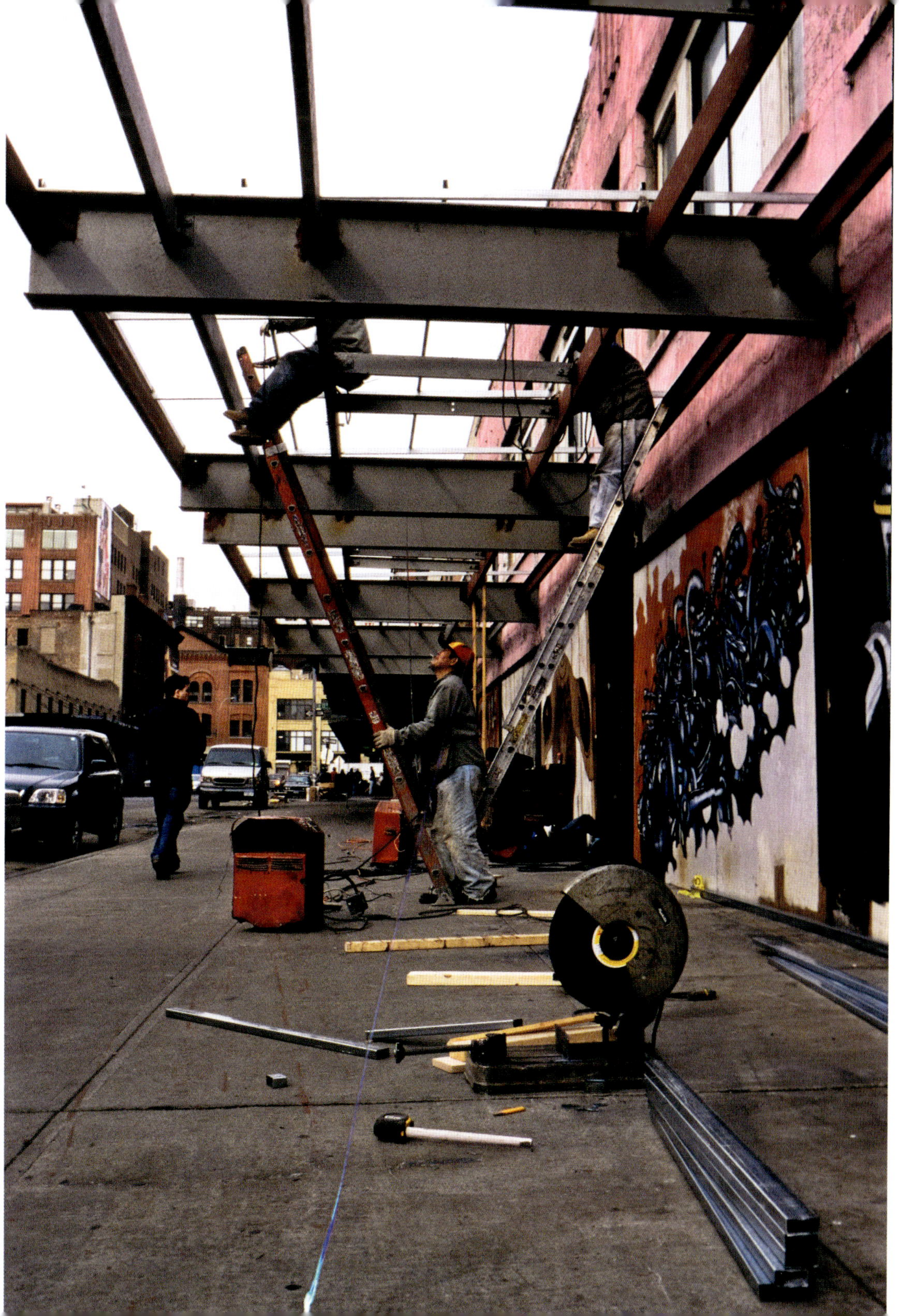

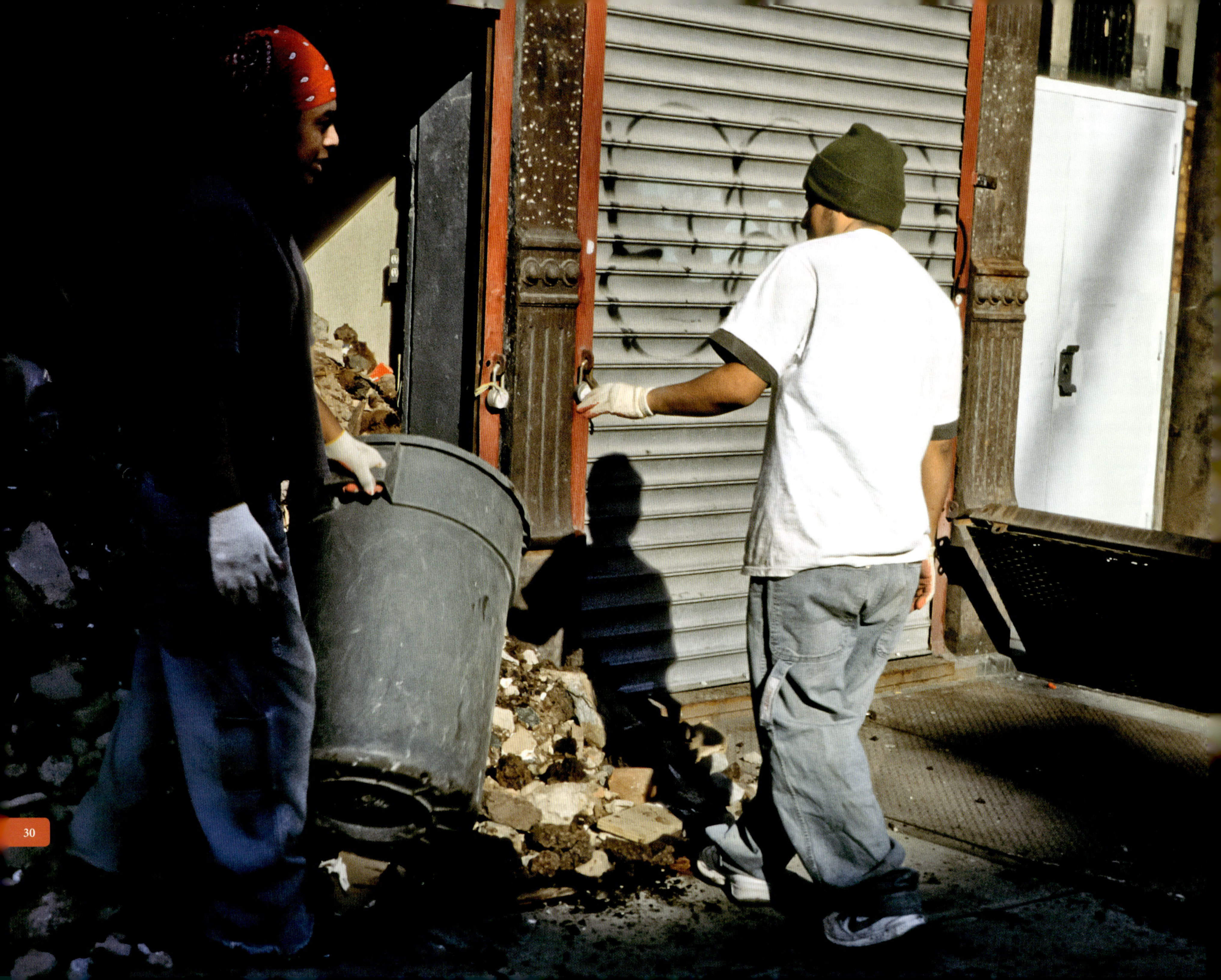

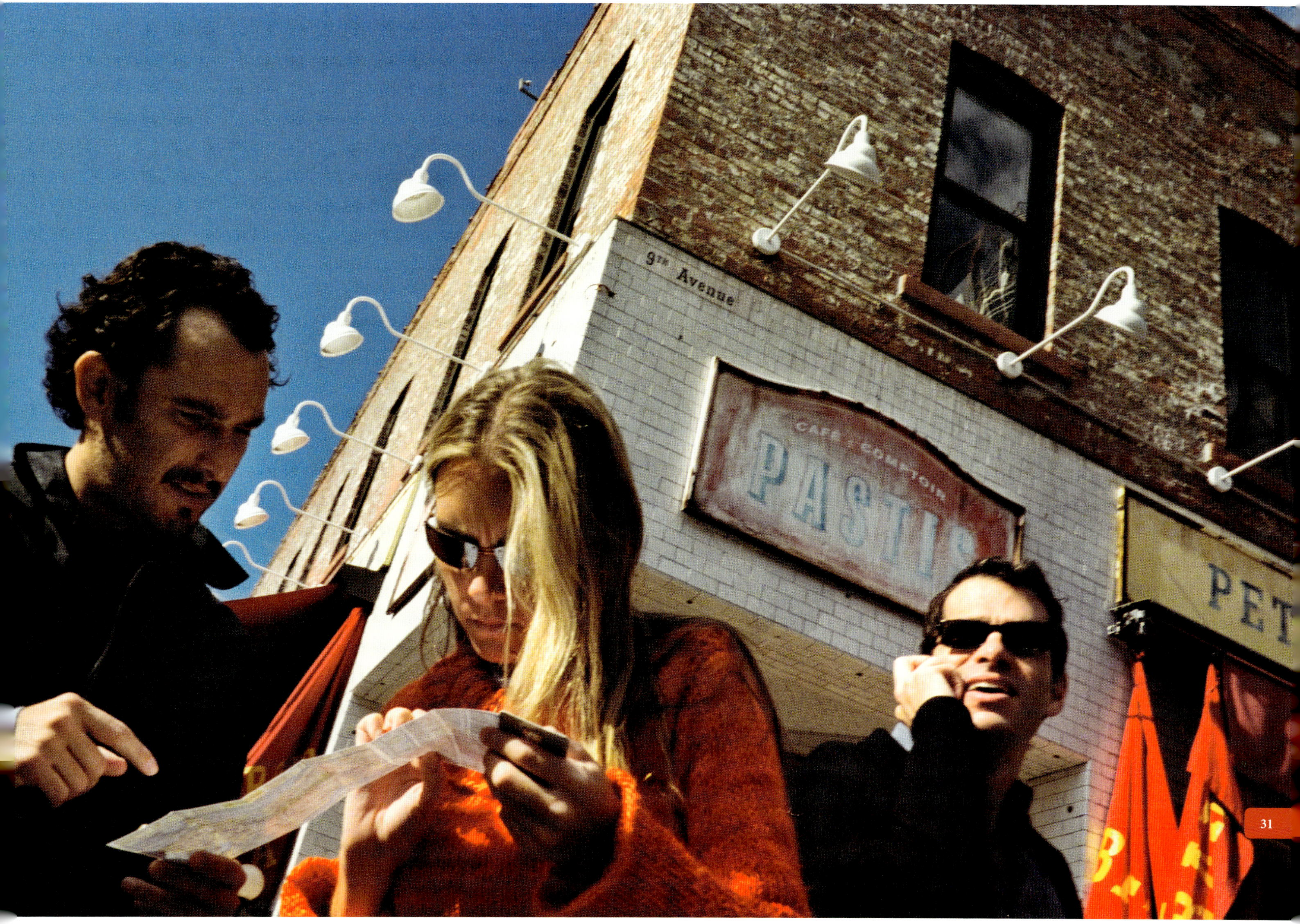
9TH Avenue
CAFE COMPTOIR
PASTIS

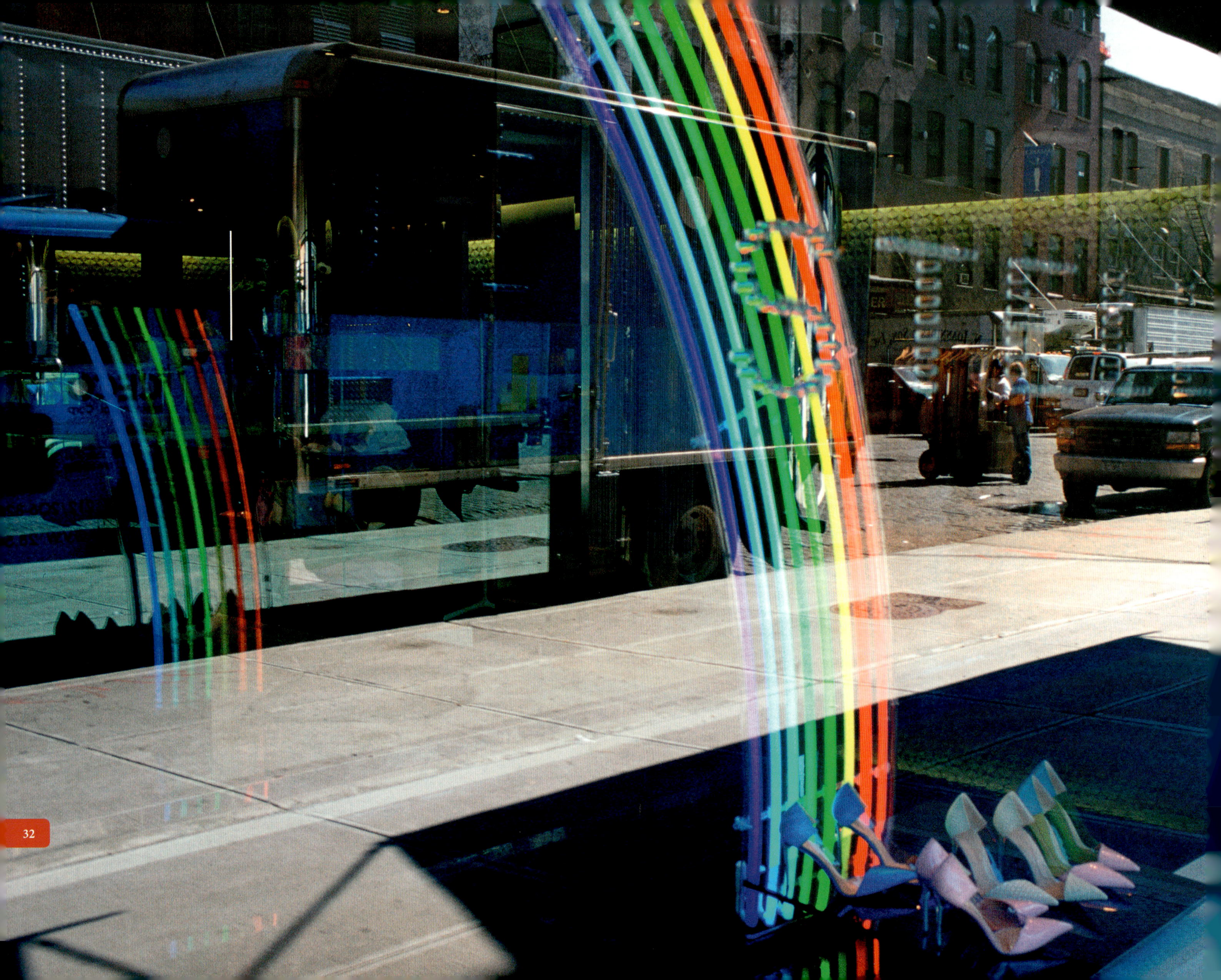

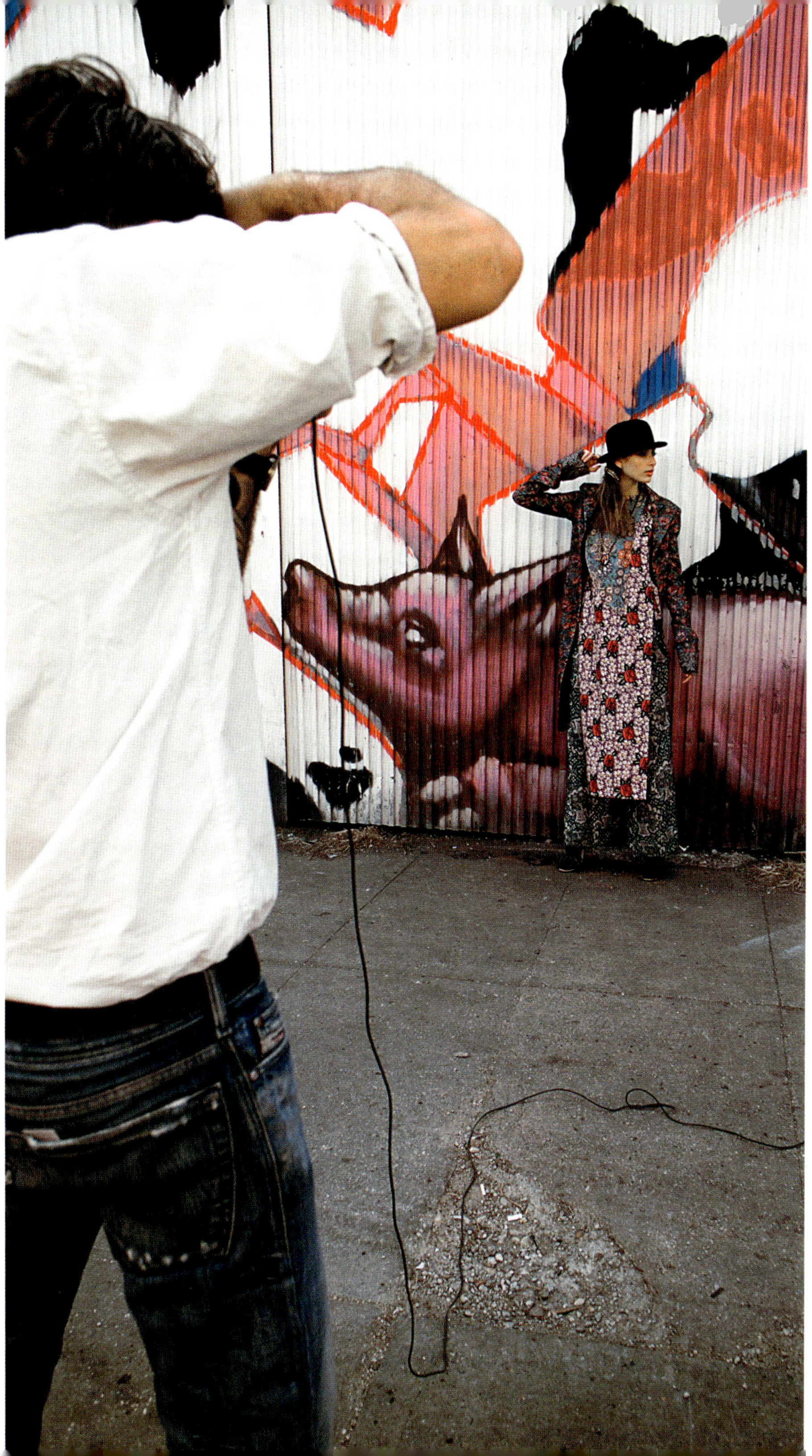

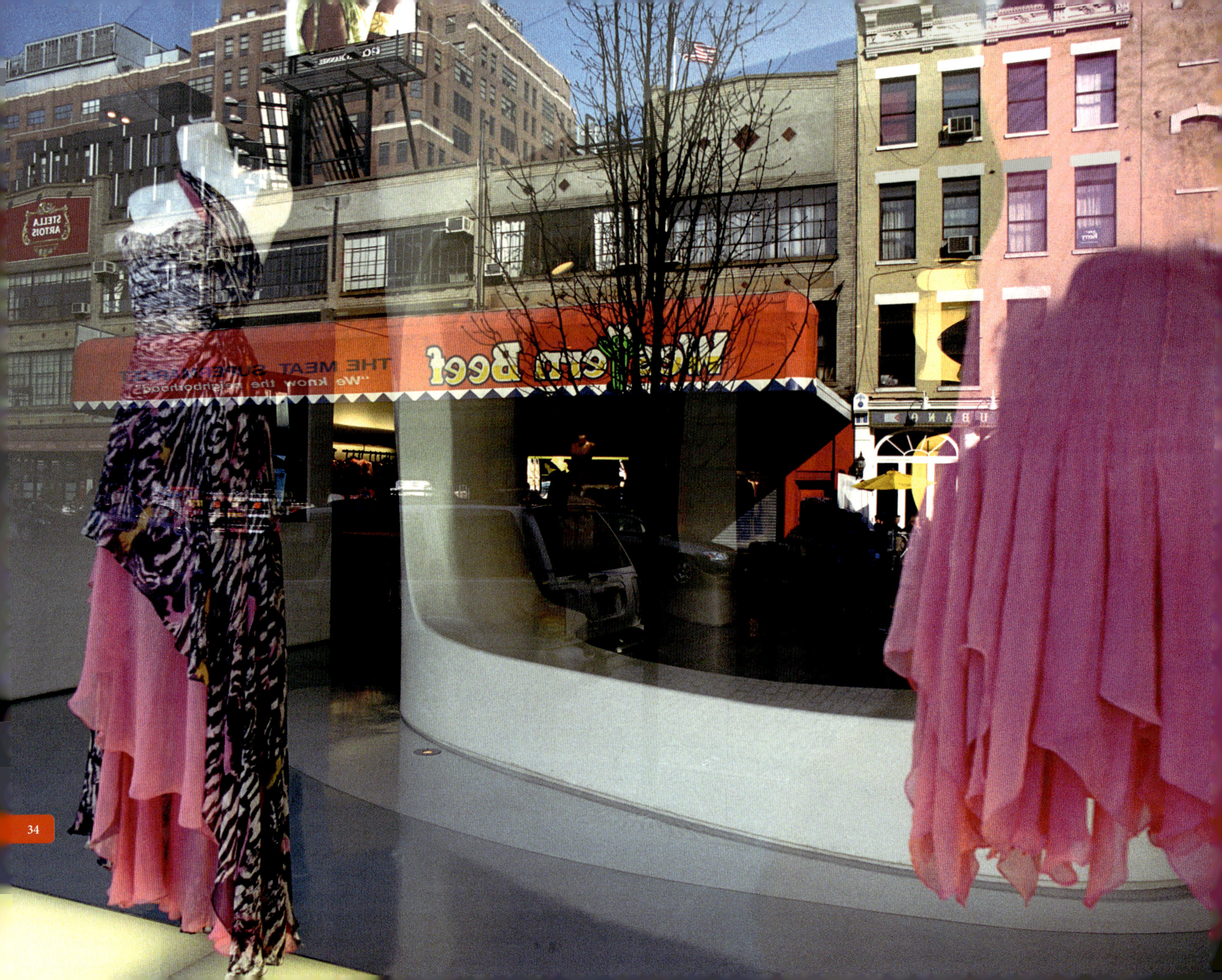

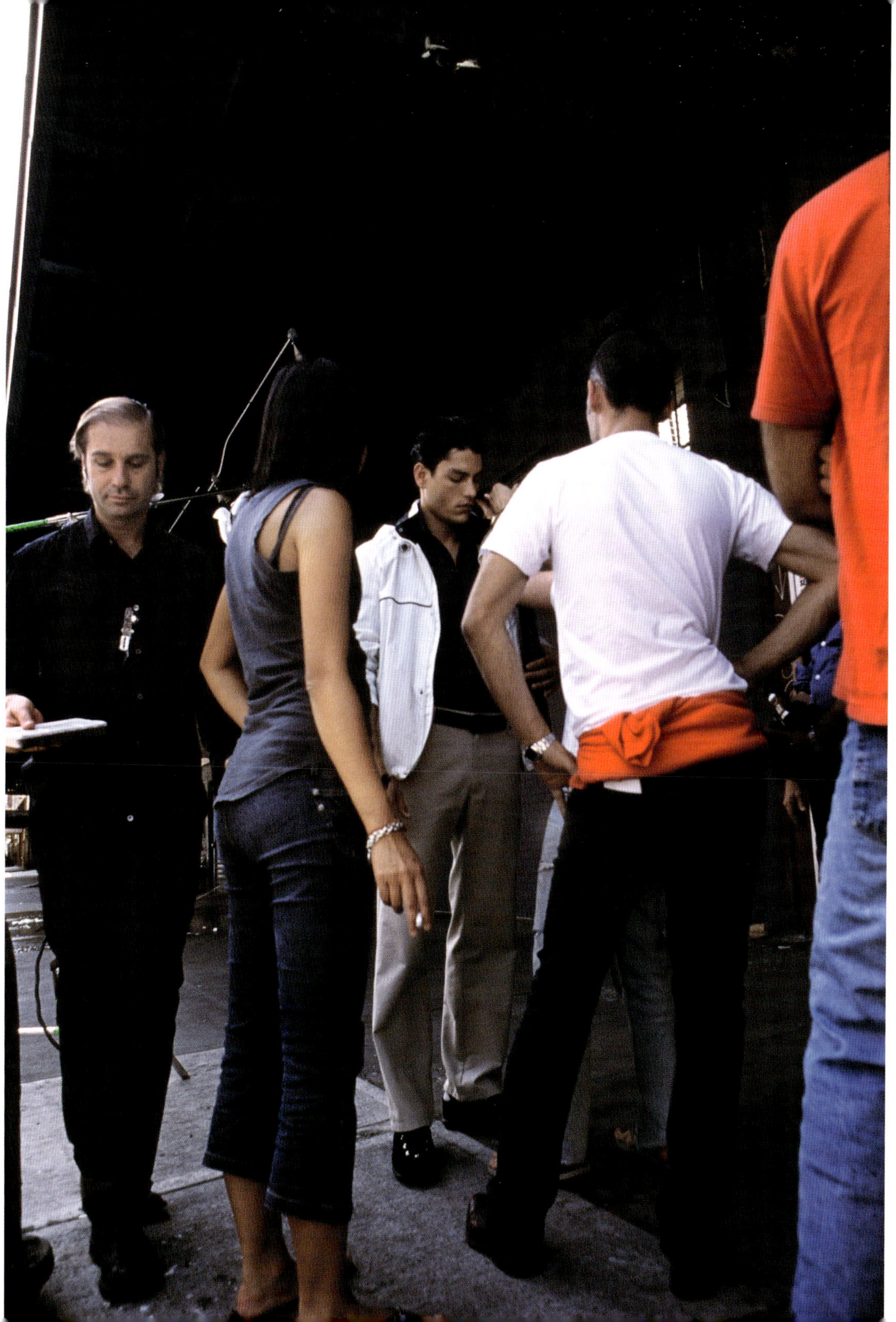

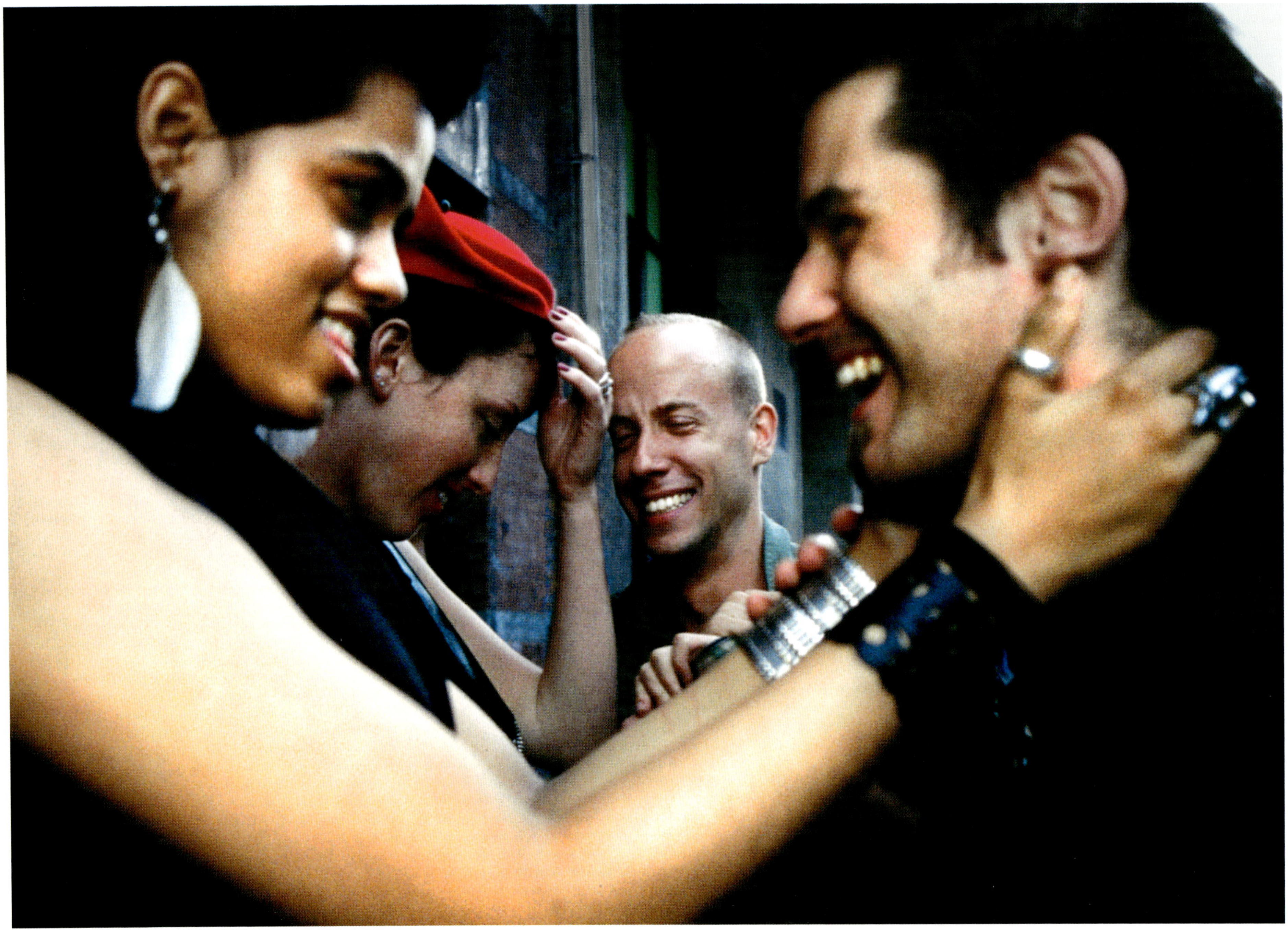

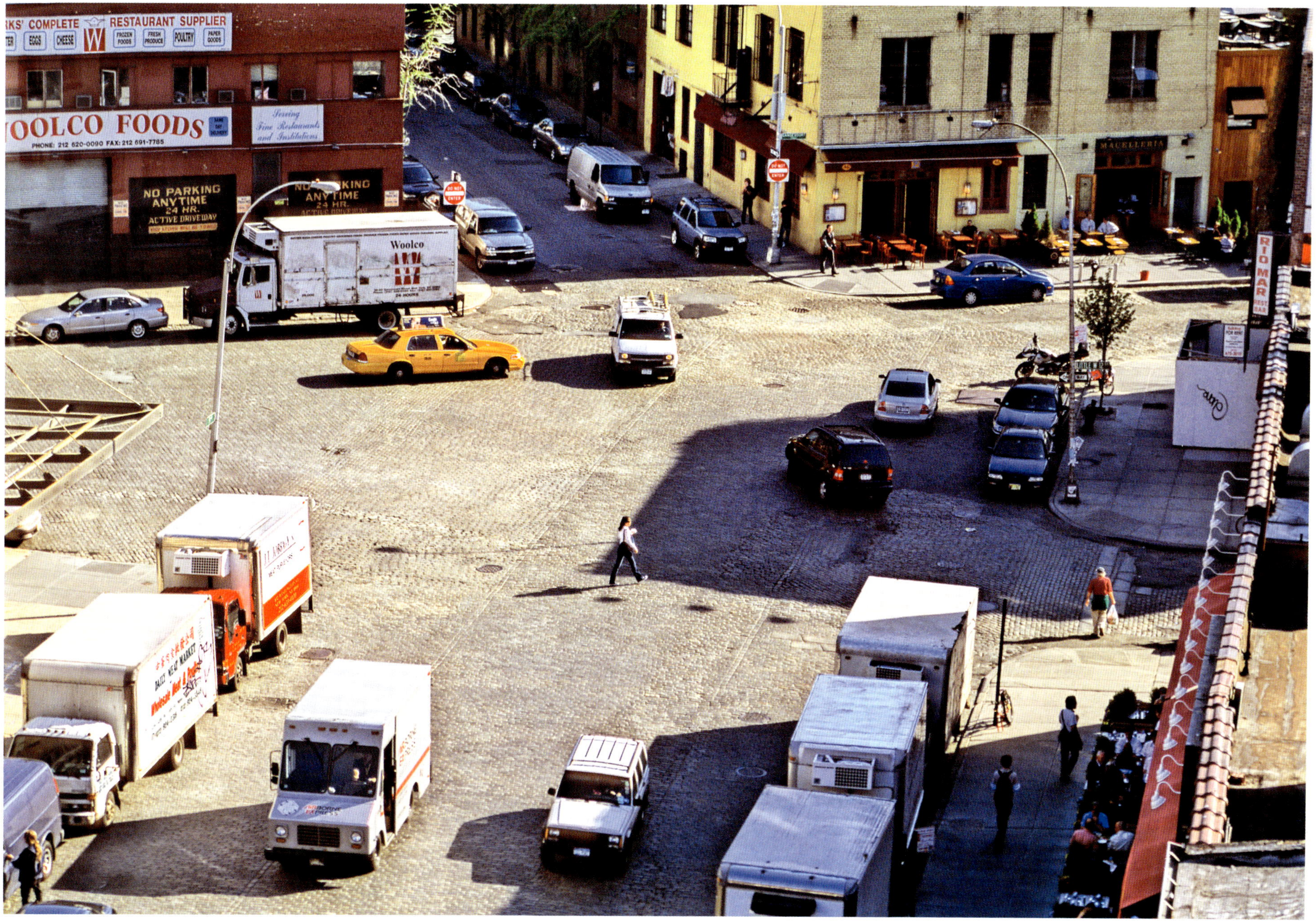
RKS' COMPLETE
RESTAURANT SUPPLIER
EGGS
CHEESE
W
FROZEN FOODS
FRESH PRODUCE
POULTRY
PAPER GOODS
OOLCO FOODS
PHONE: 212 620-0090 FAX: 212 691-7785
Serving Fine Restaurants and Institutions
NO PARKING ANYTIME 24 HR. ACTIVE DRIVEWAY
ANYTIME 24 HR.
Woolco
DO NOT ENTER
RIO MAR

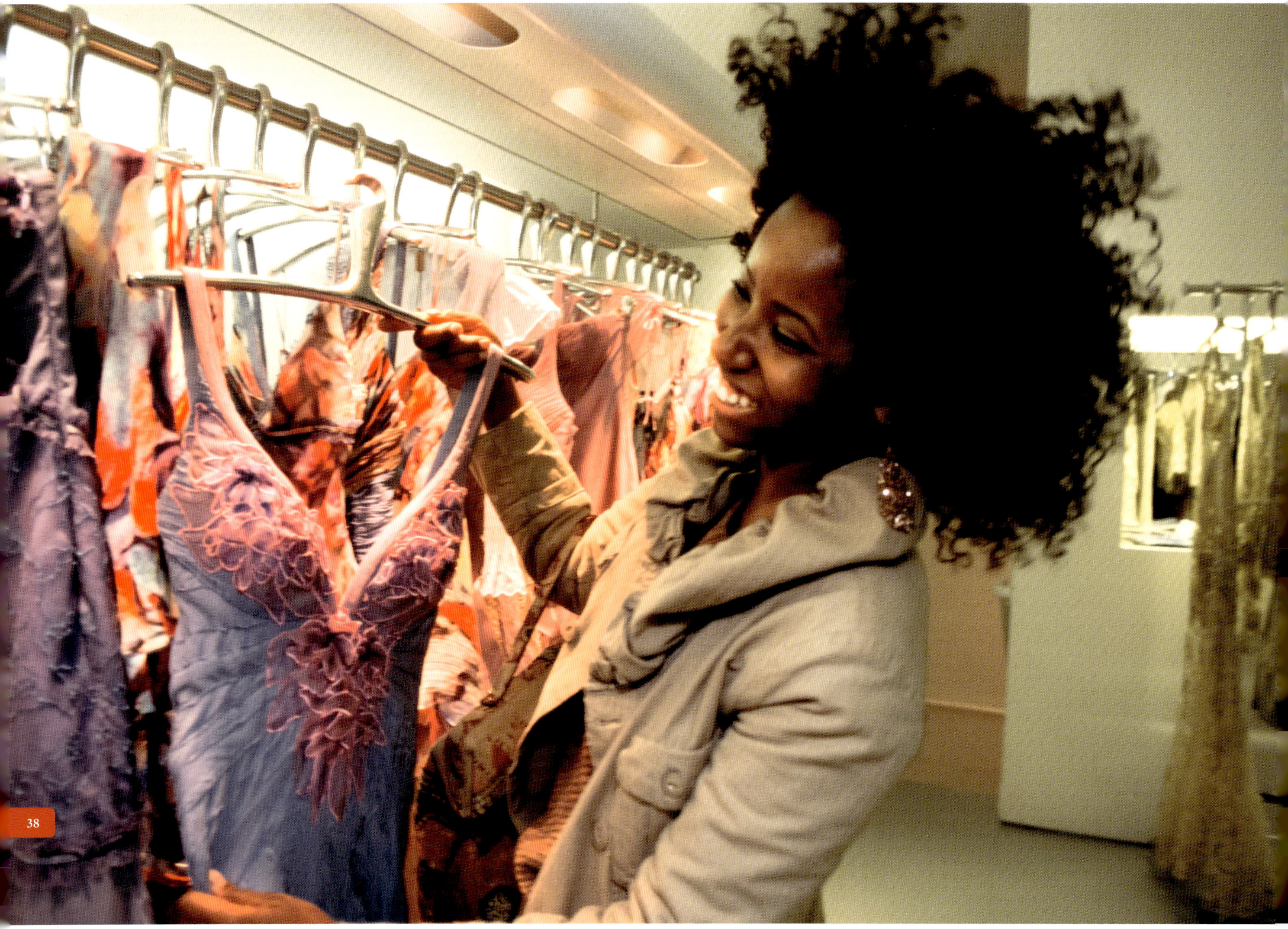

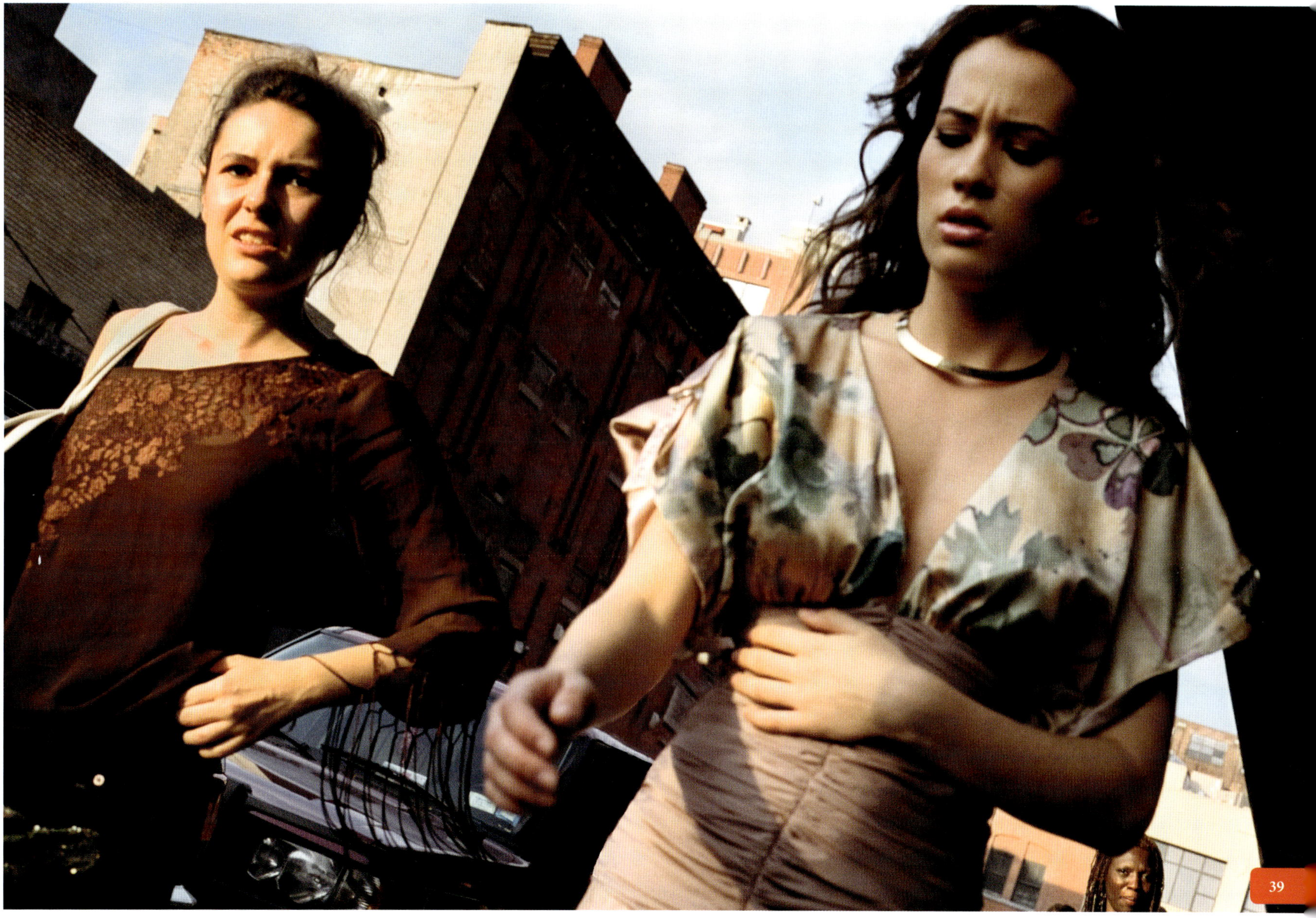

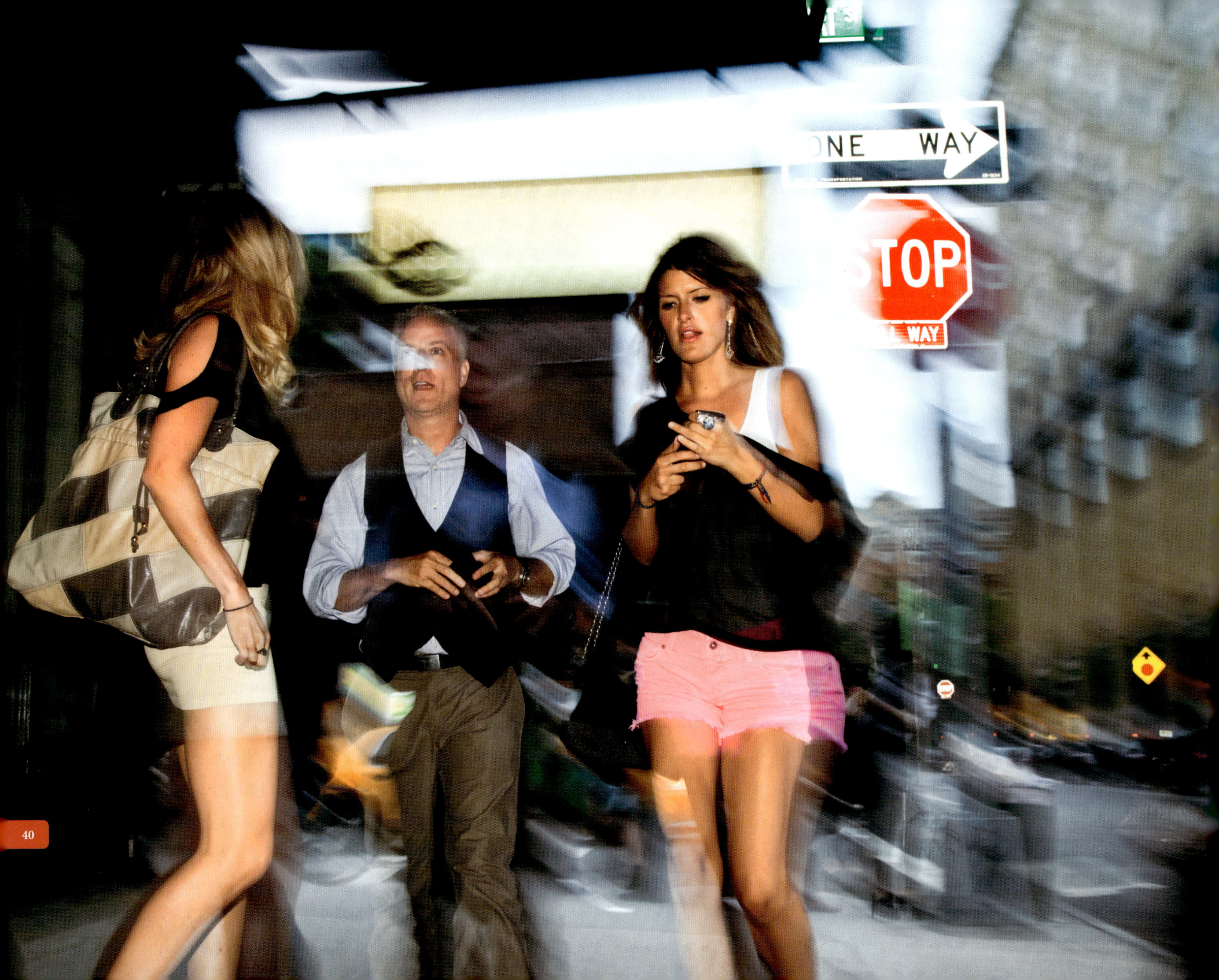
ONE WAY
STOP

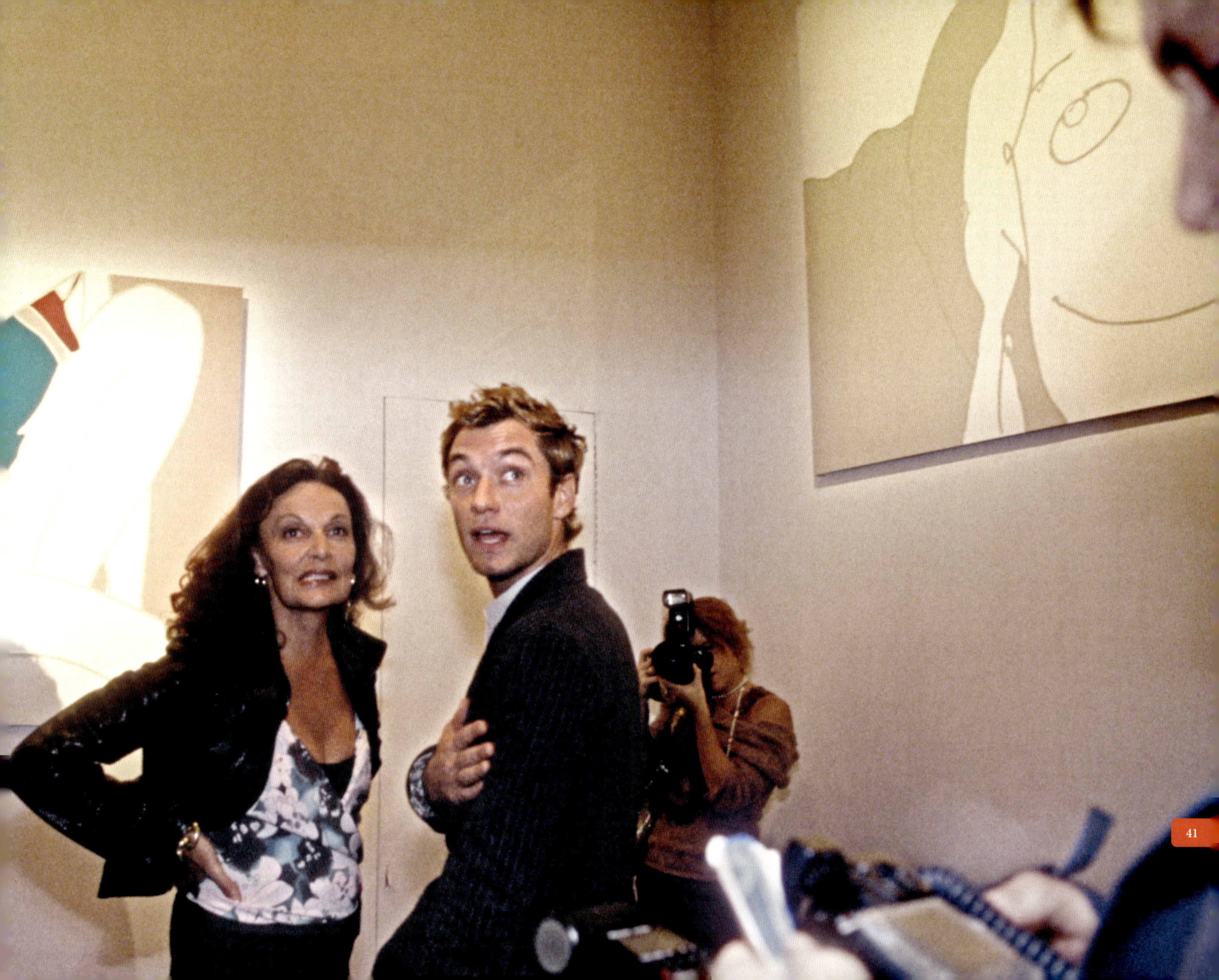

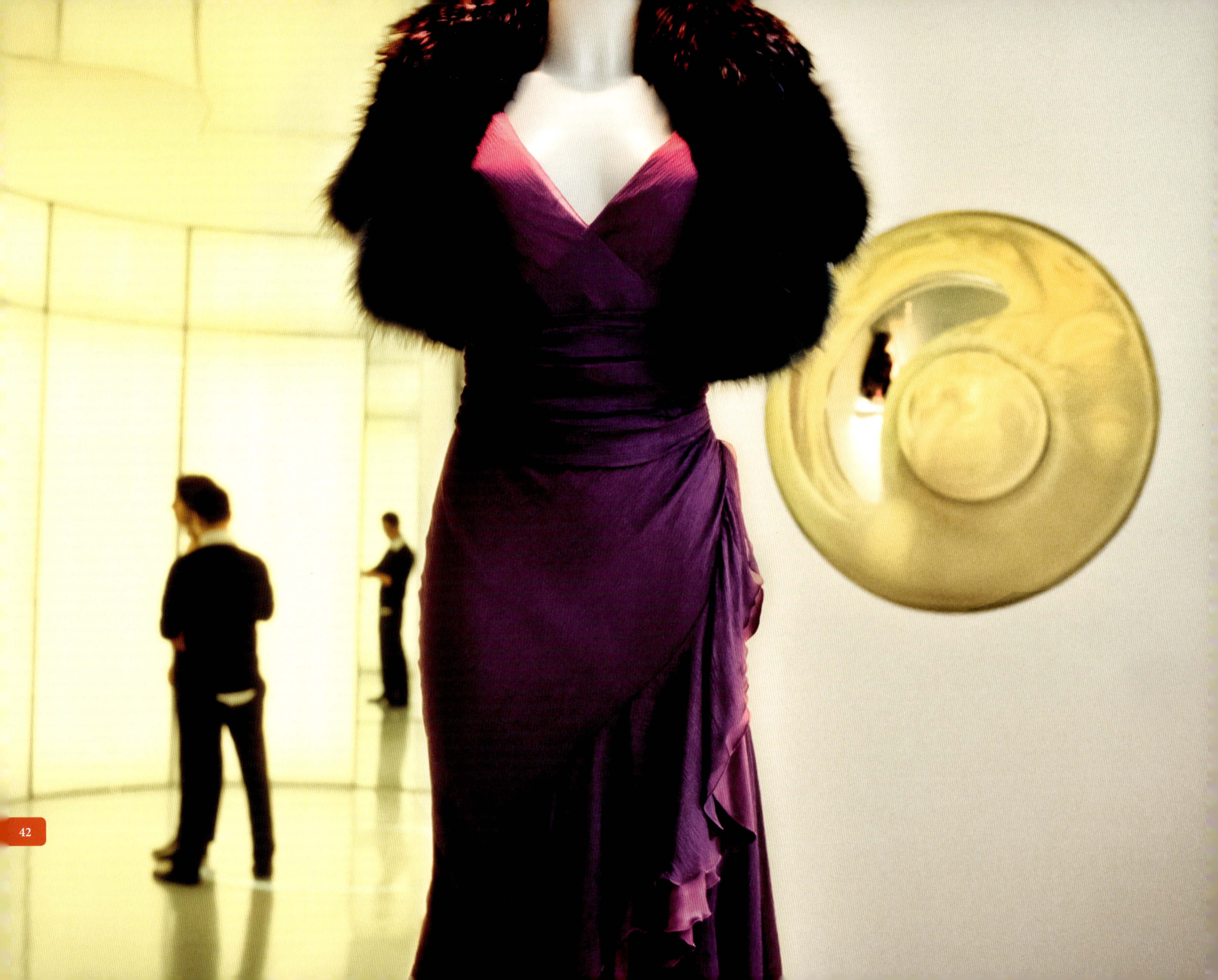

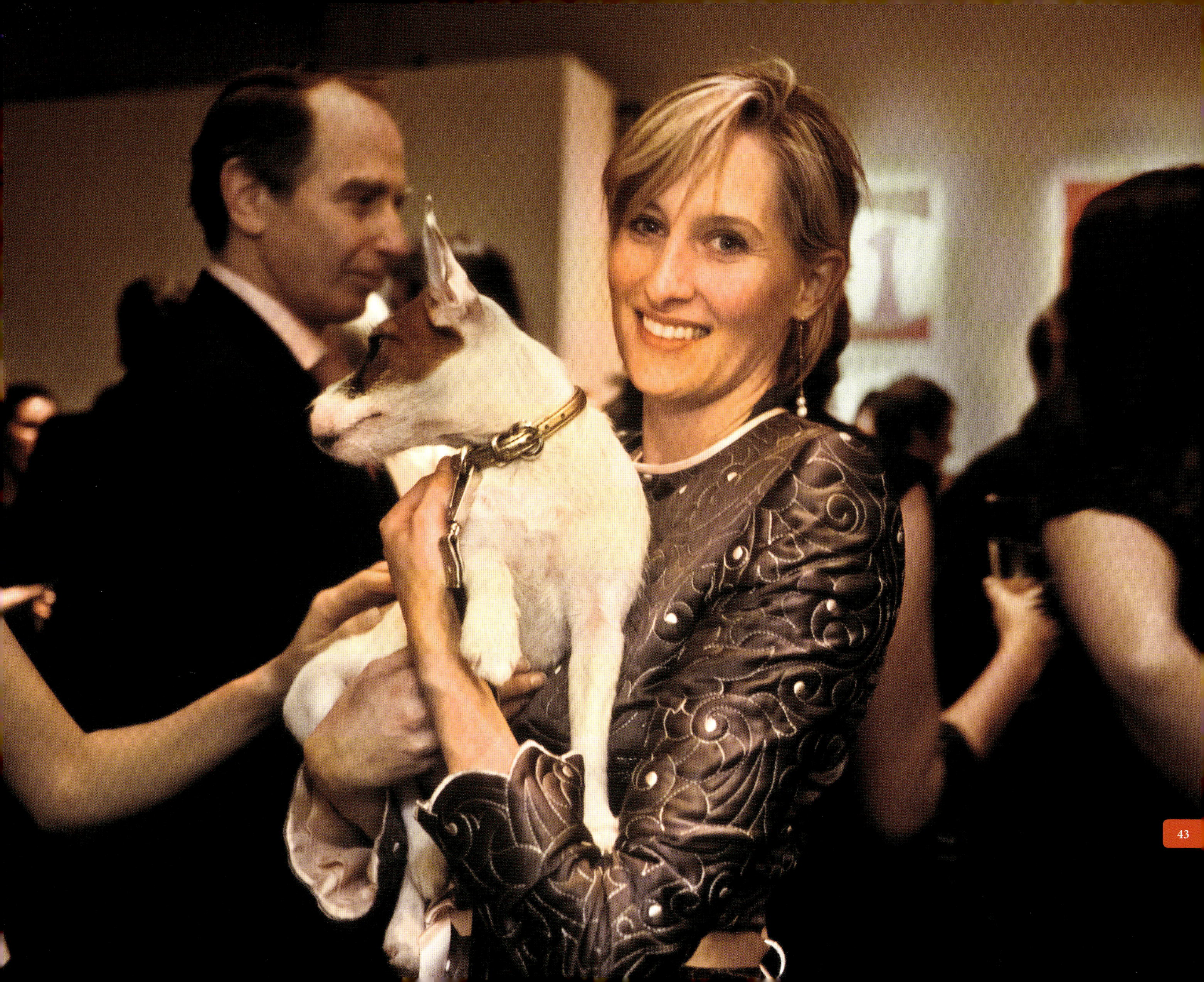

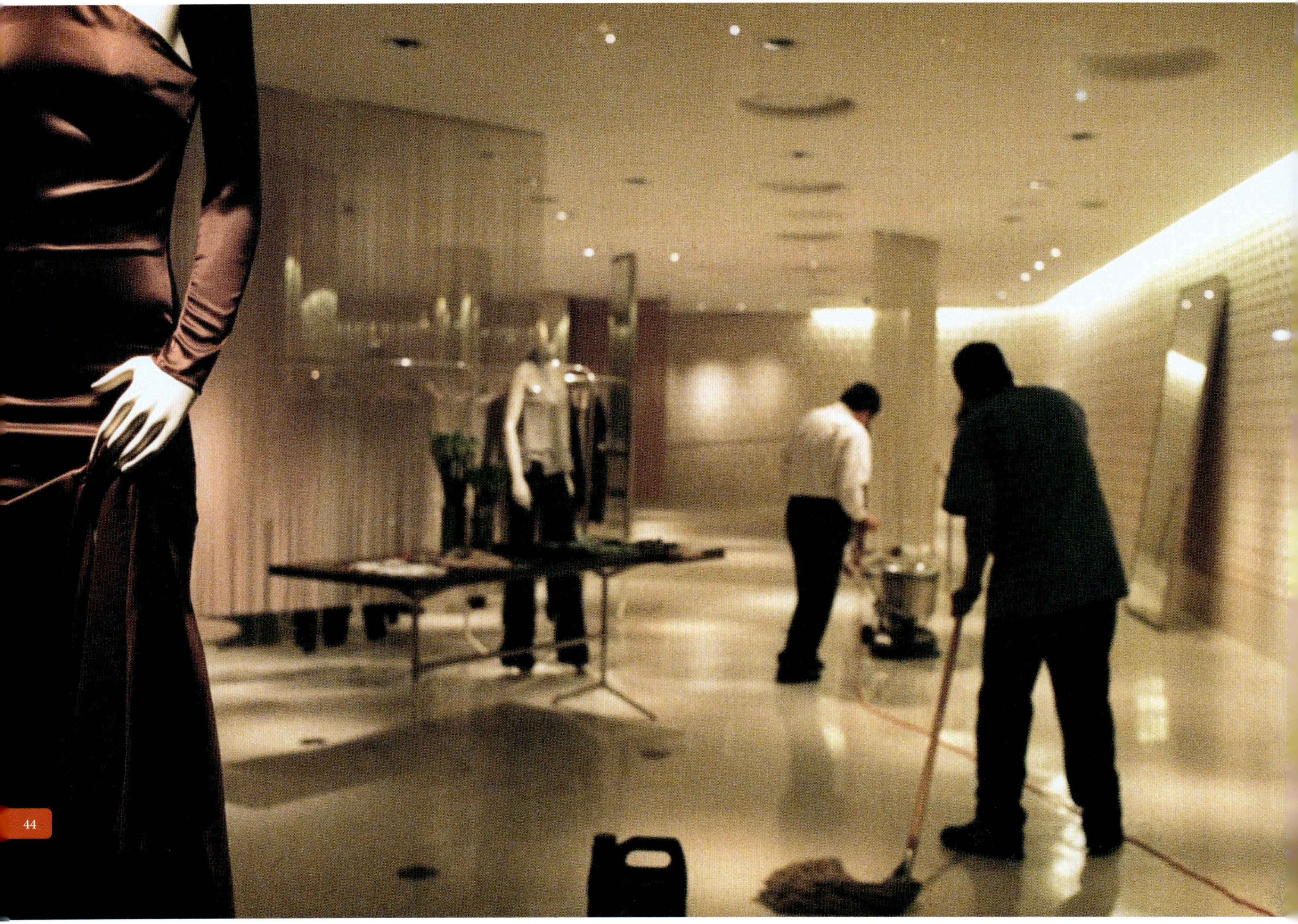

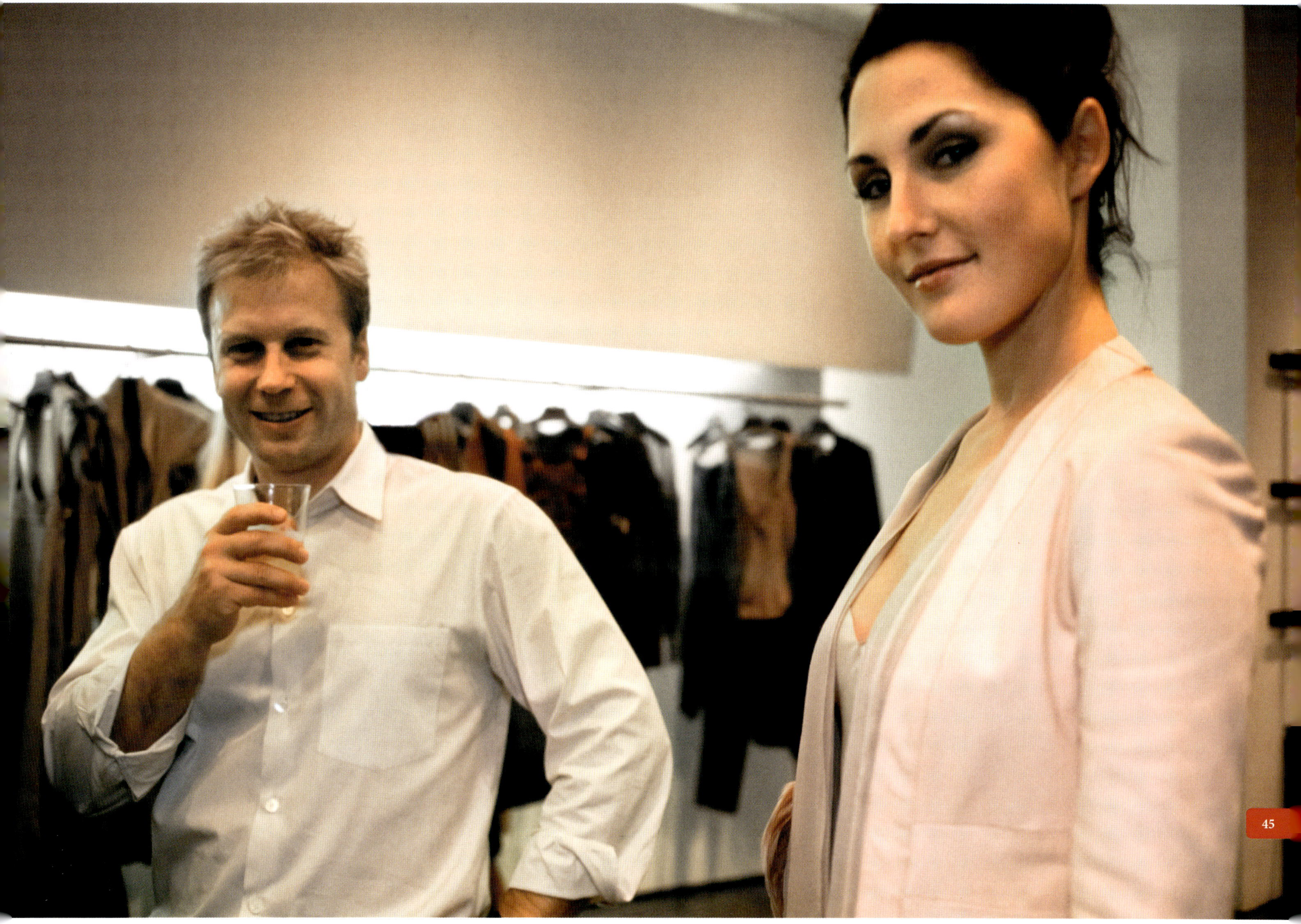

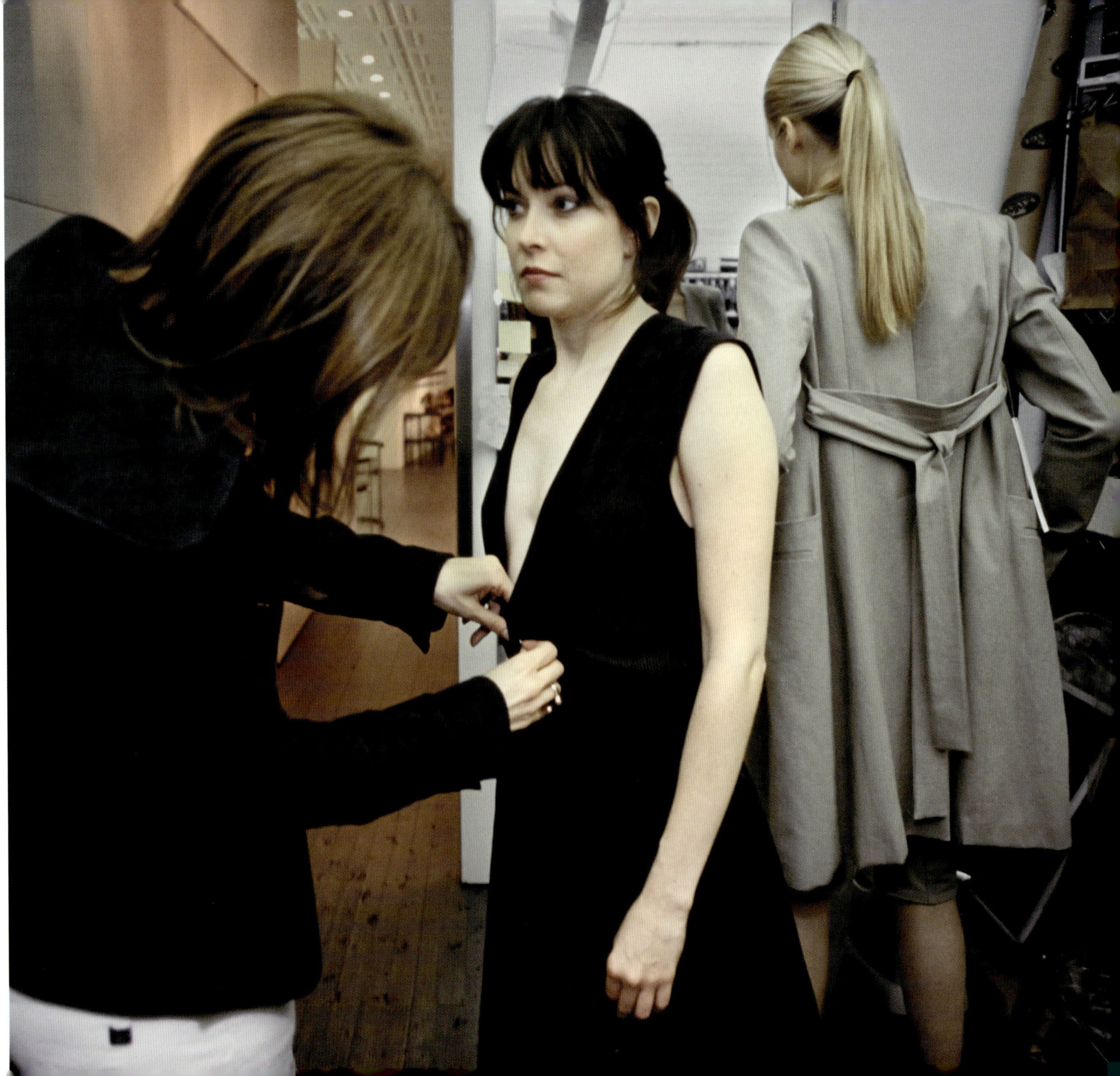

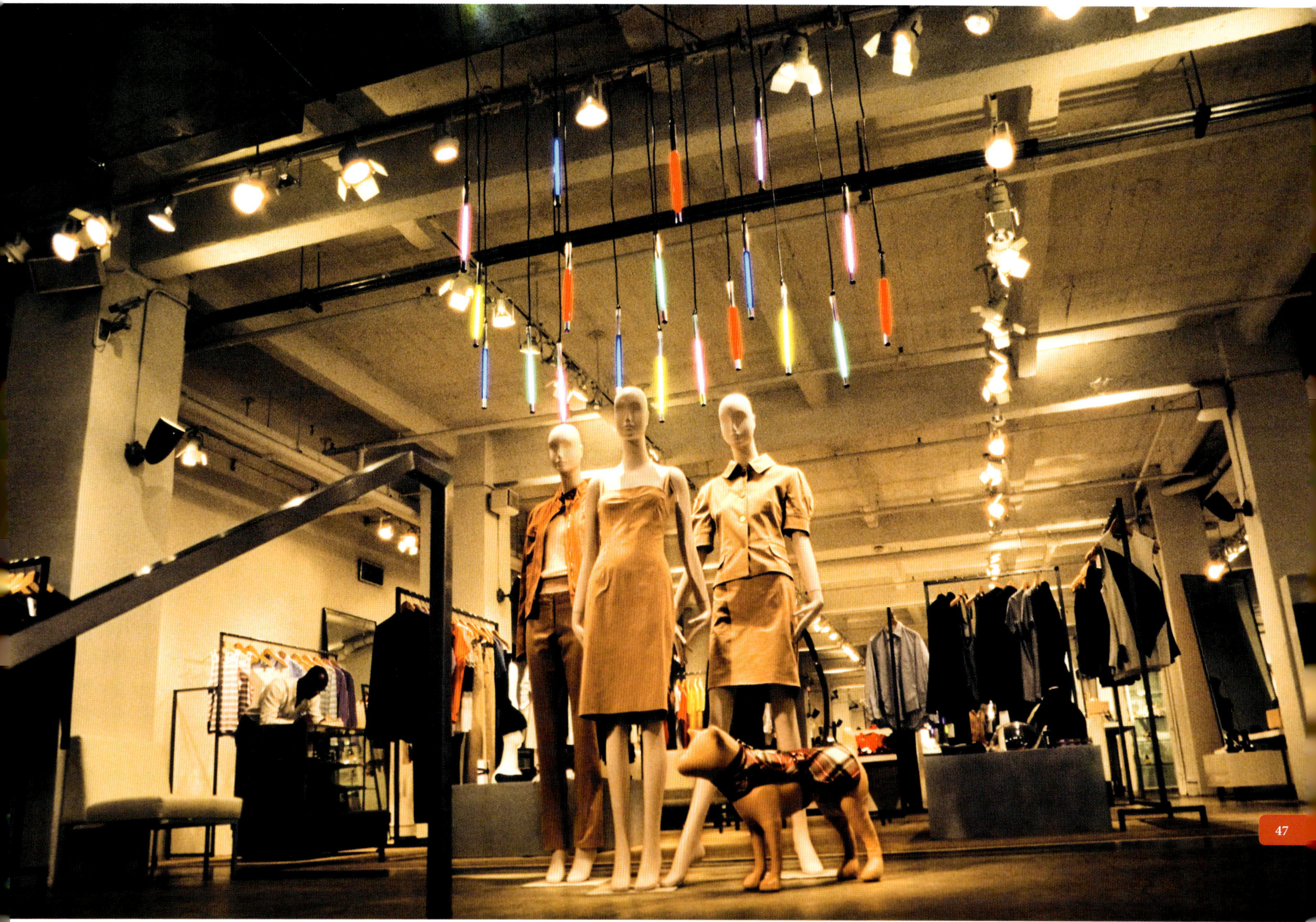

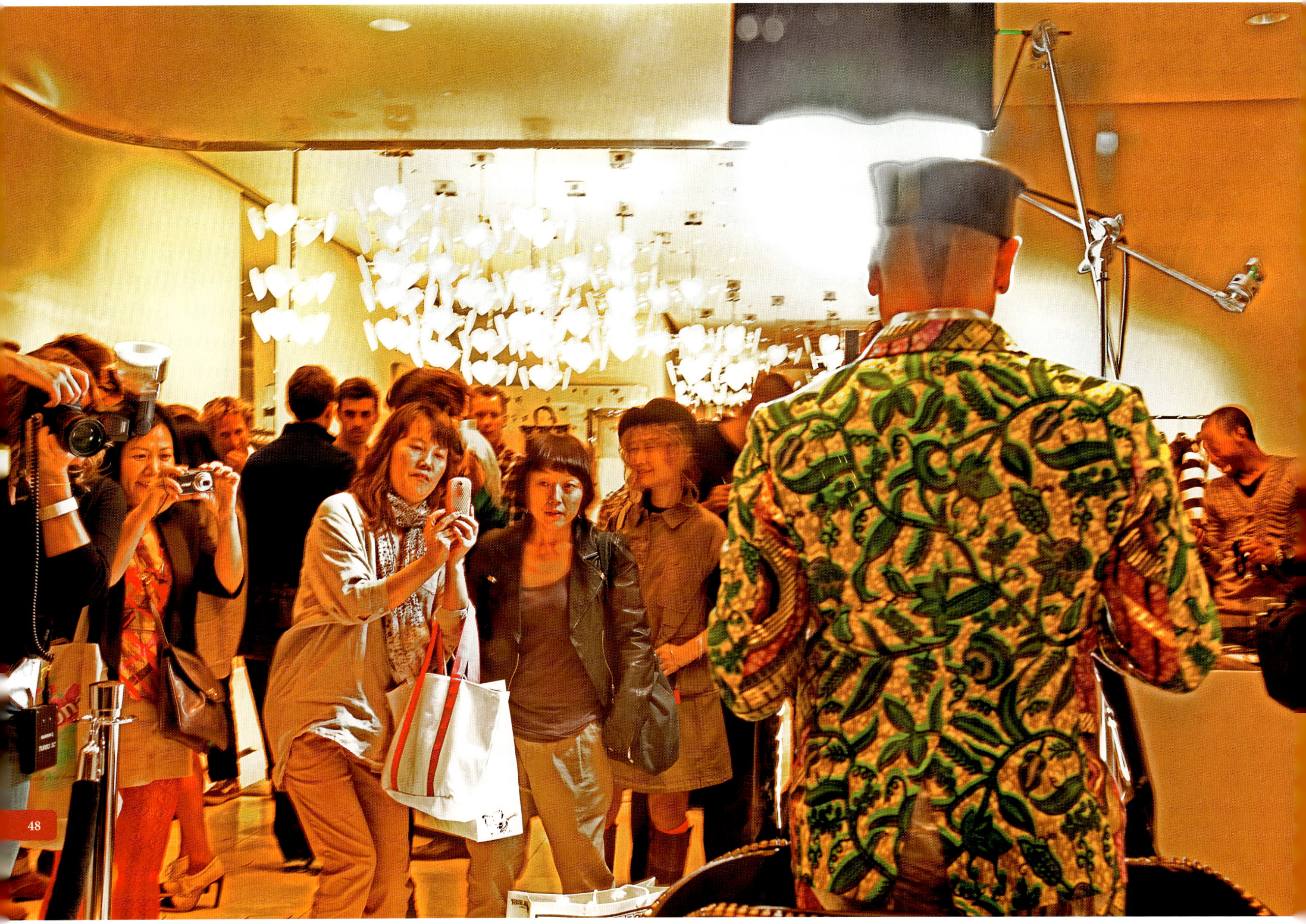

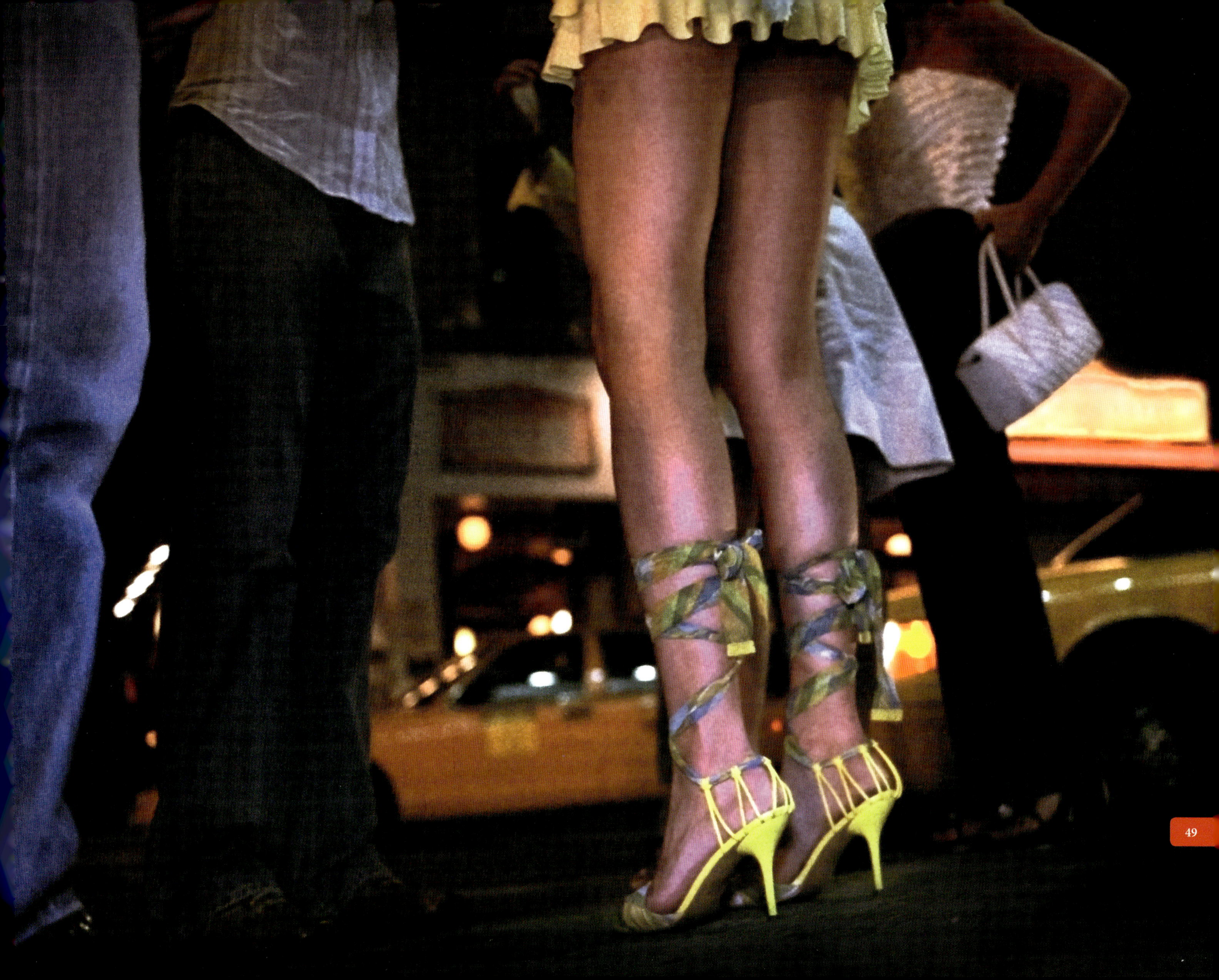

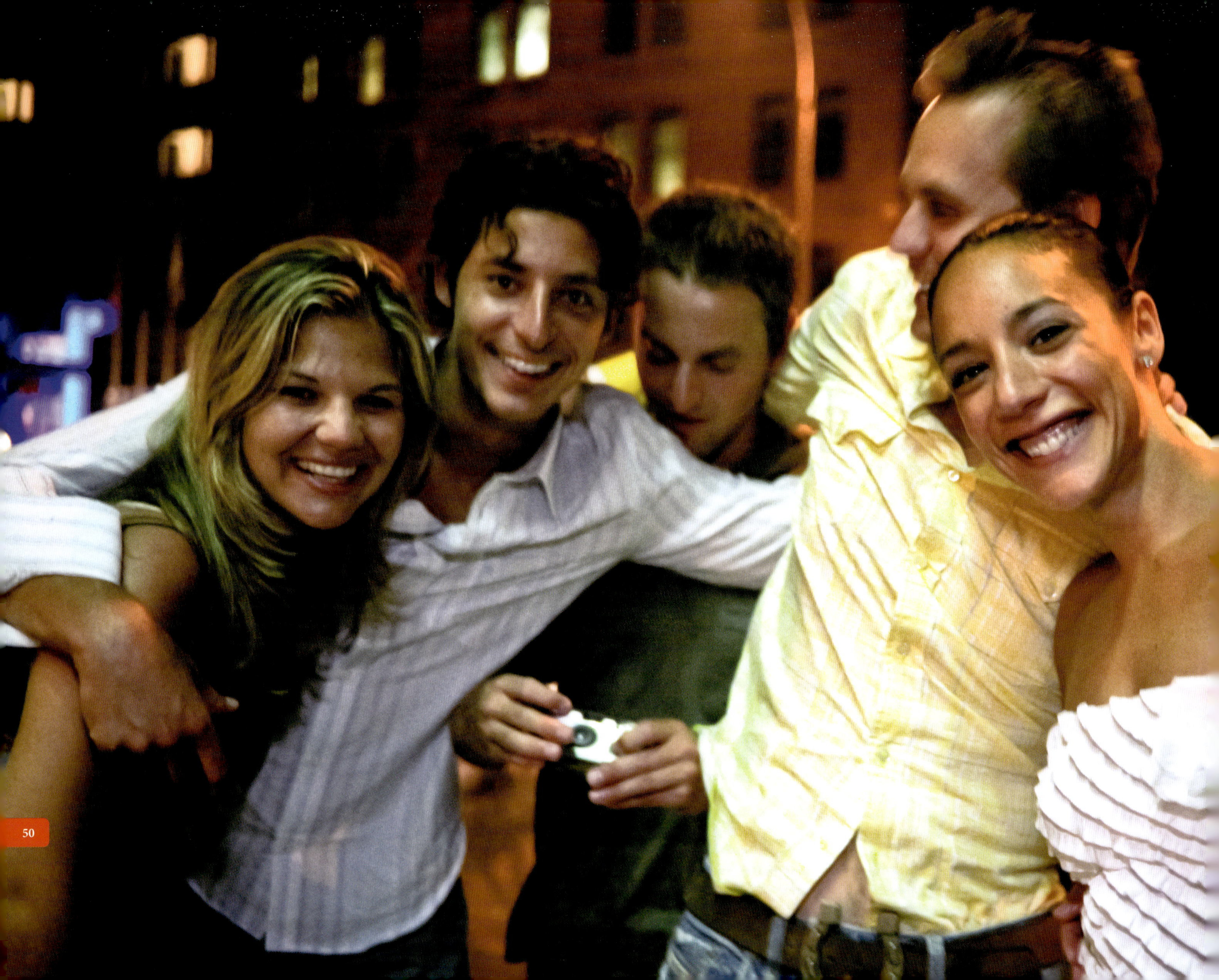

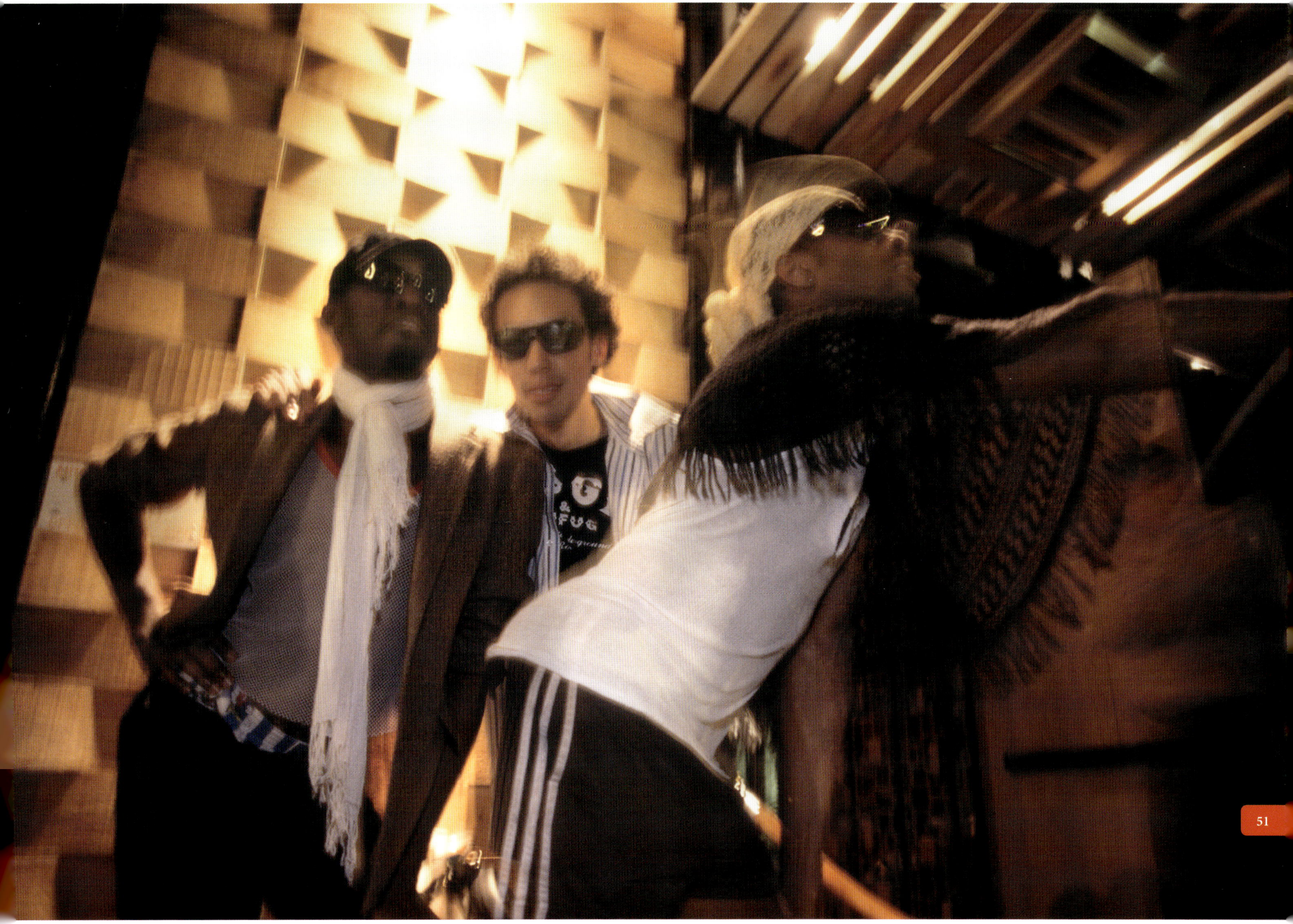

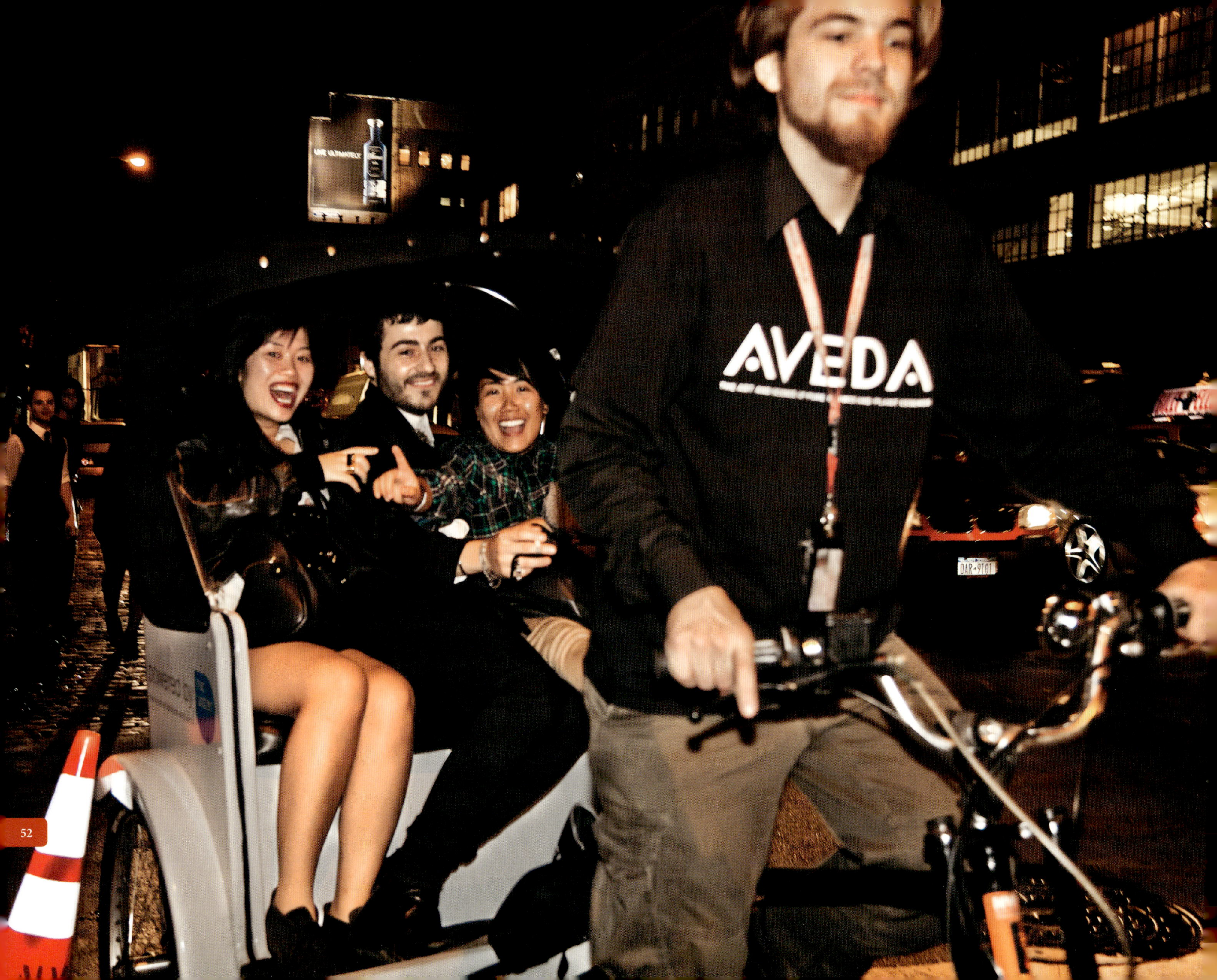
AVEDA

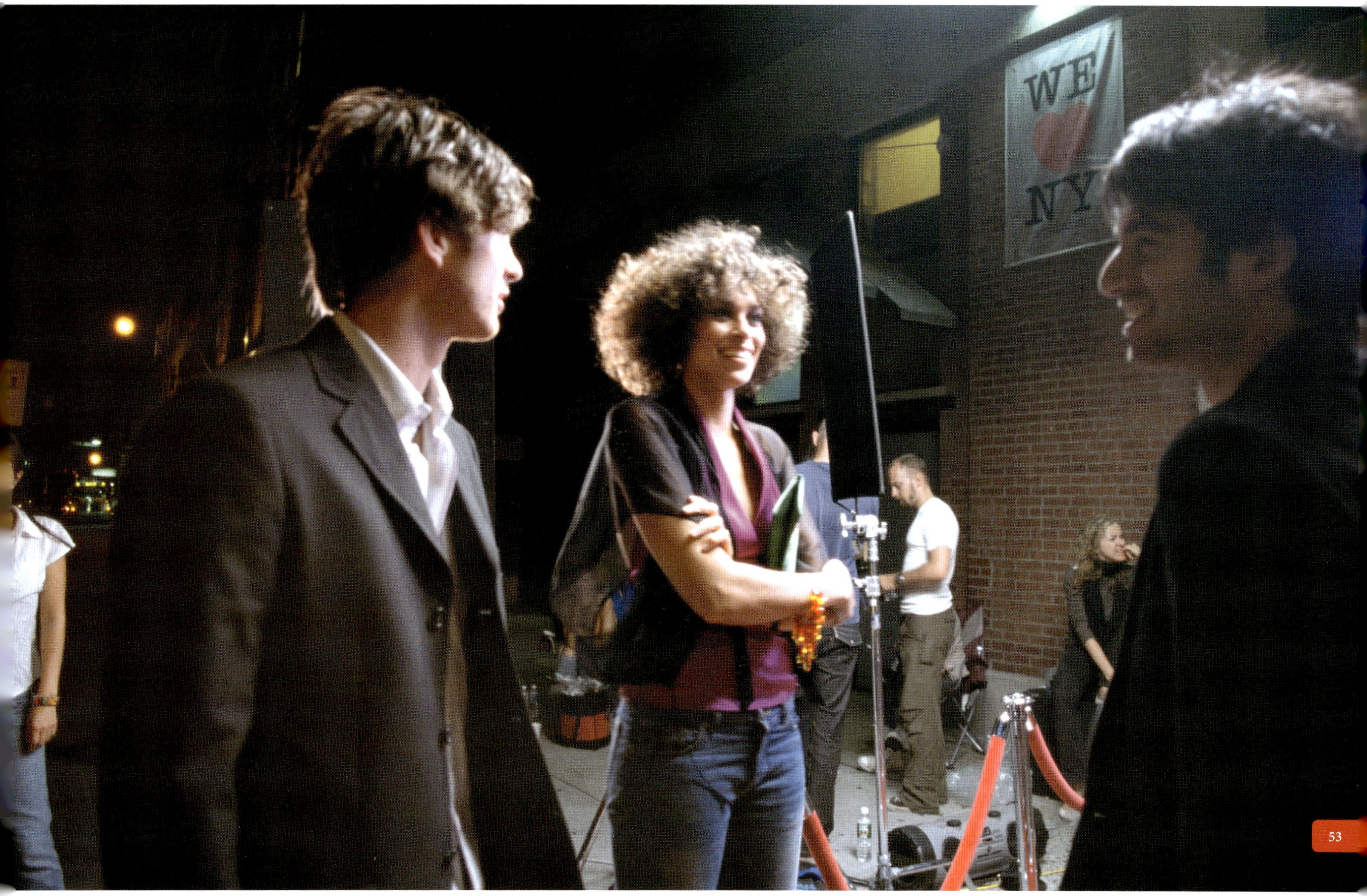
WE
NY

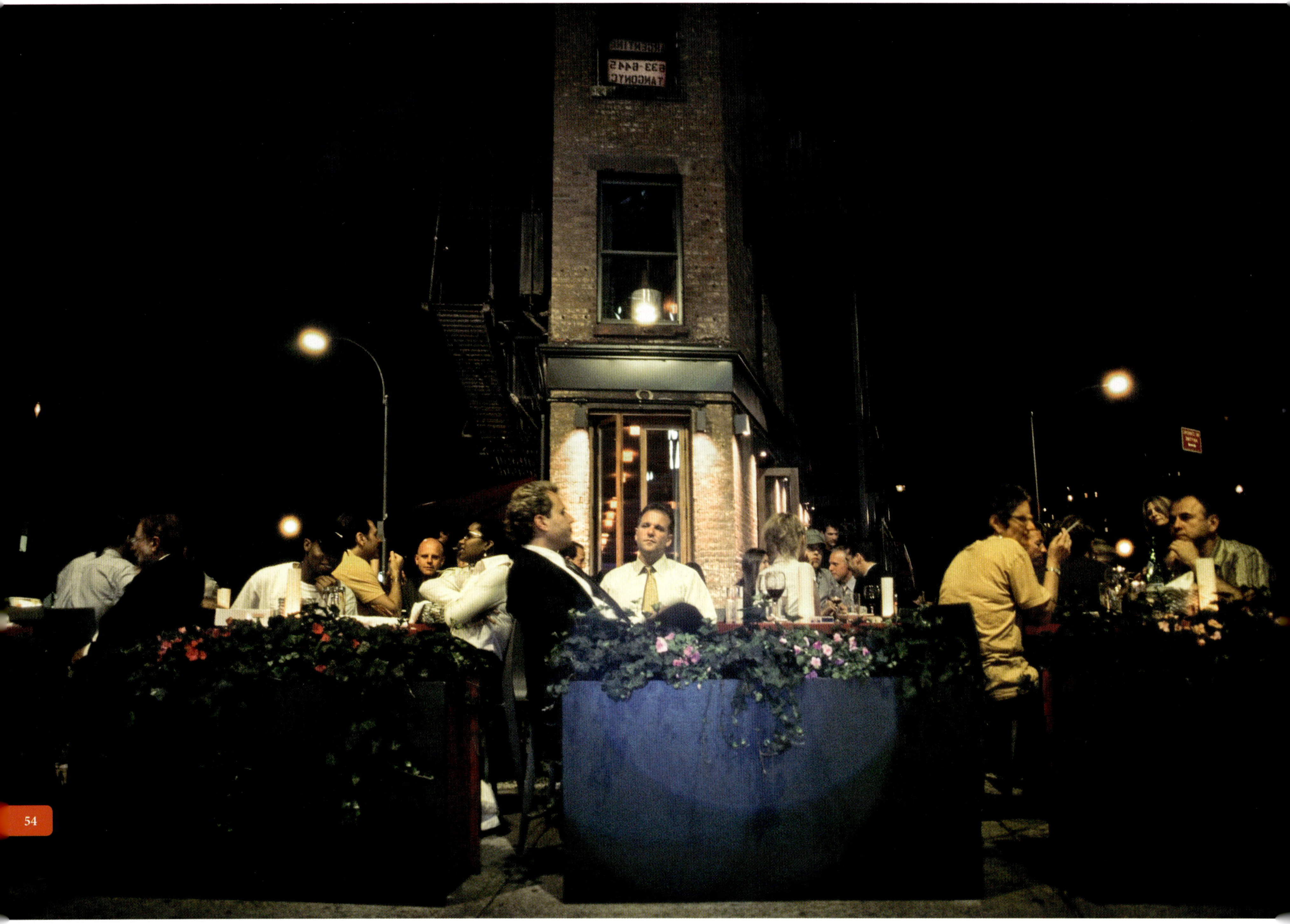

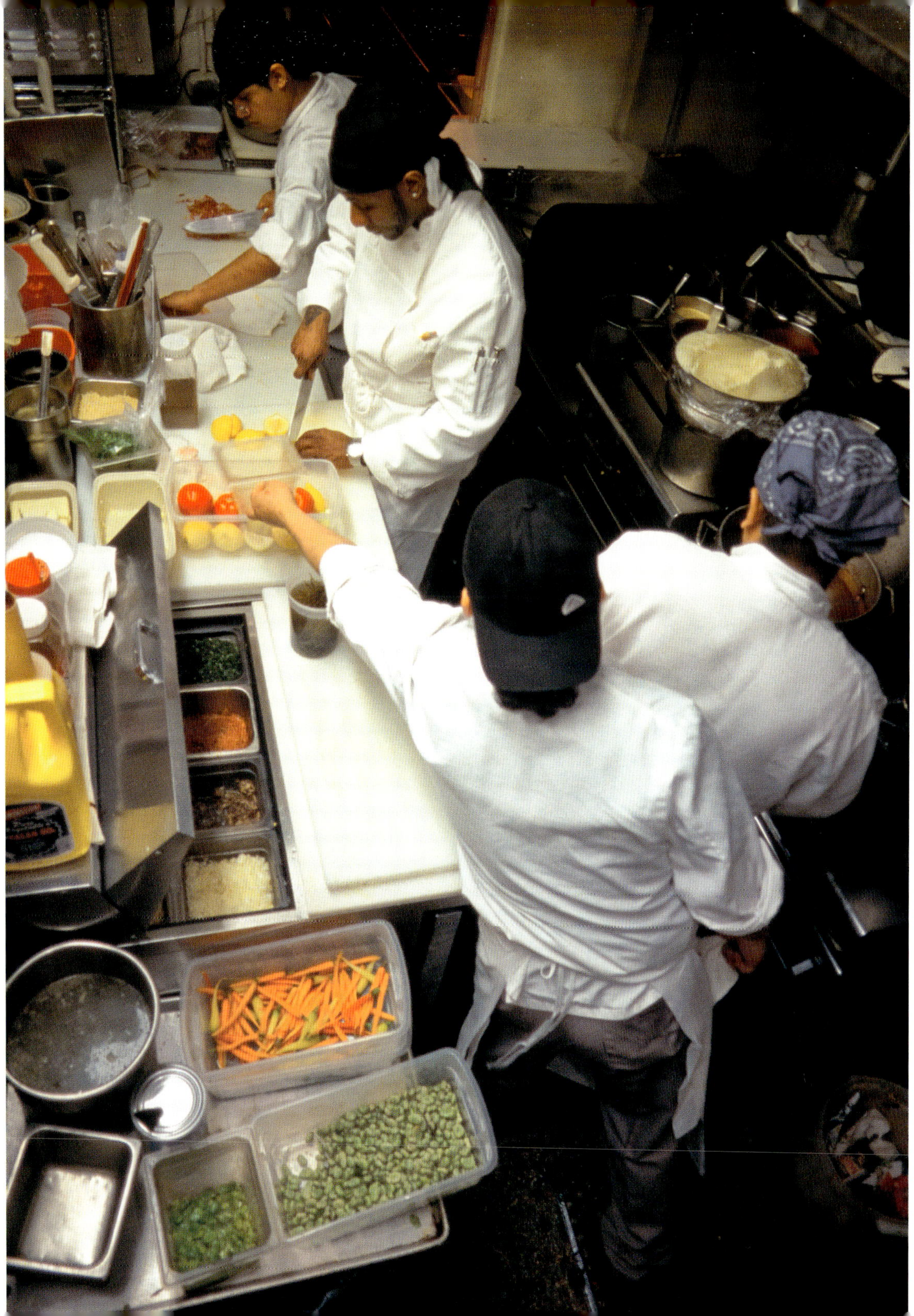

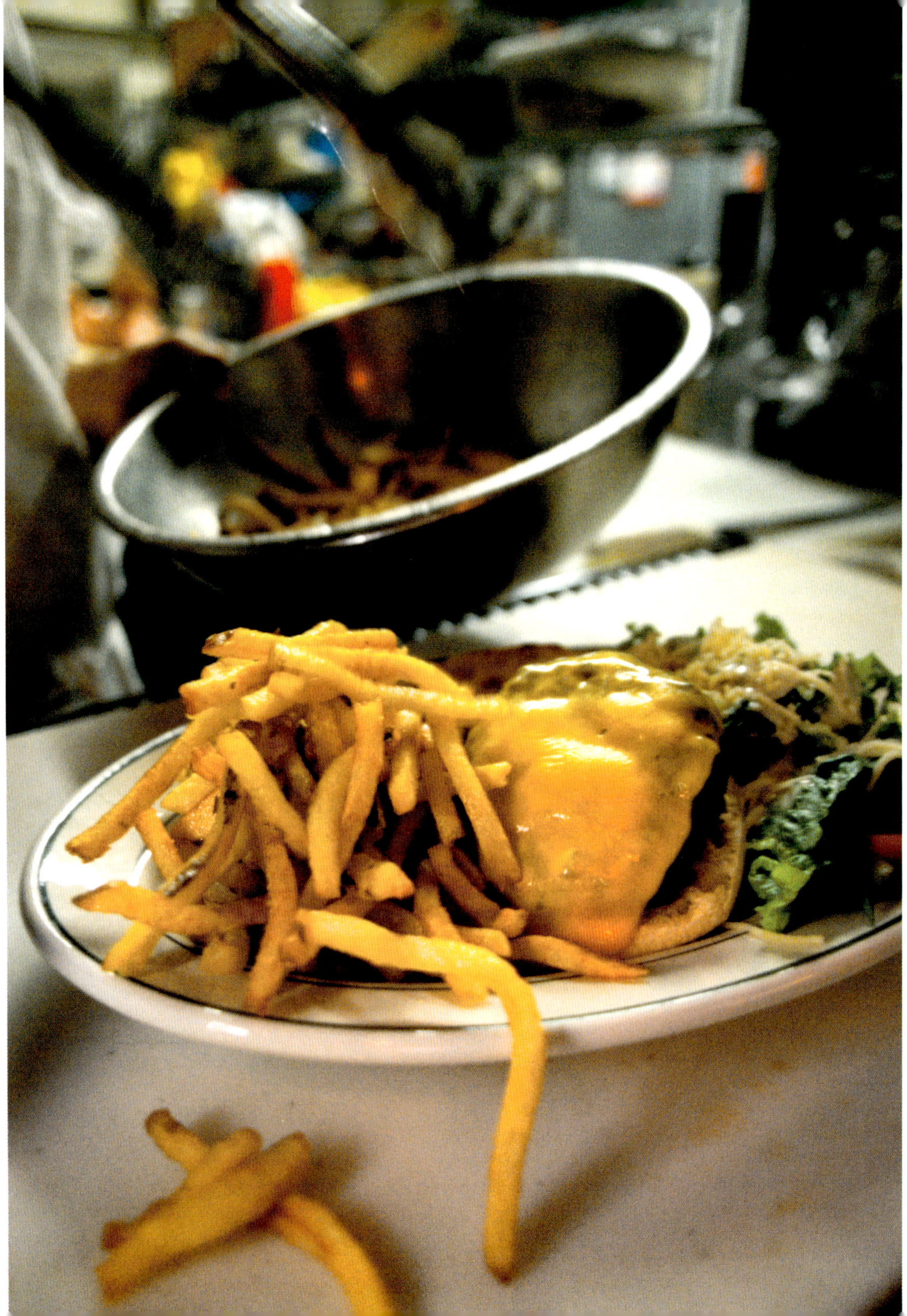

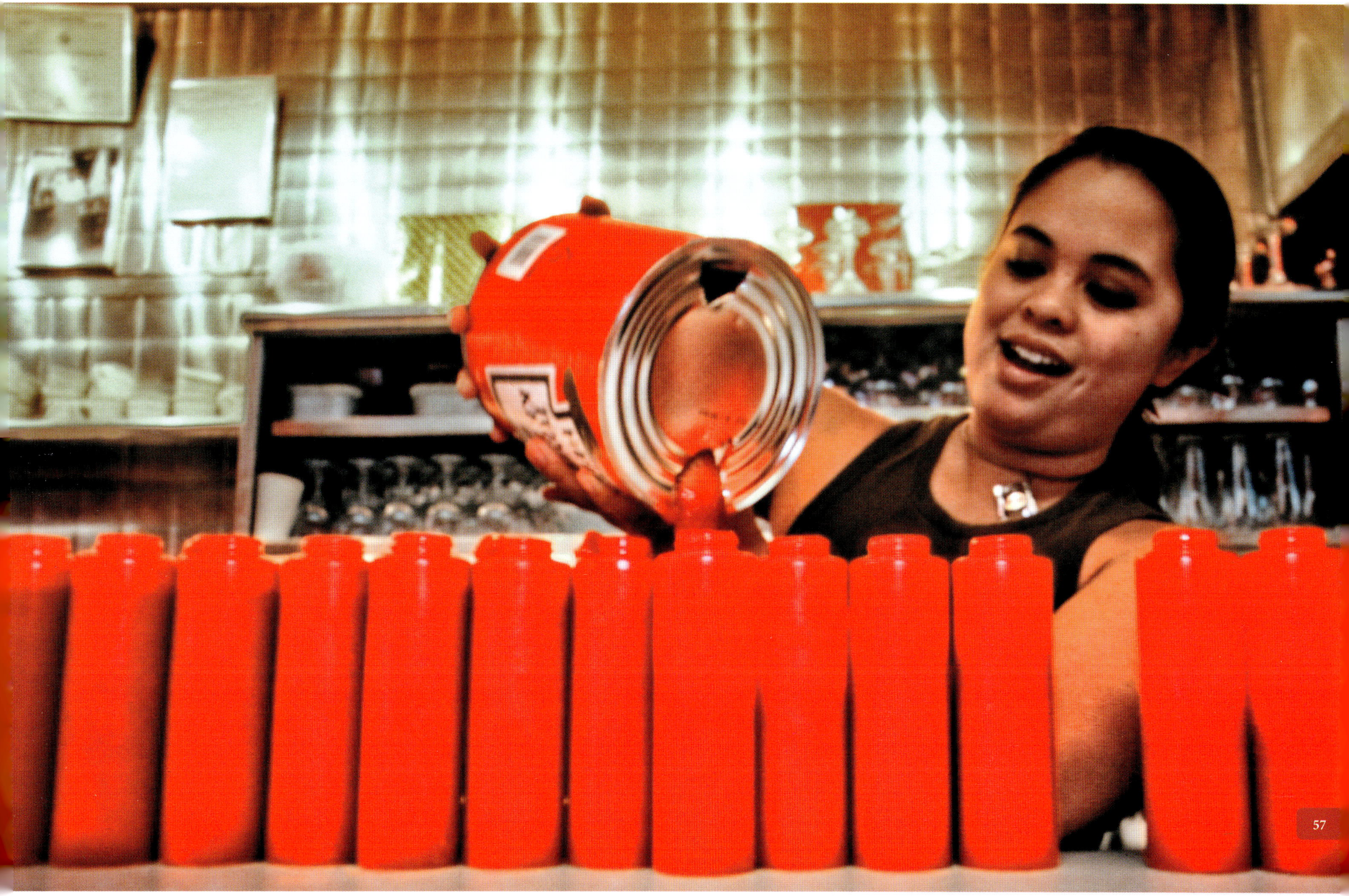

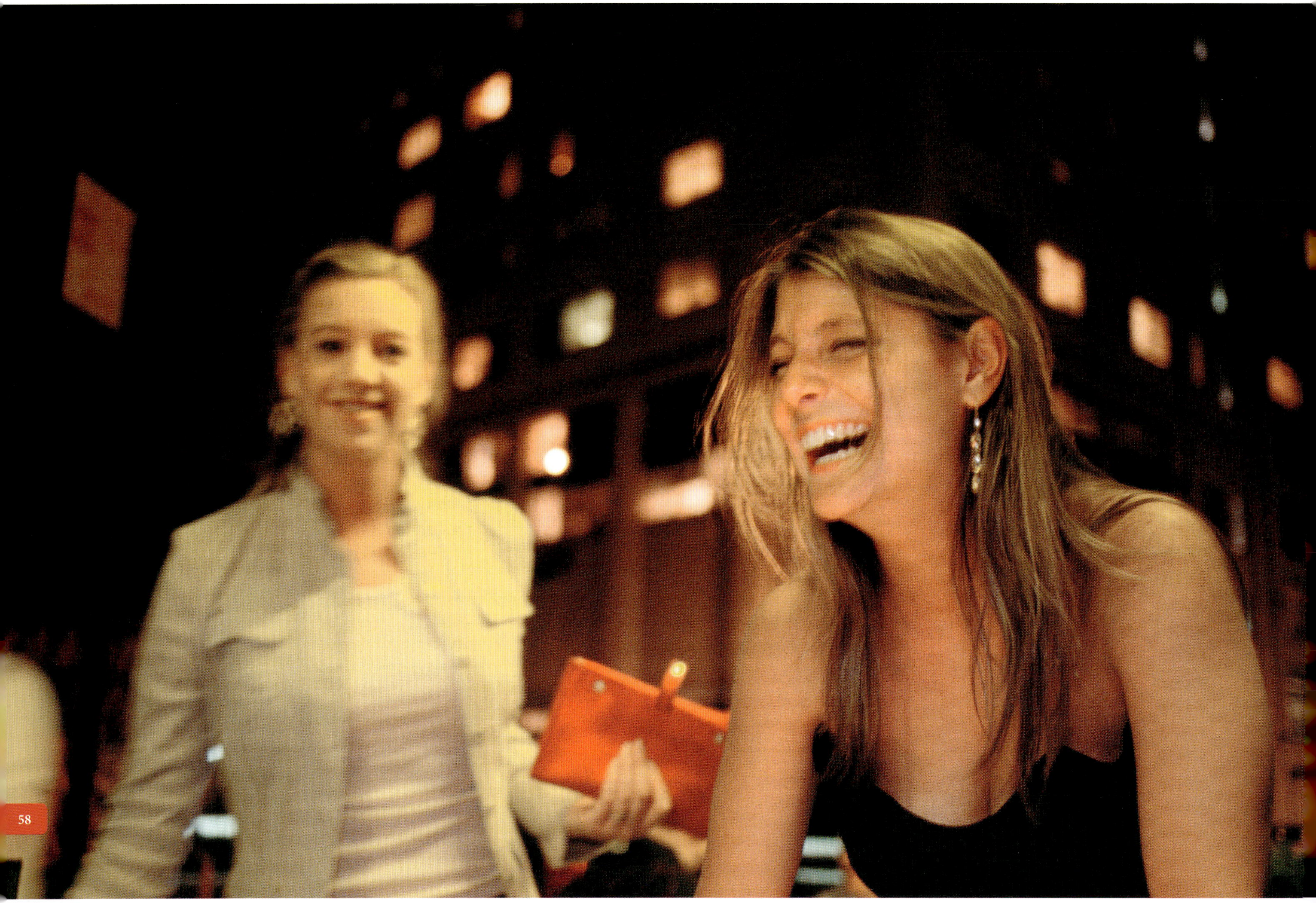

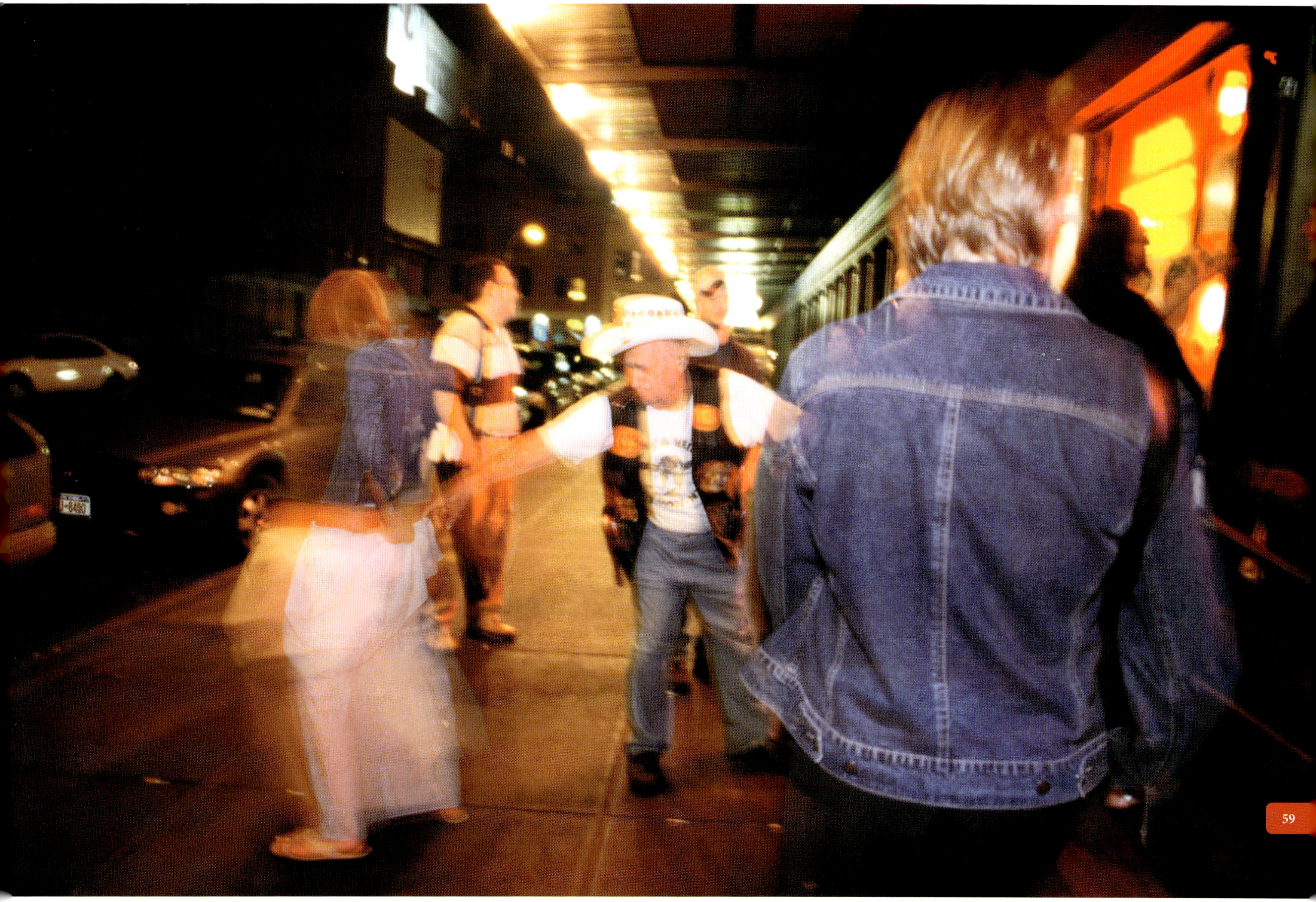

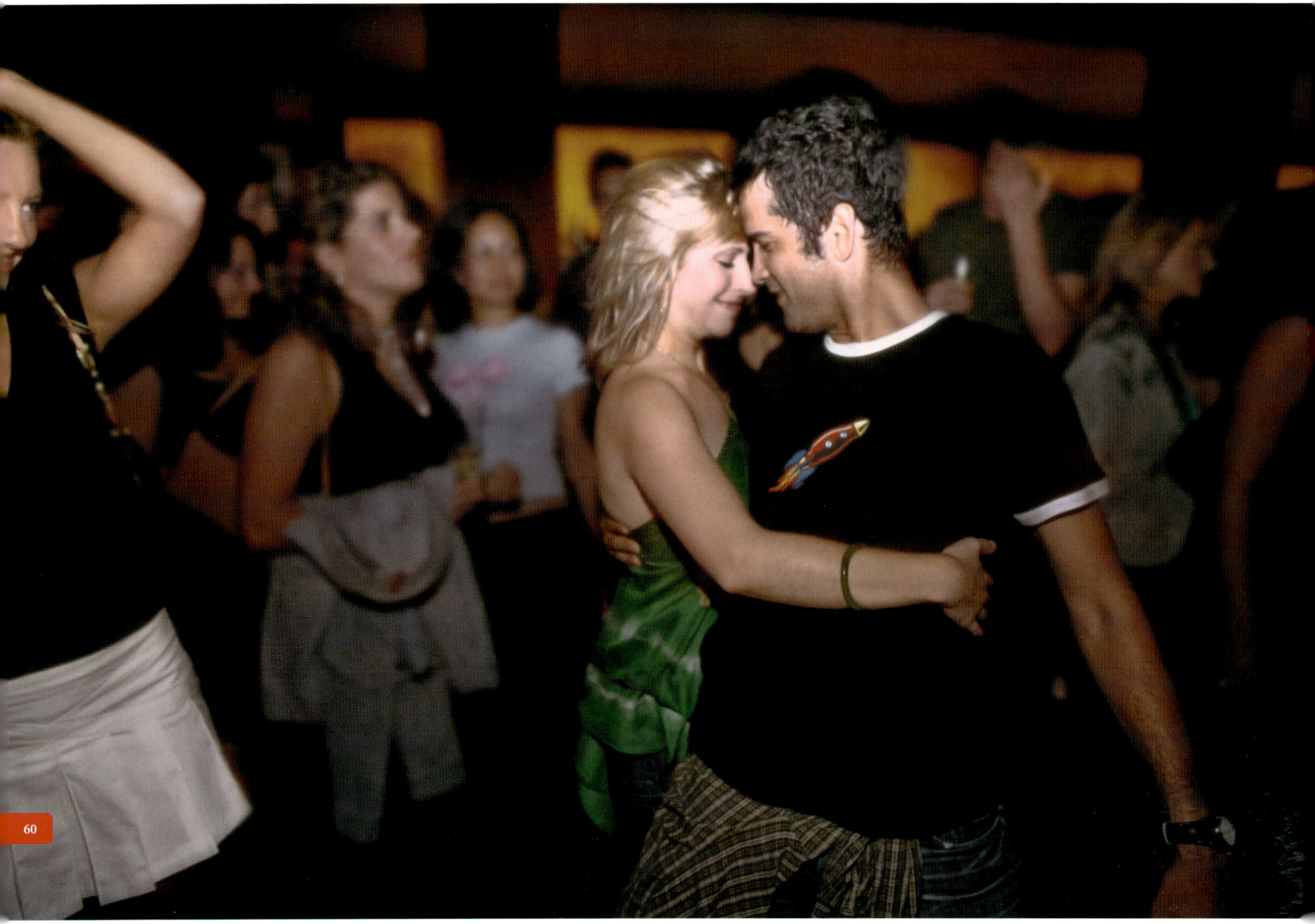

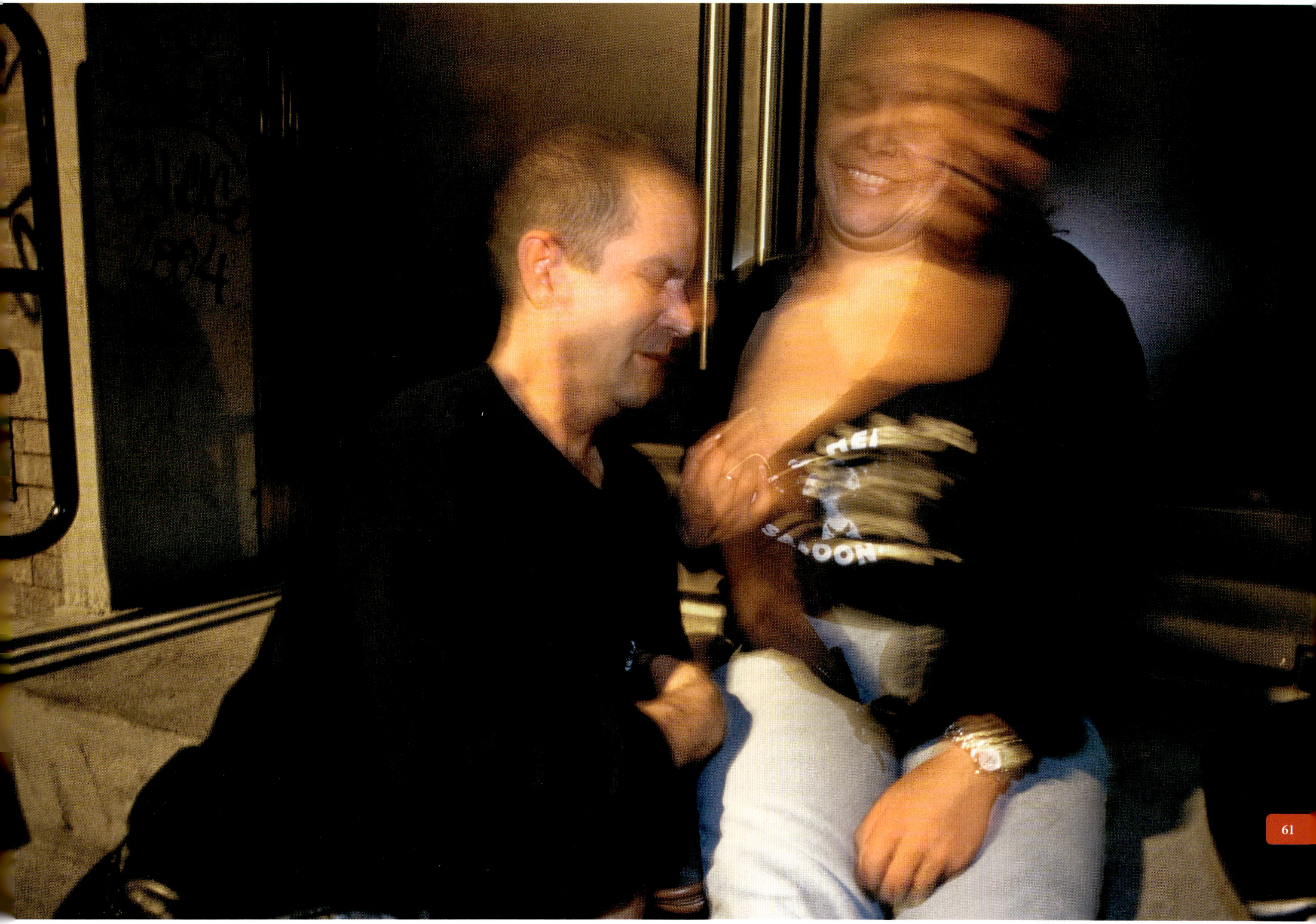

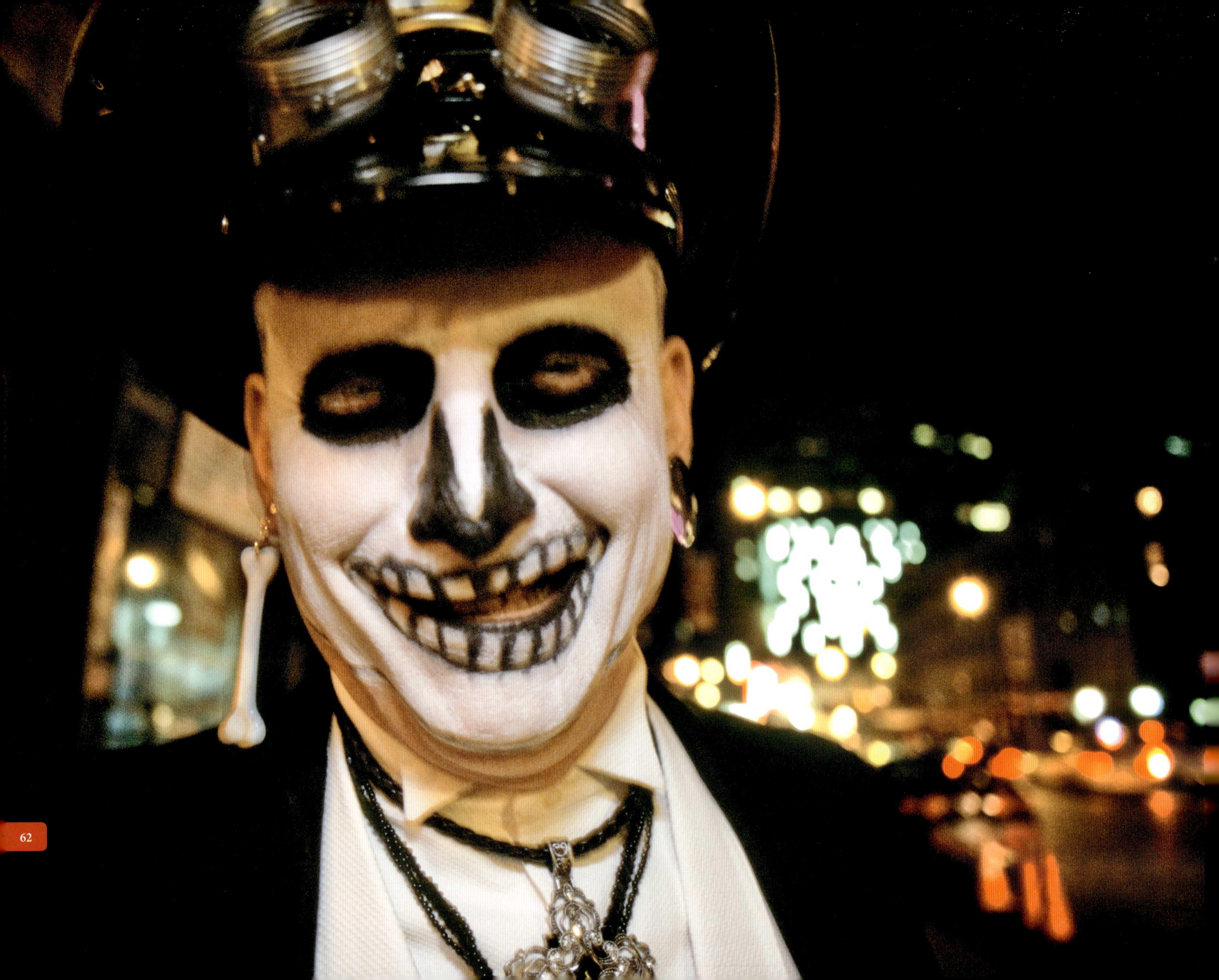

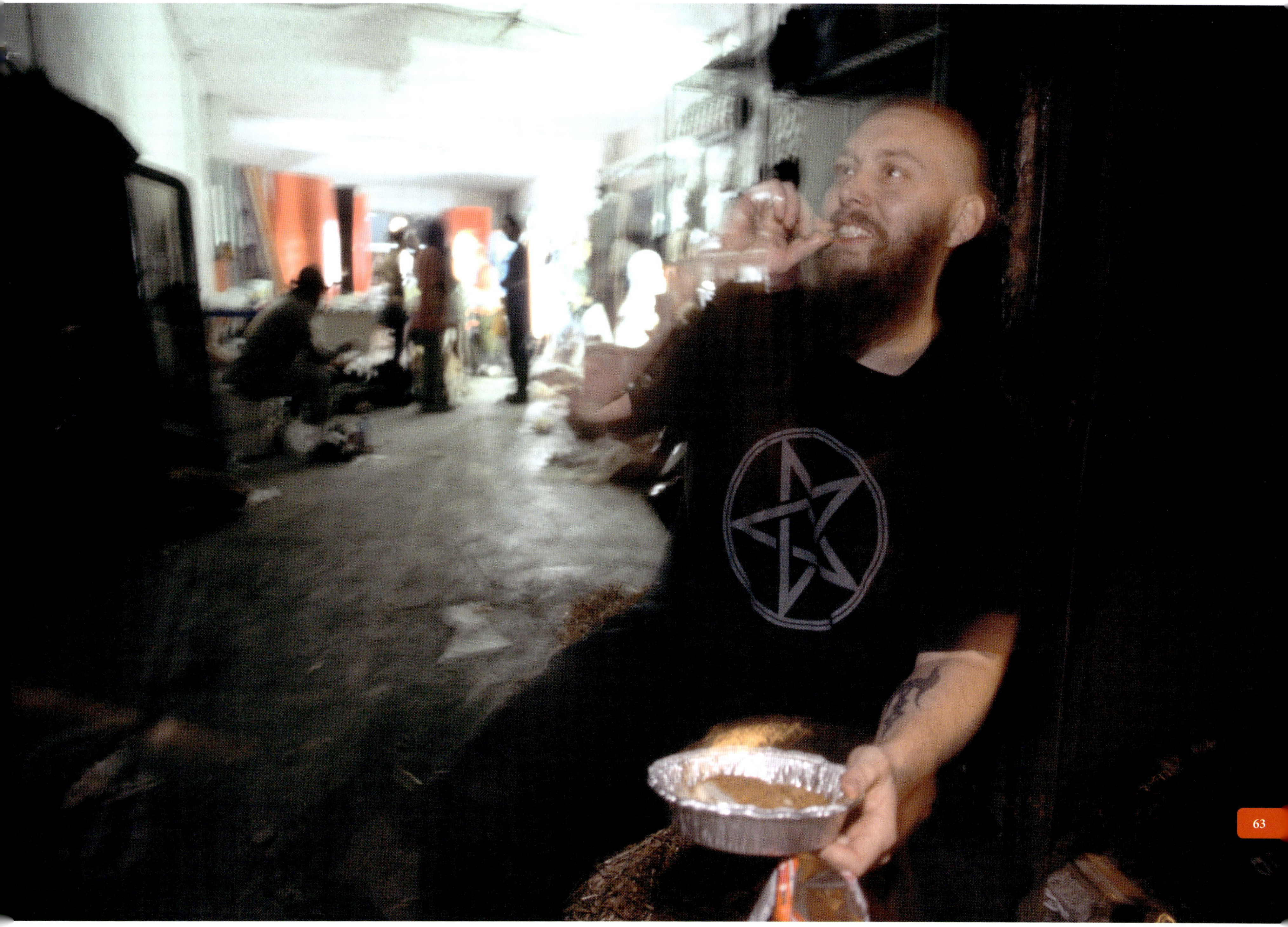

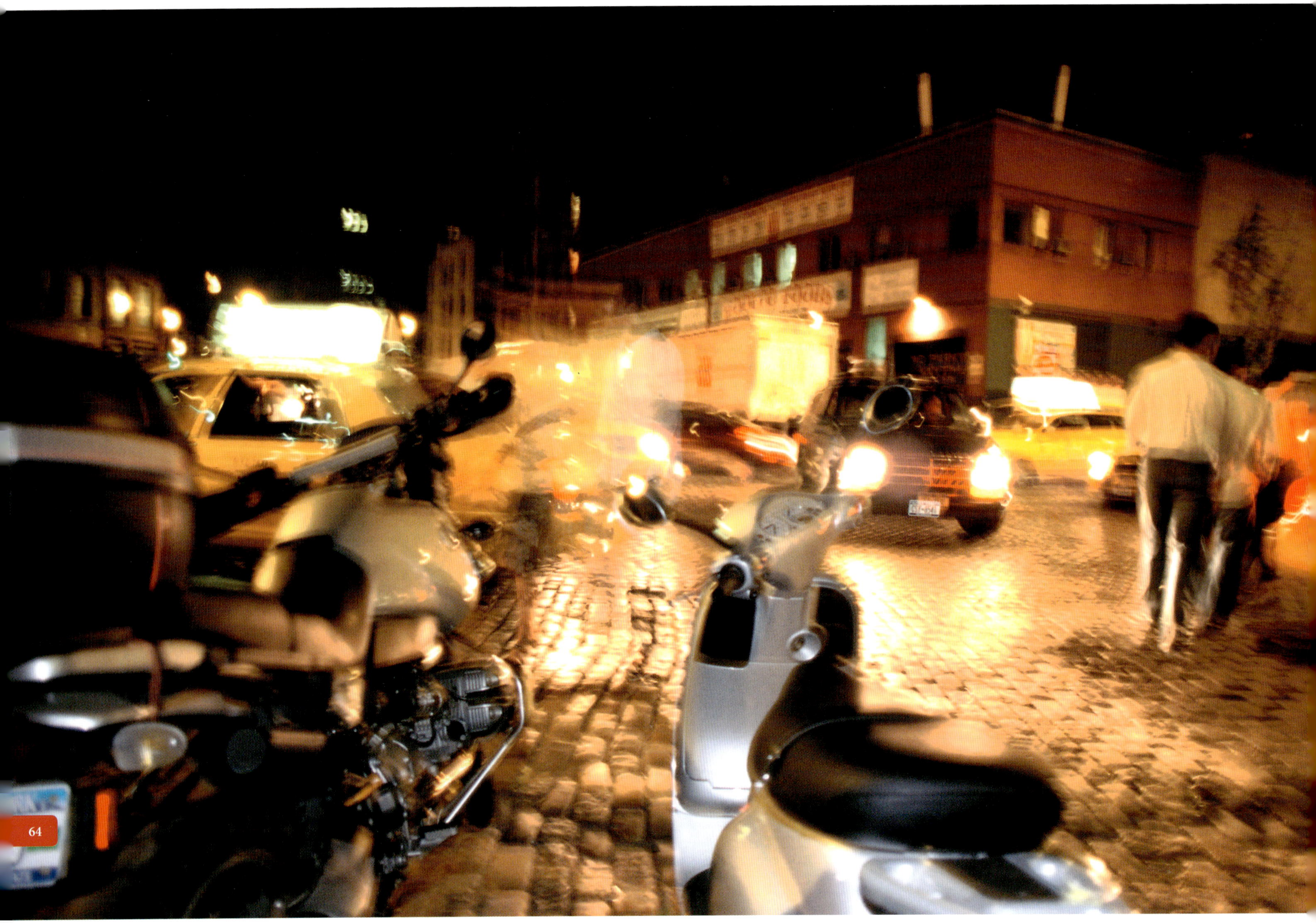

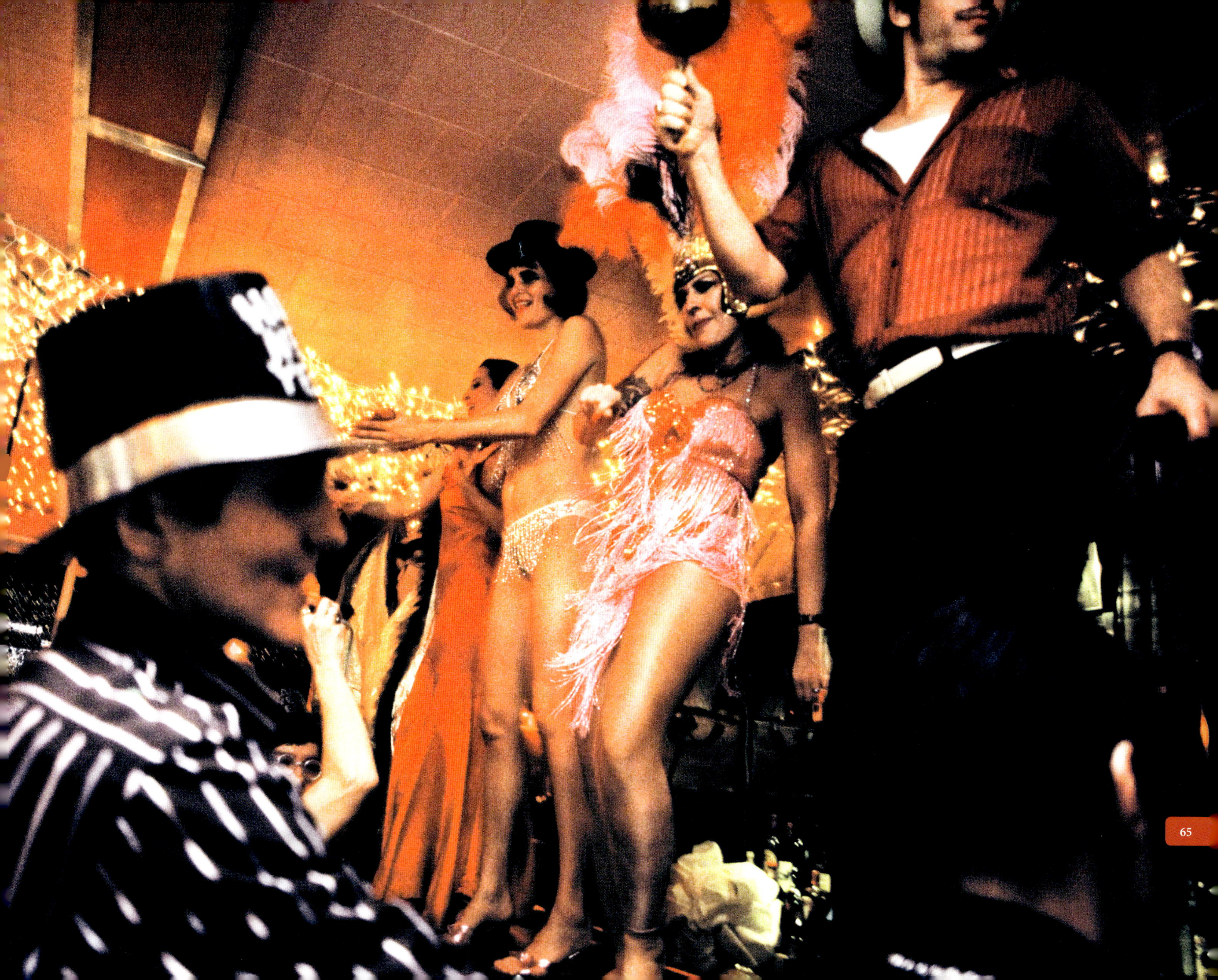

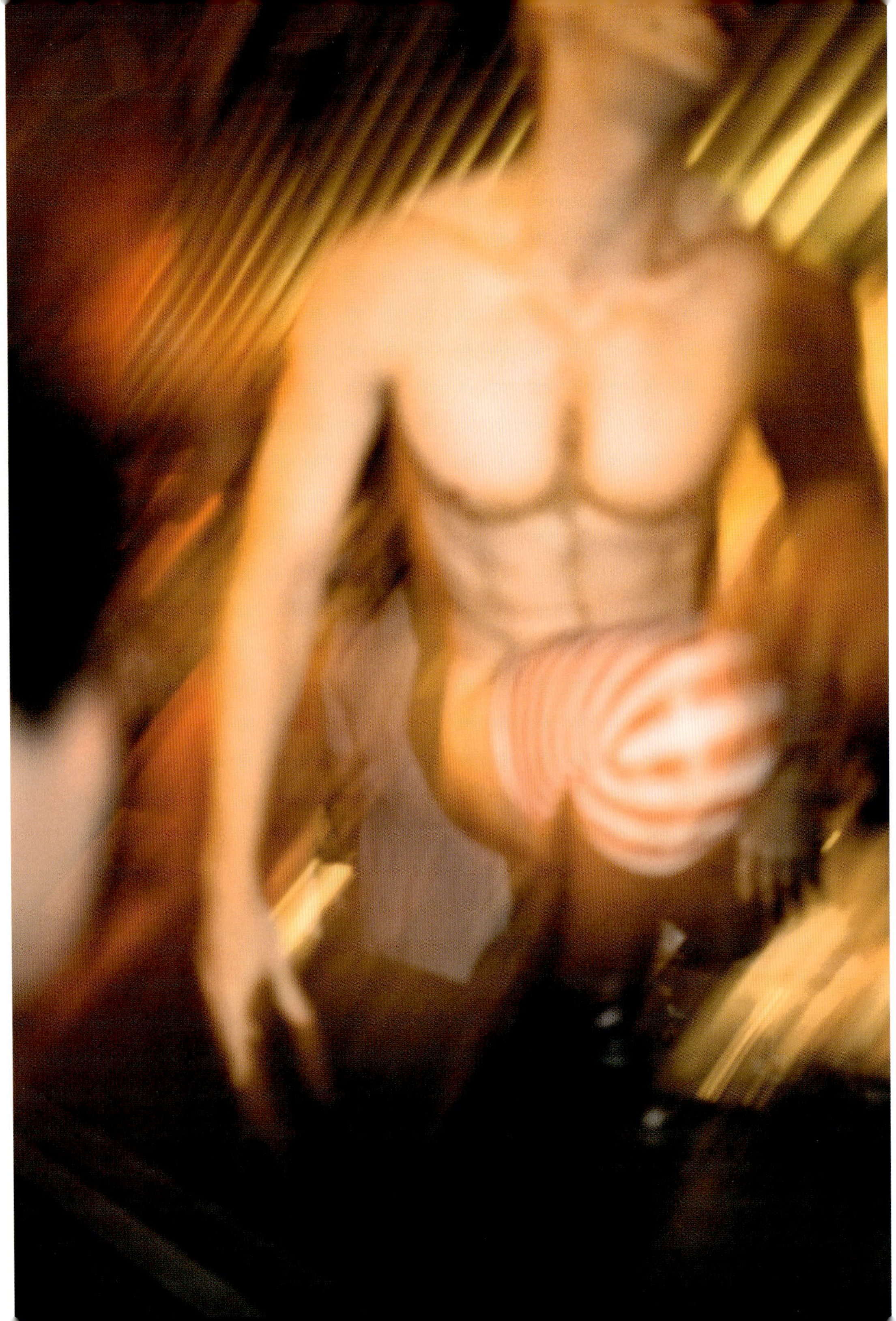

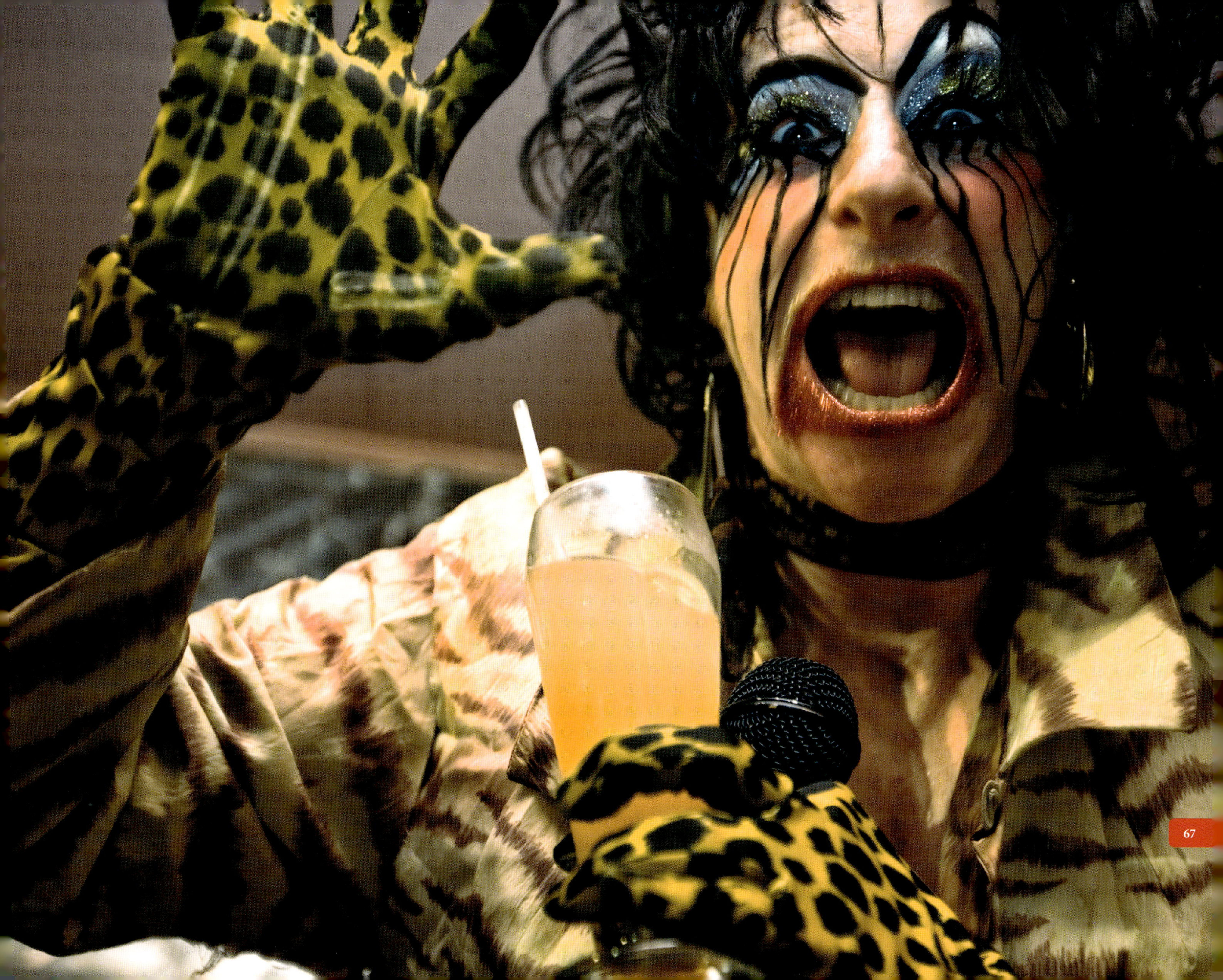

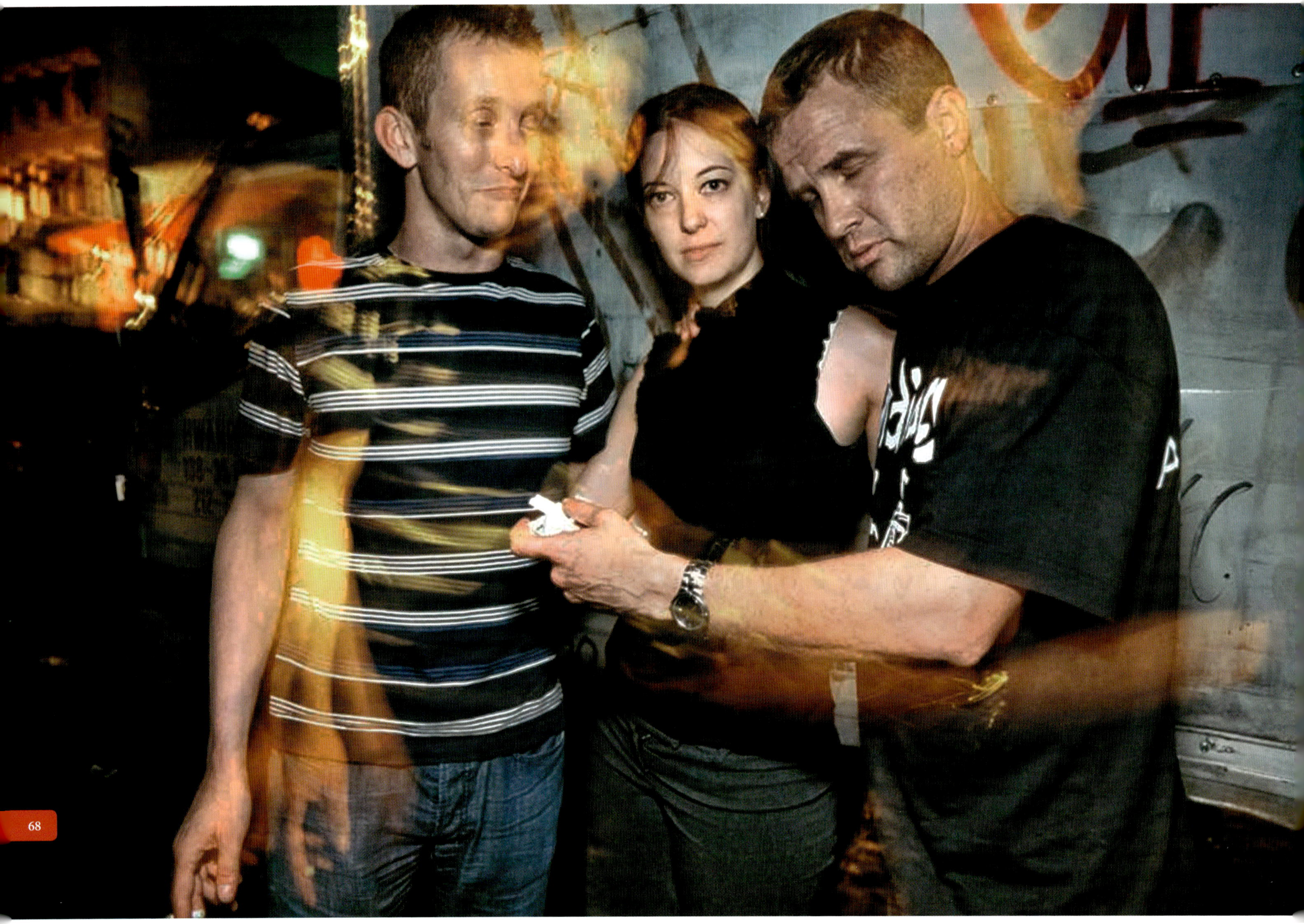

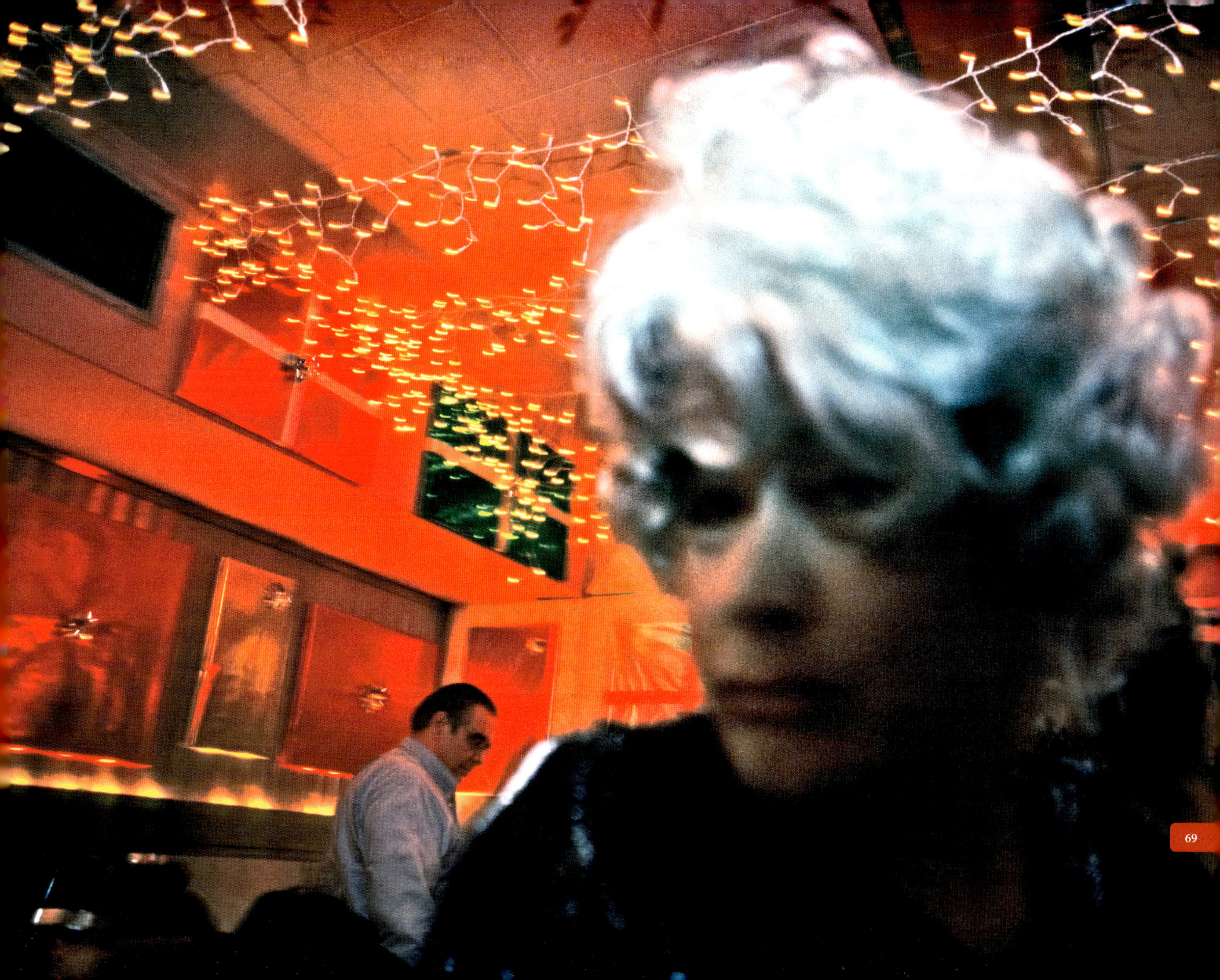

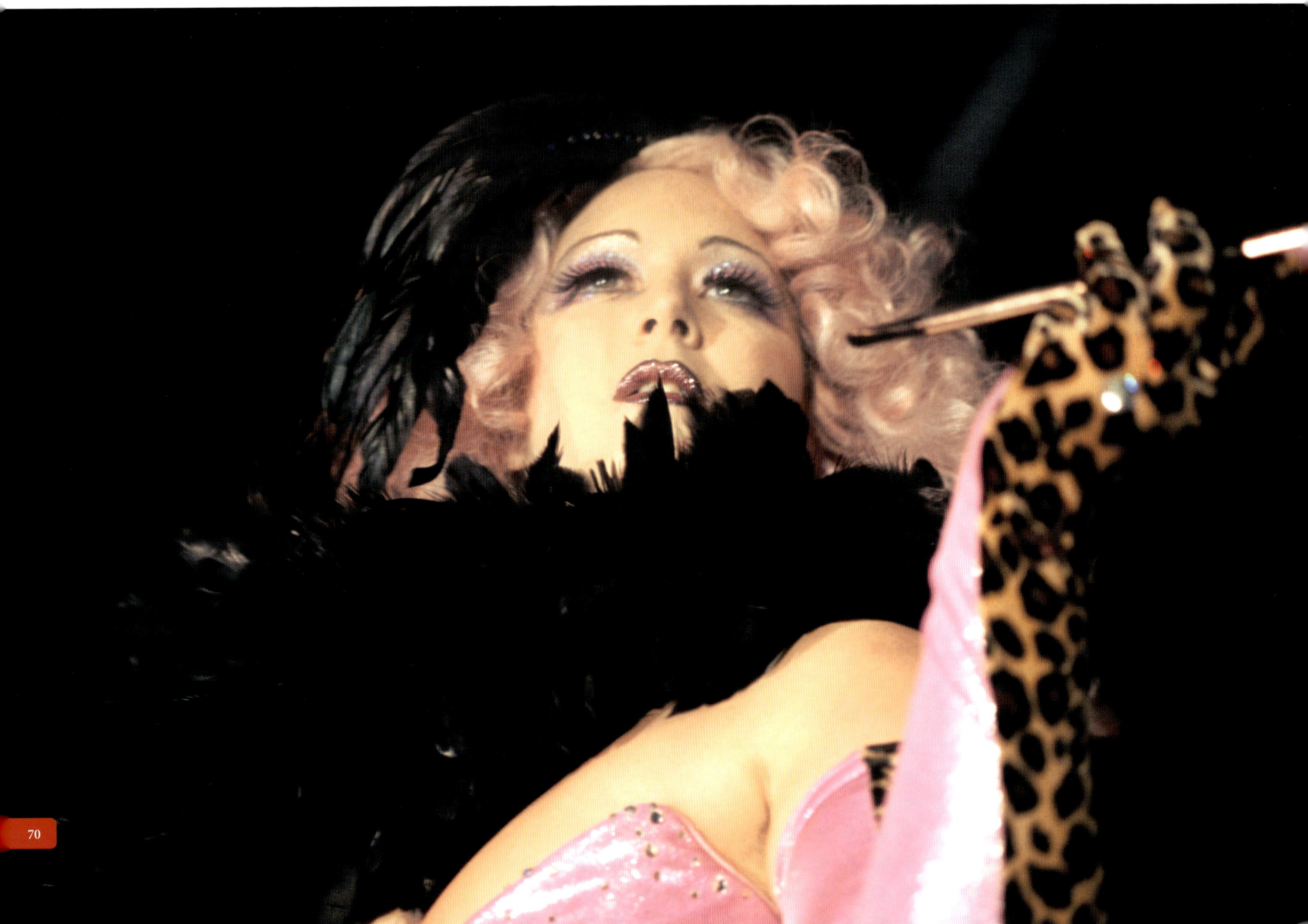

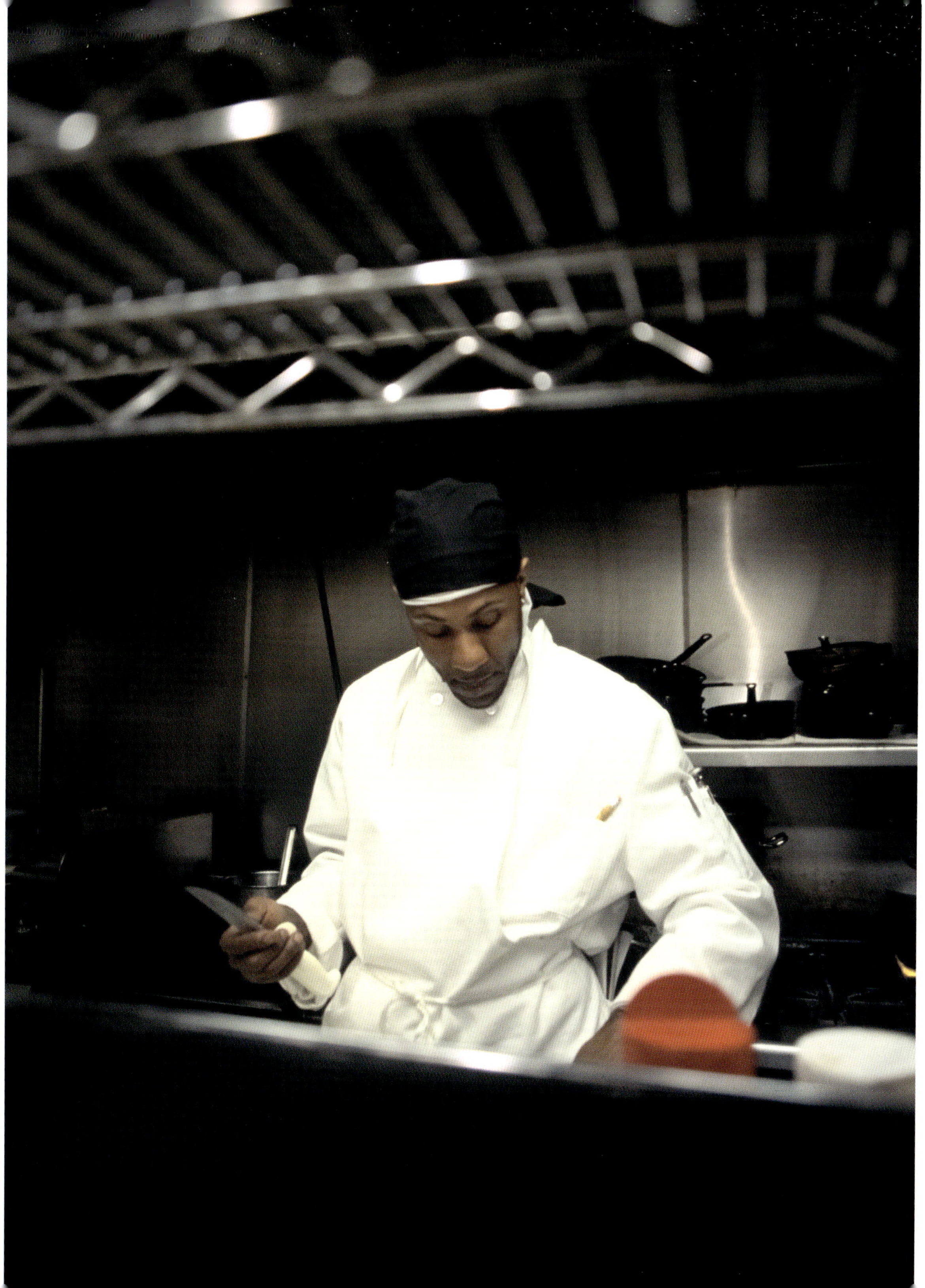

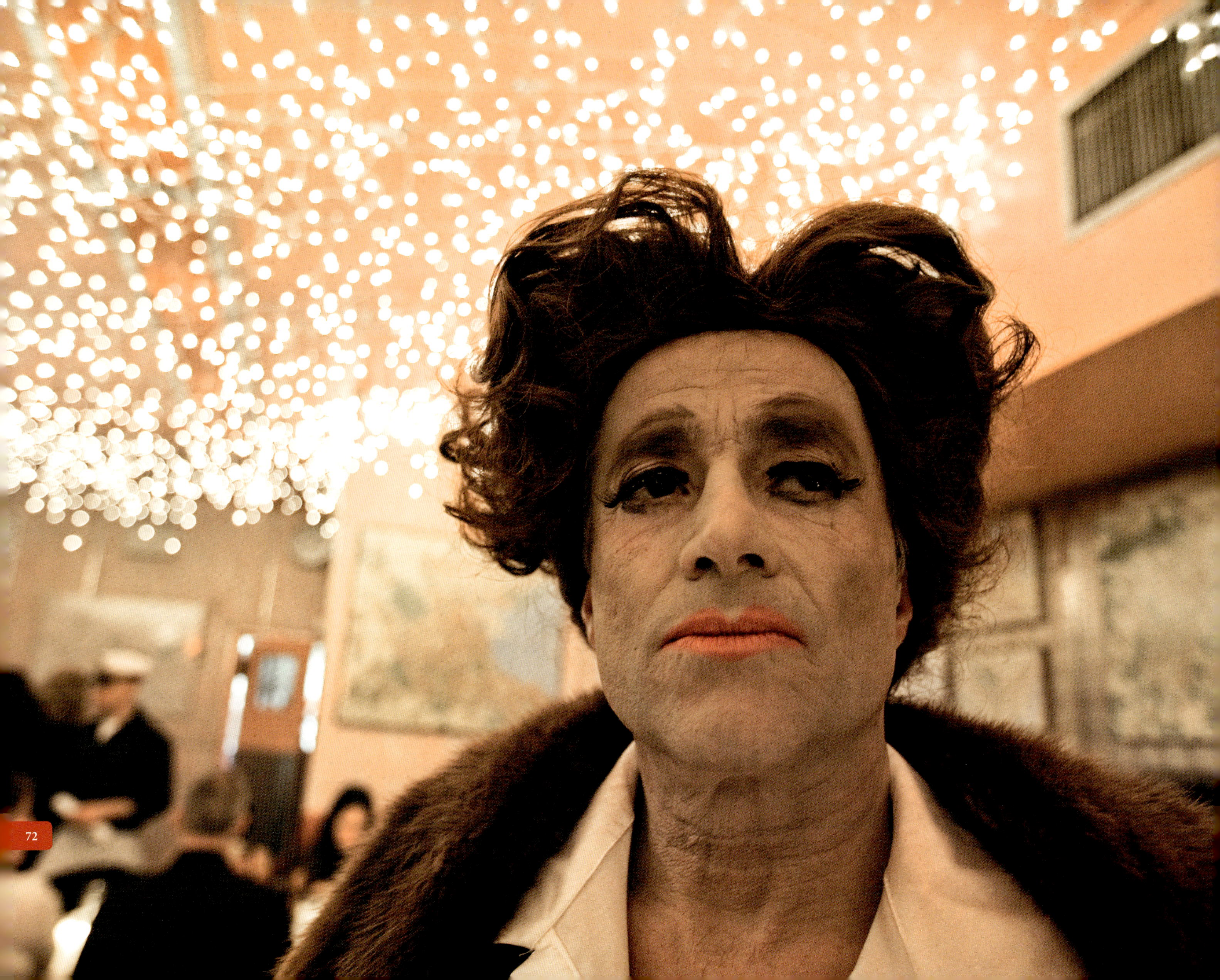

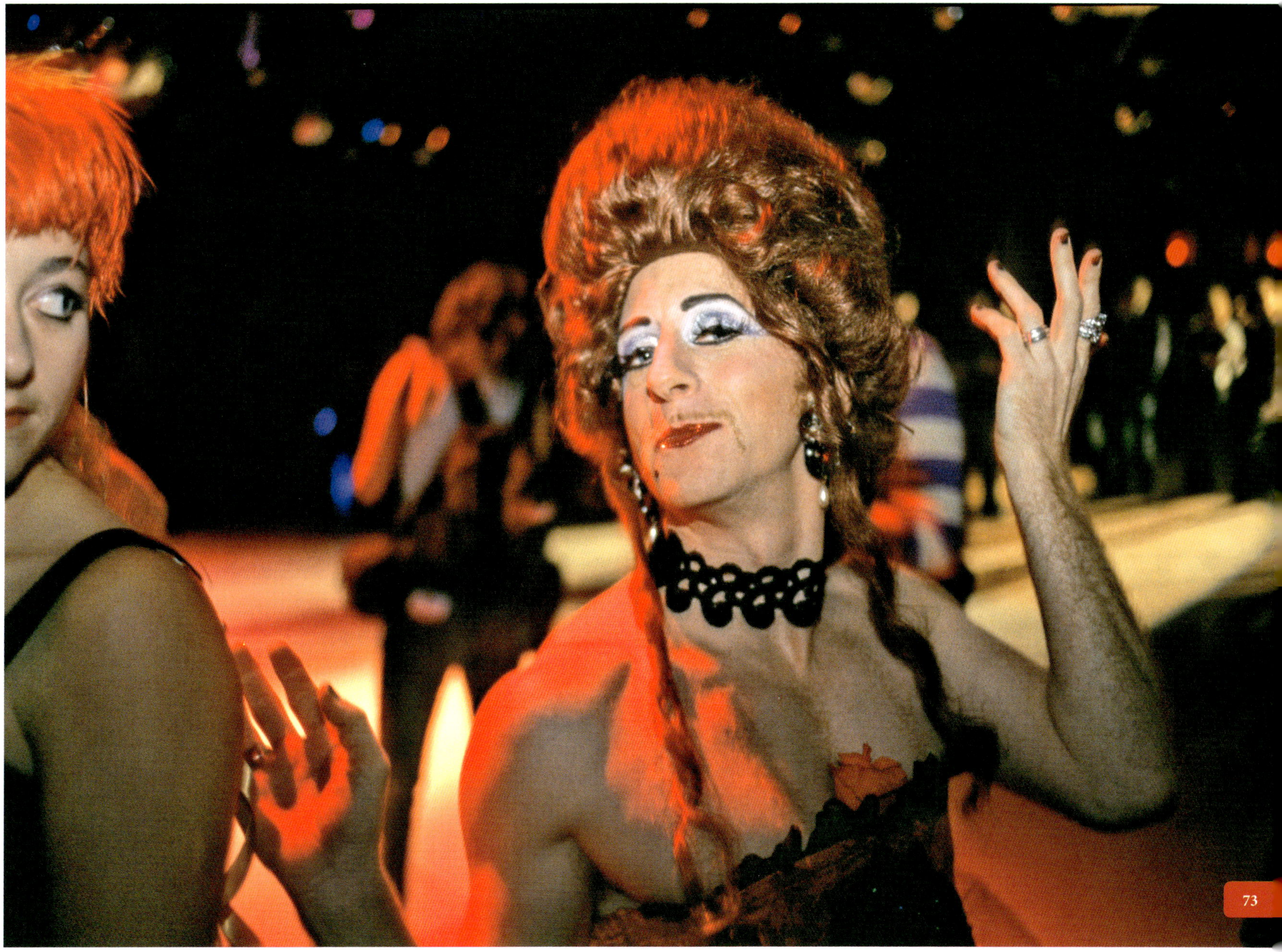

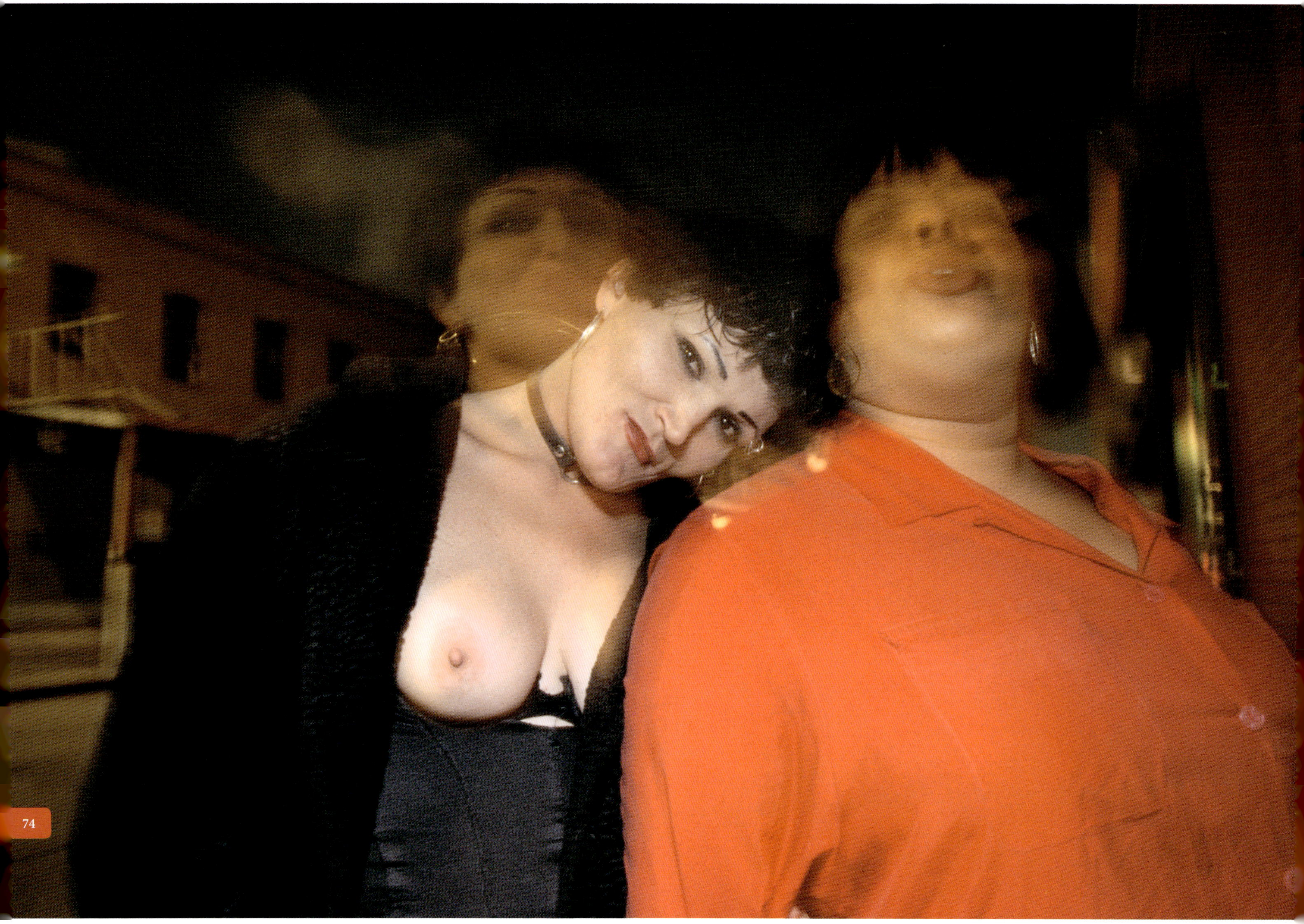

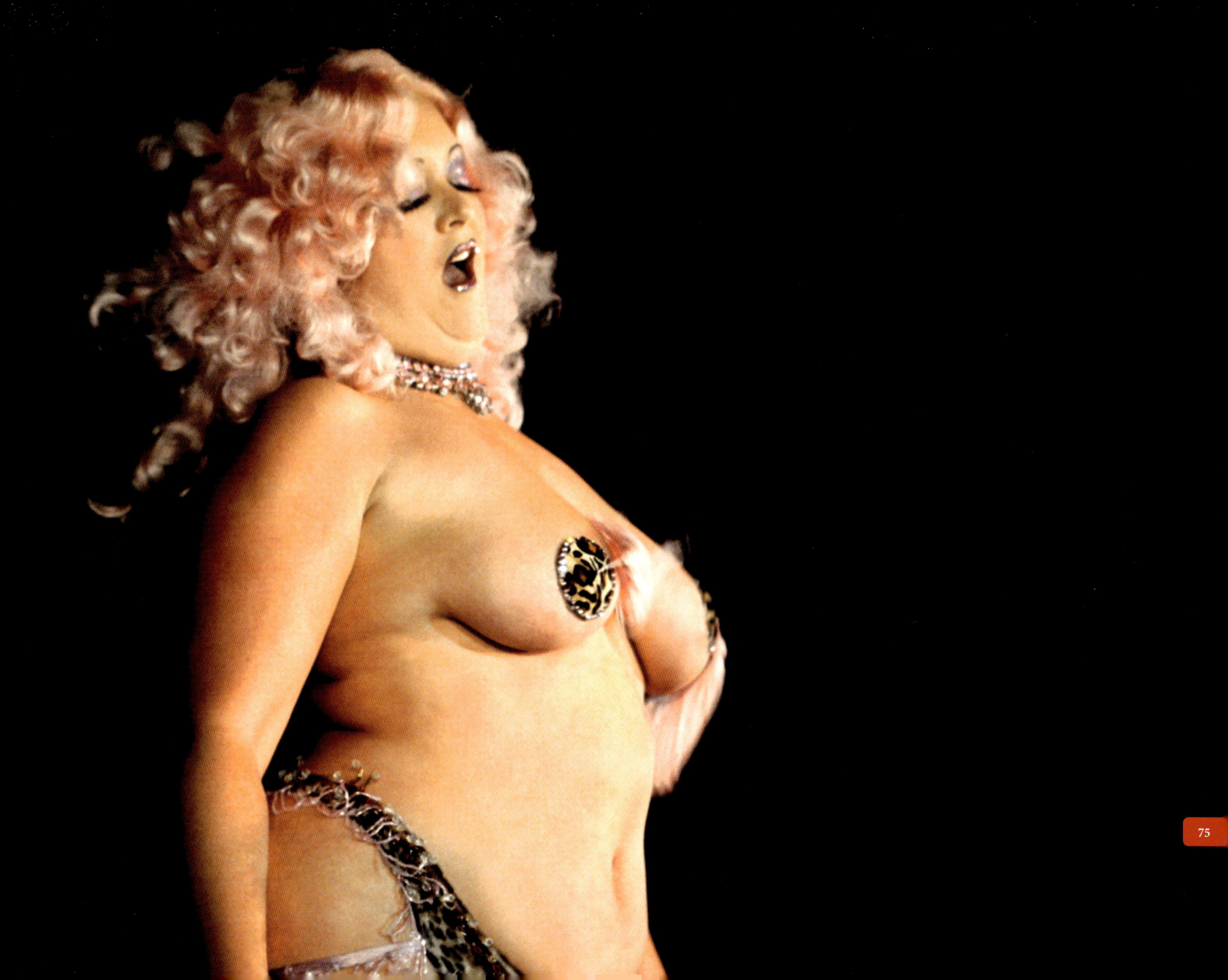

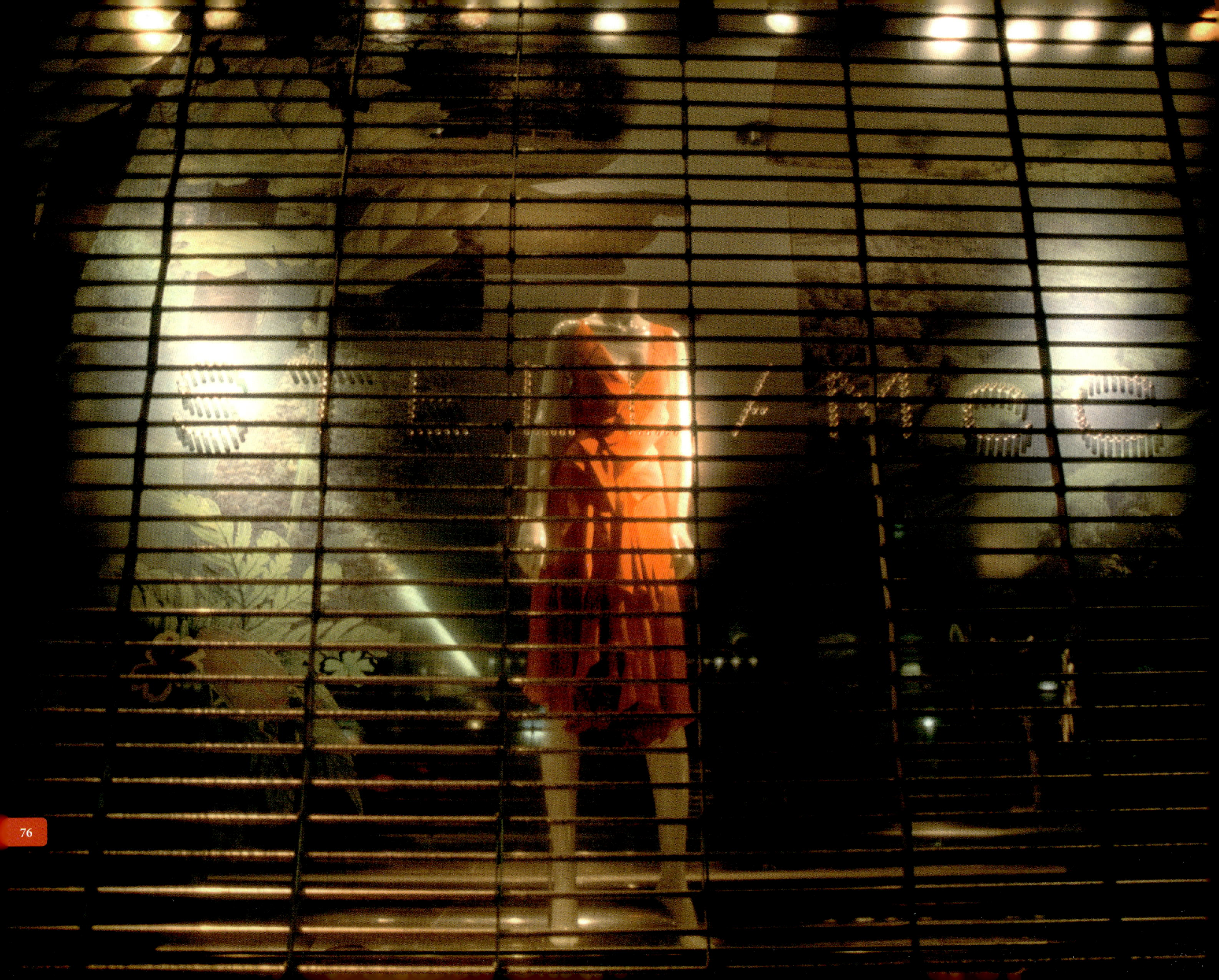

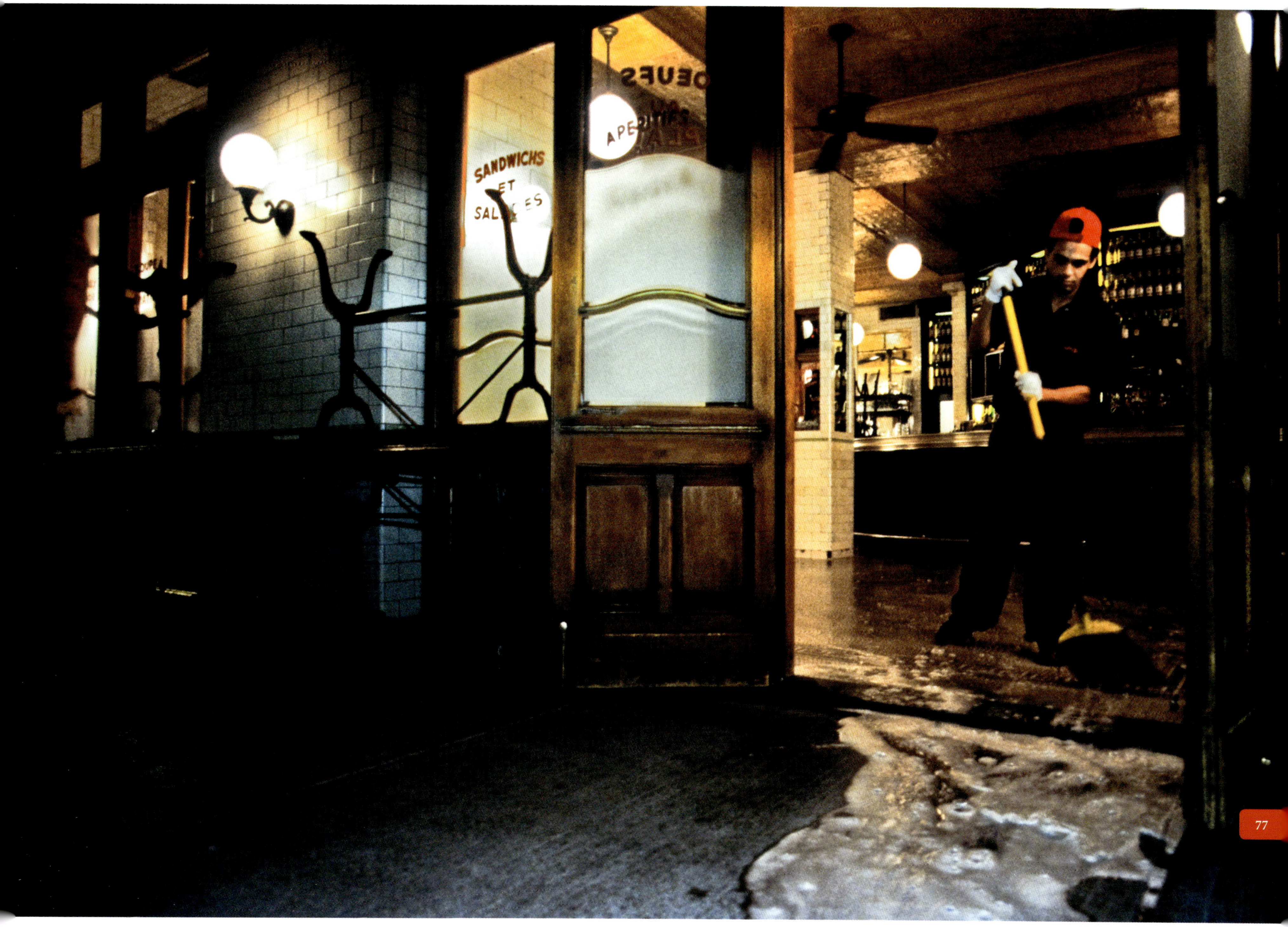
SANDWICHS
ET

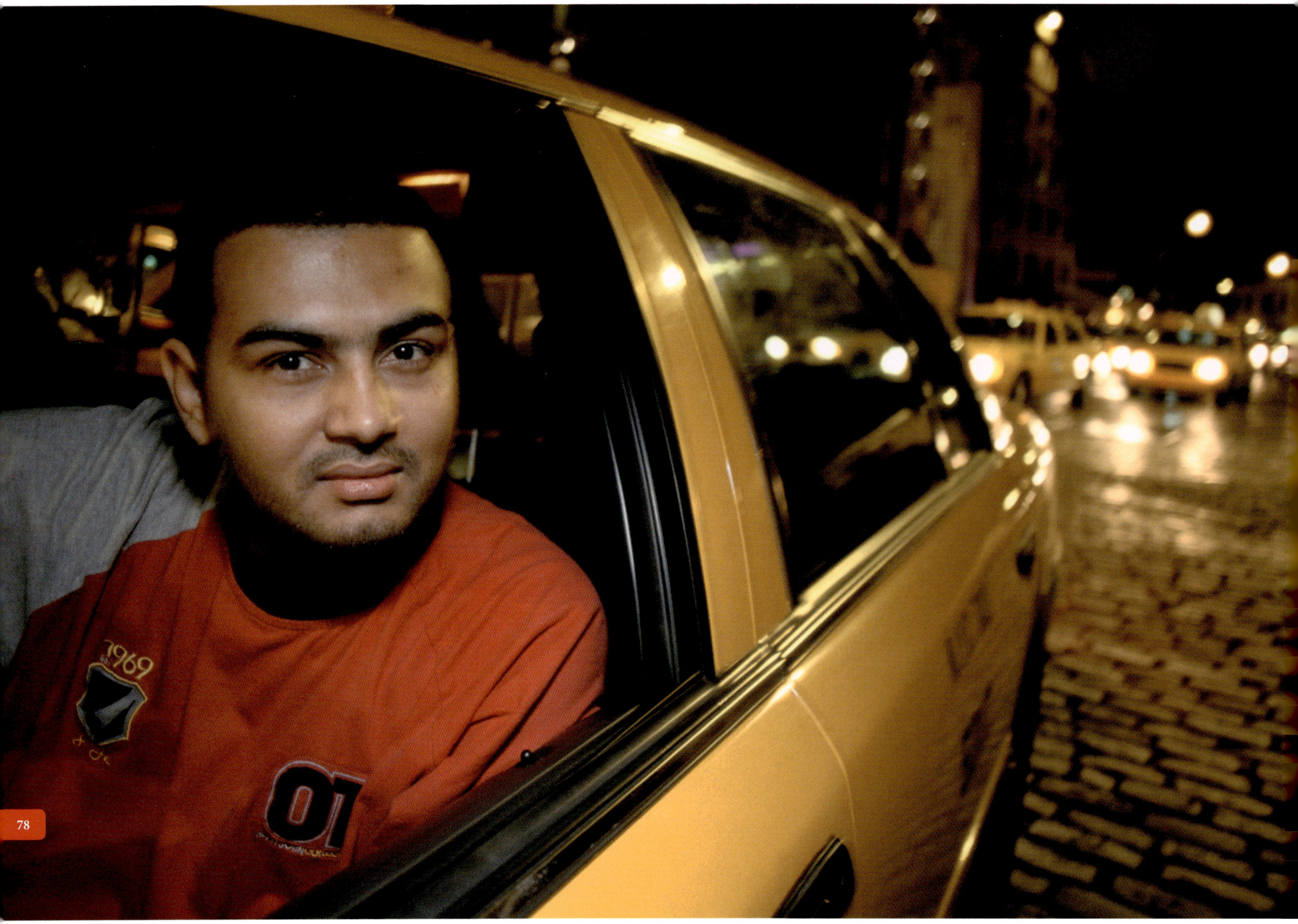
1969

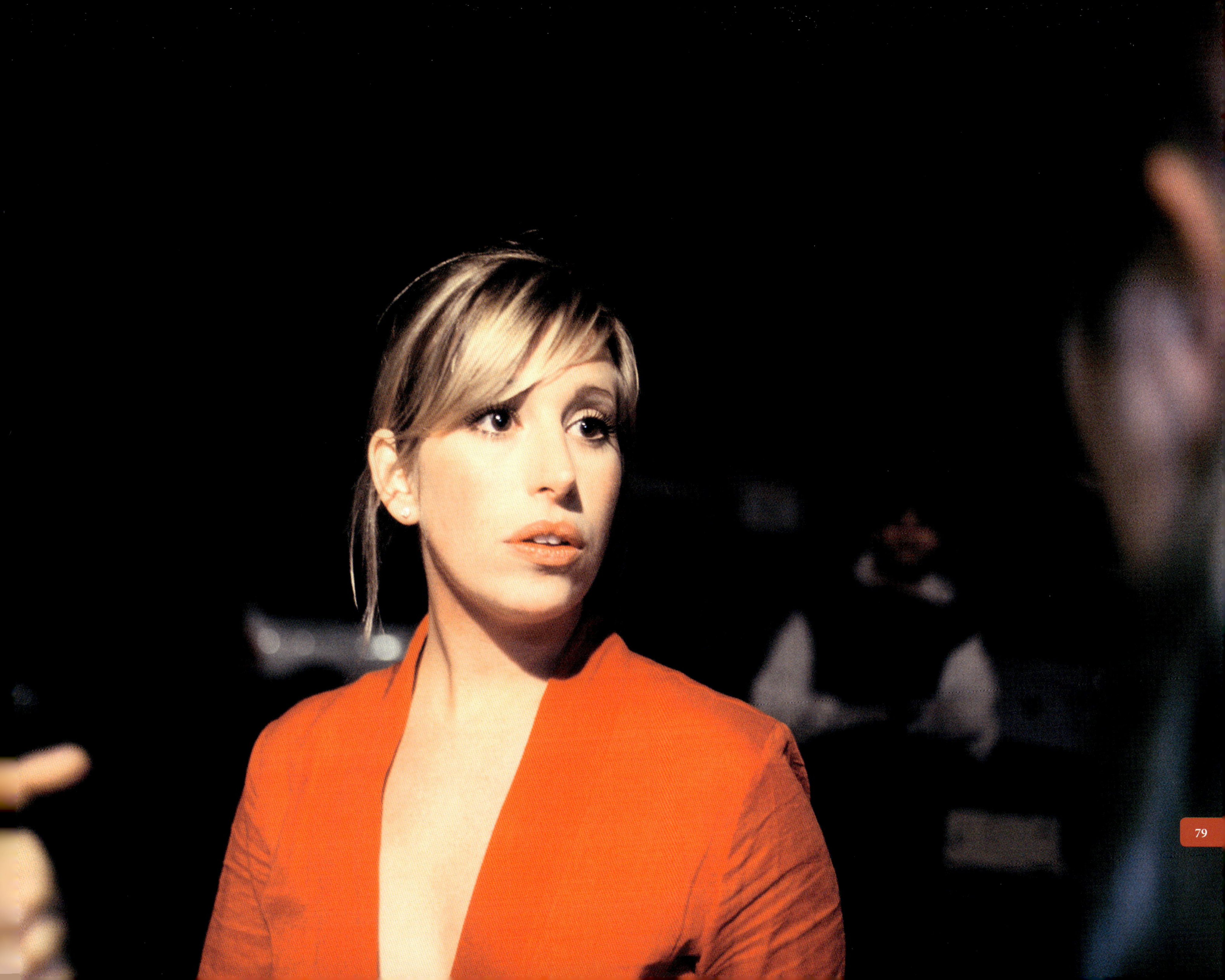

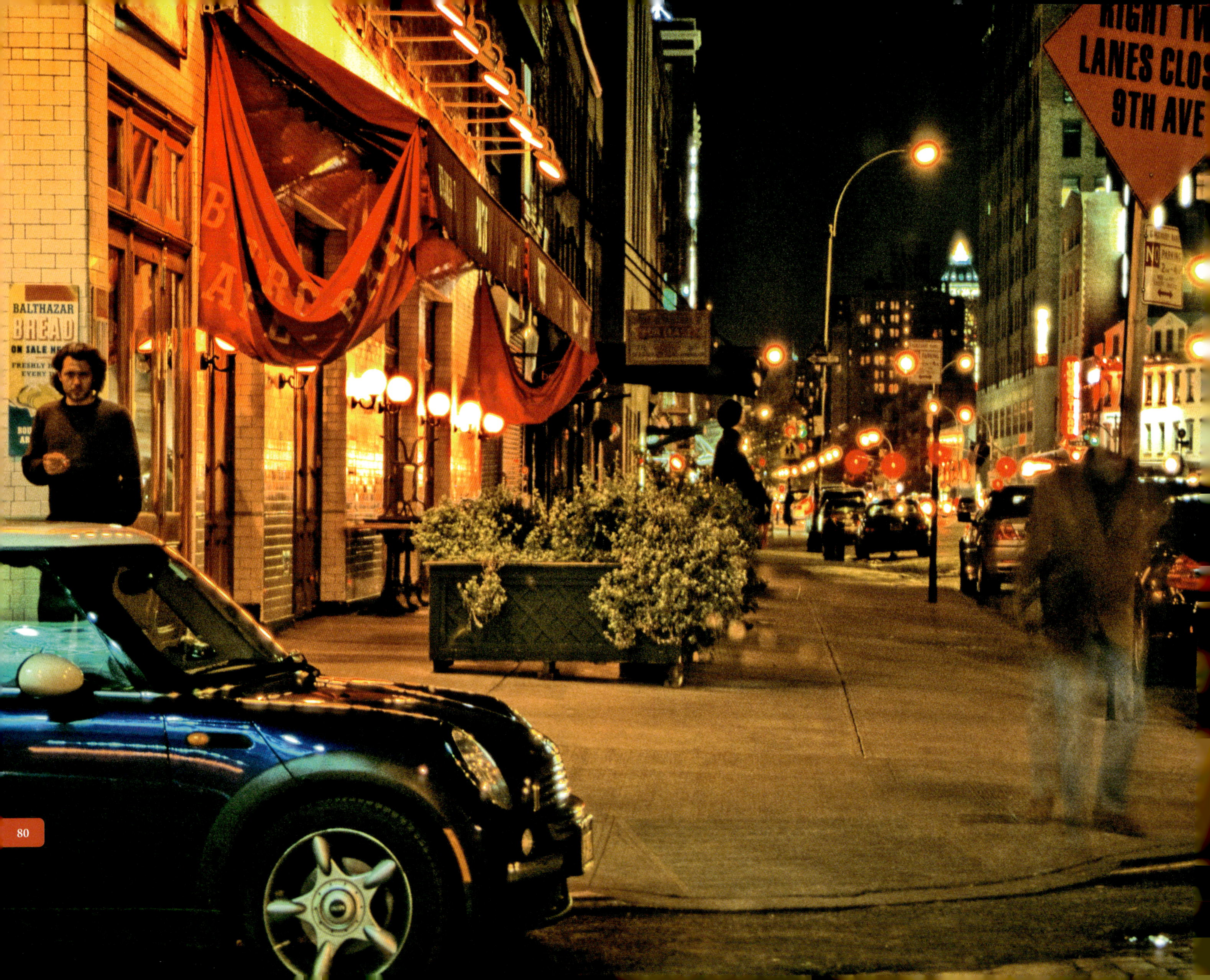
RIGHT TW
LANES CLOS
9TH AVE
BALTHAZAR
BREAD
ON SALE HE

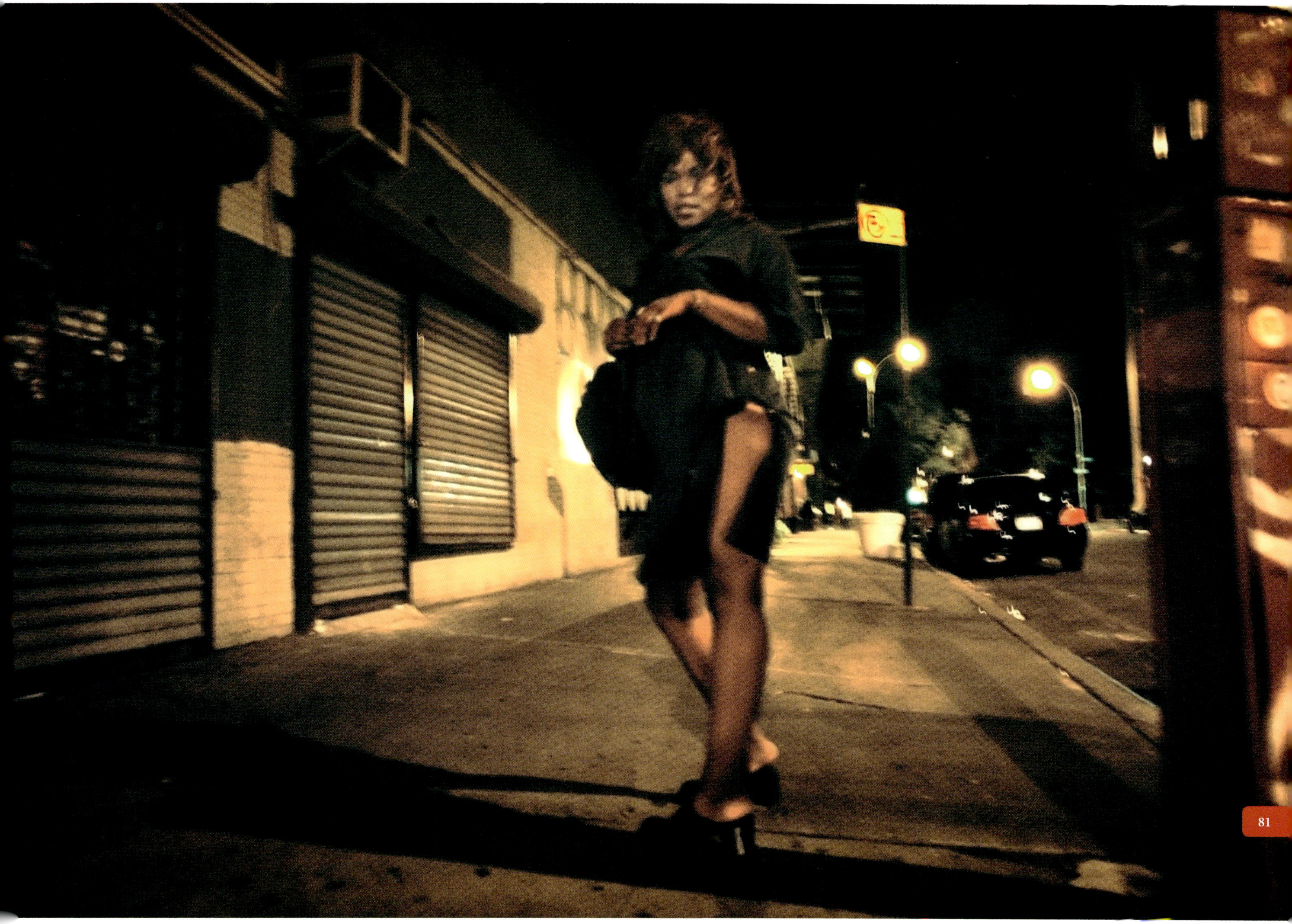

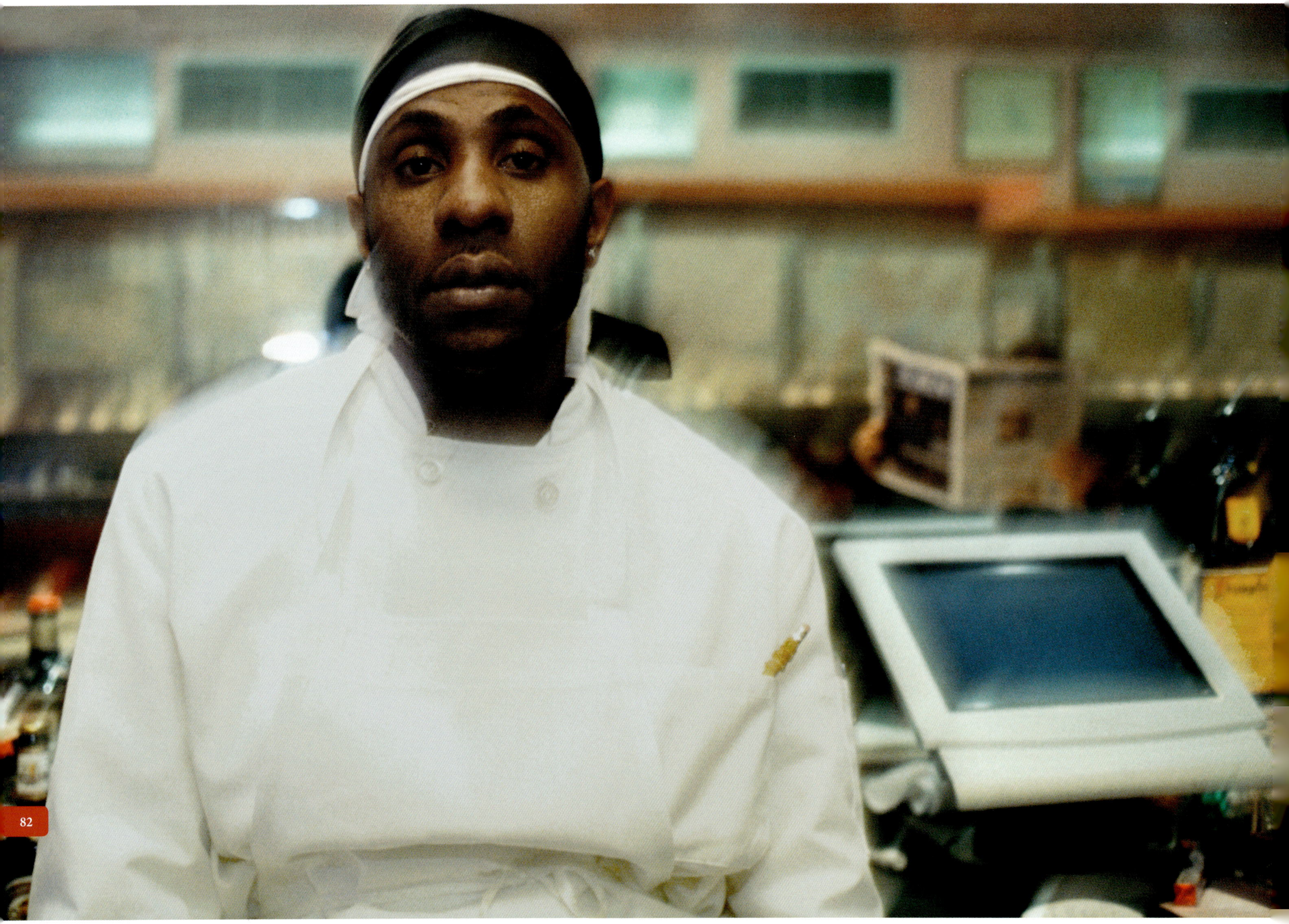

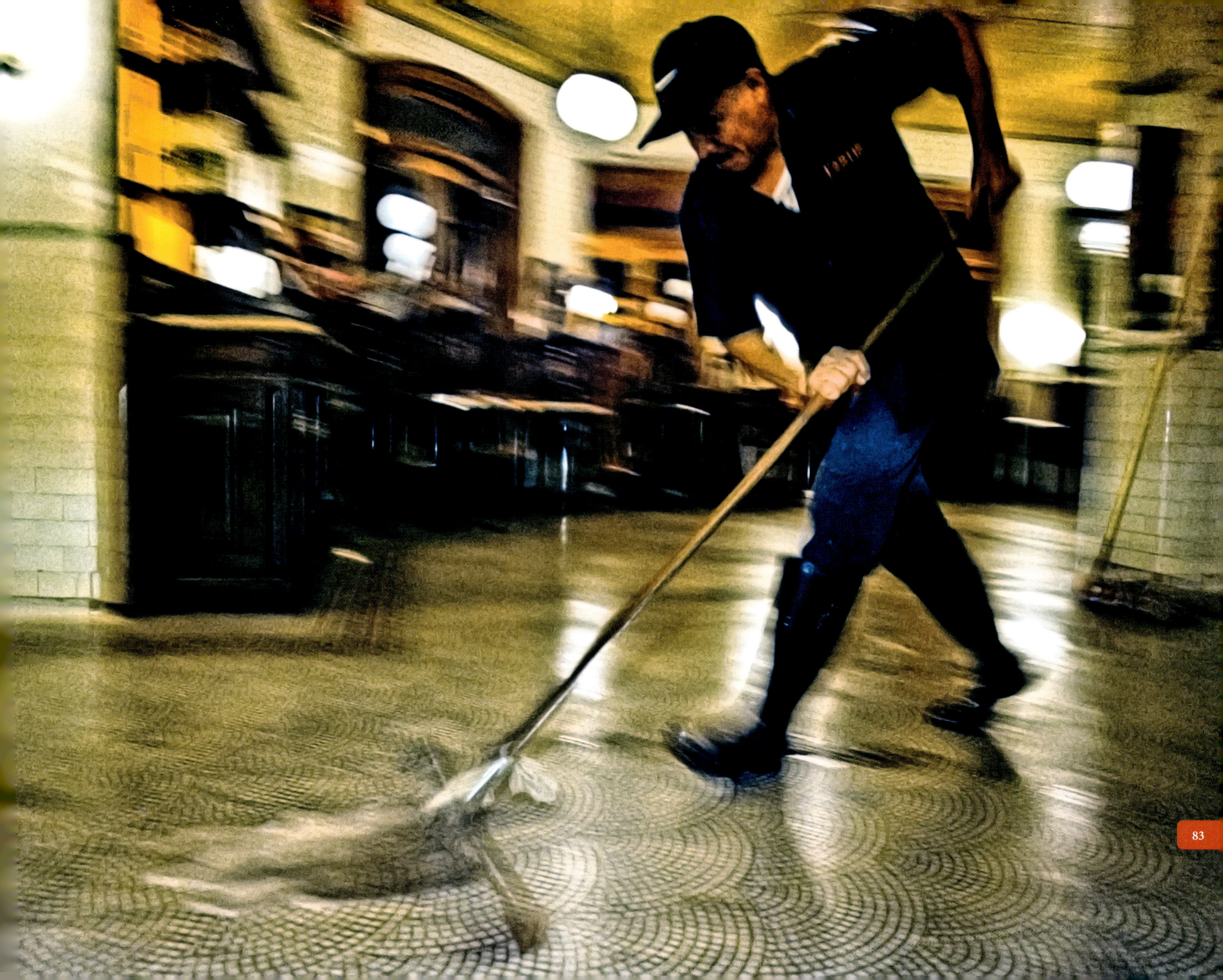

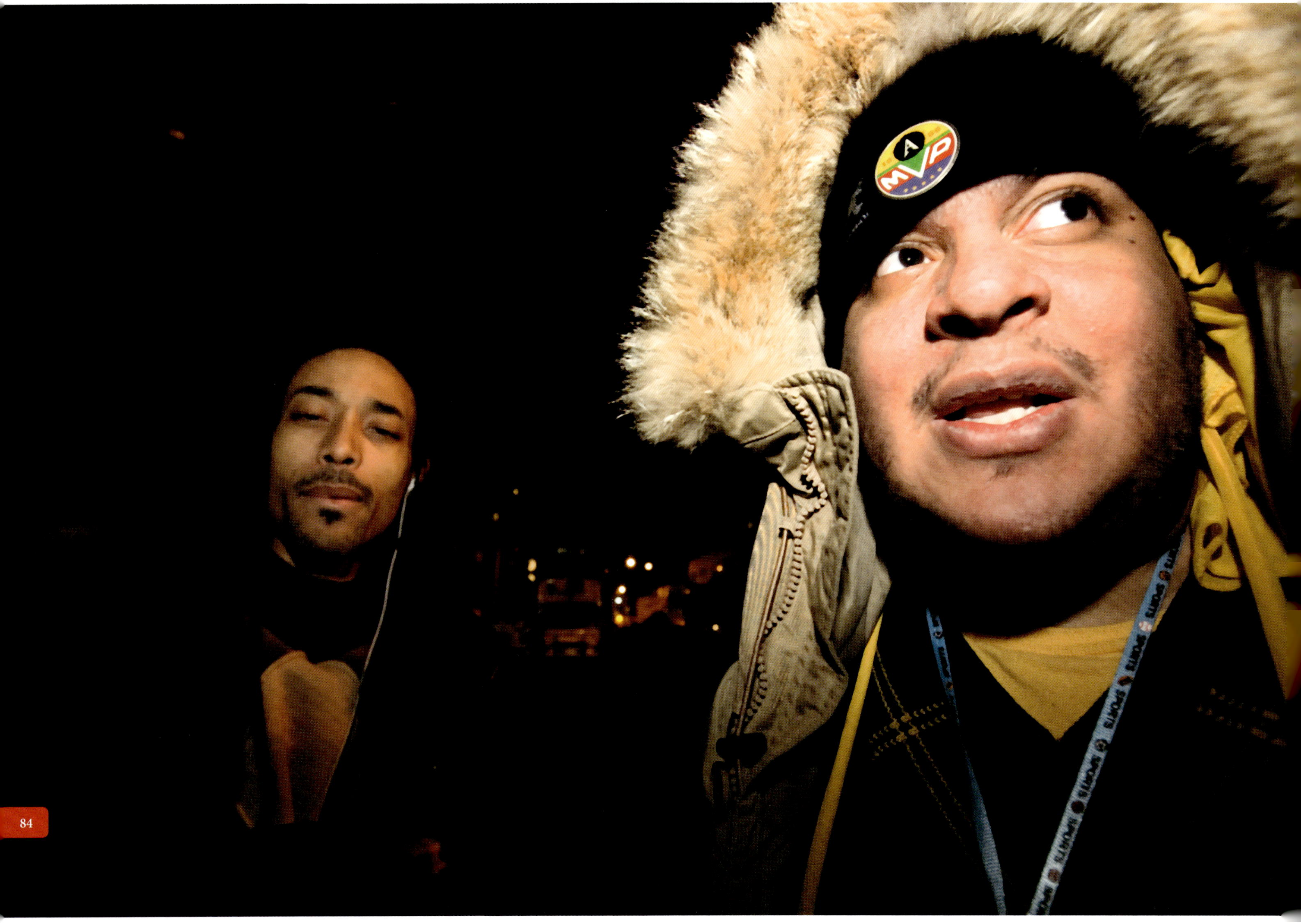
MVP
SPORTS

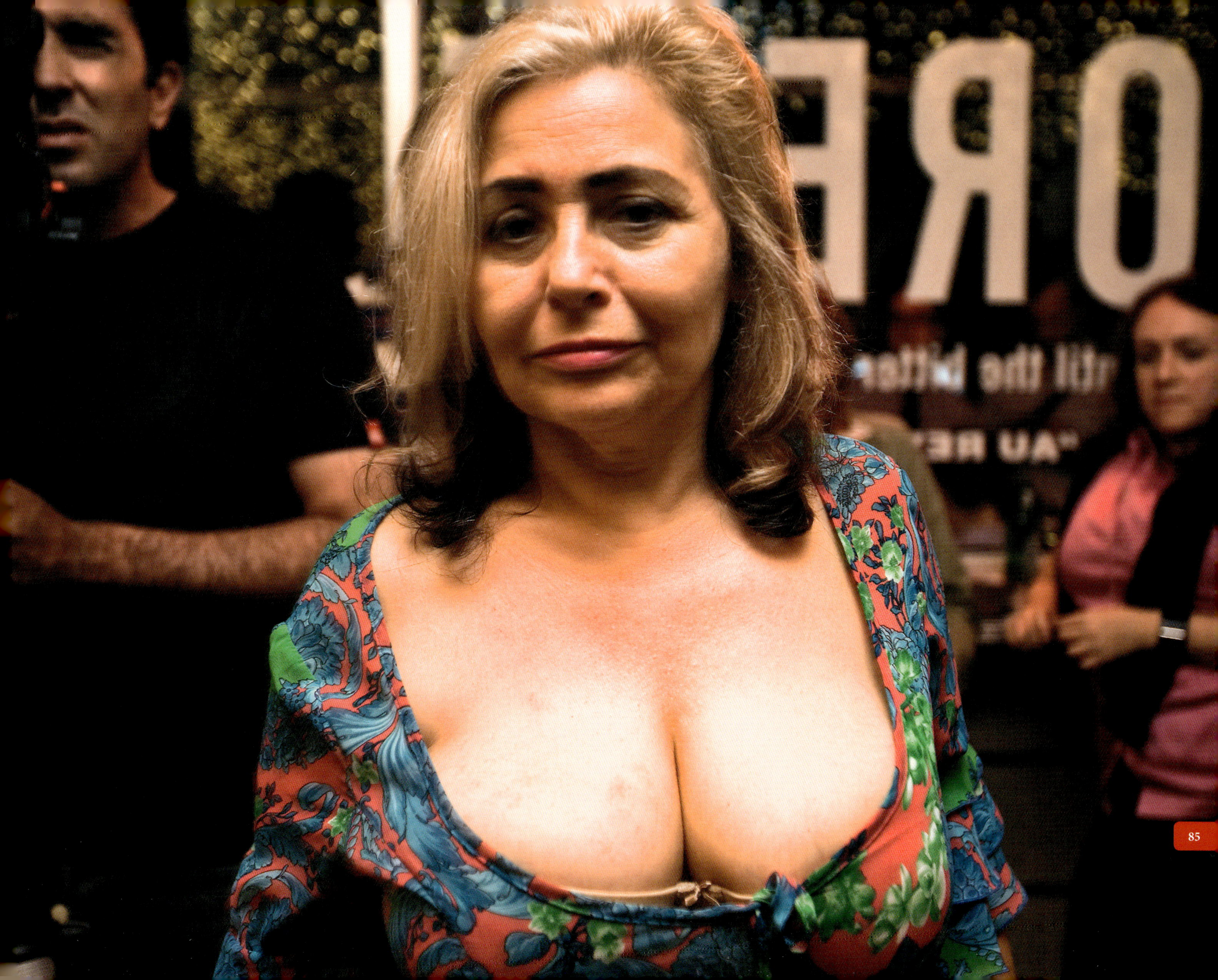

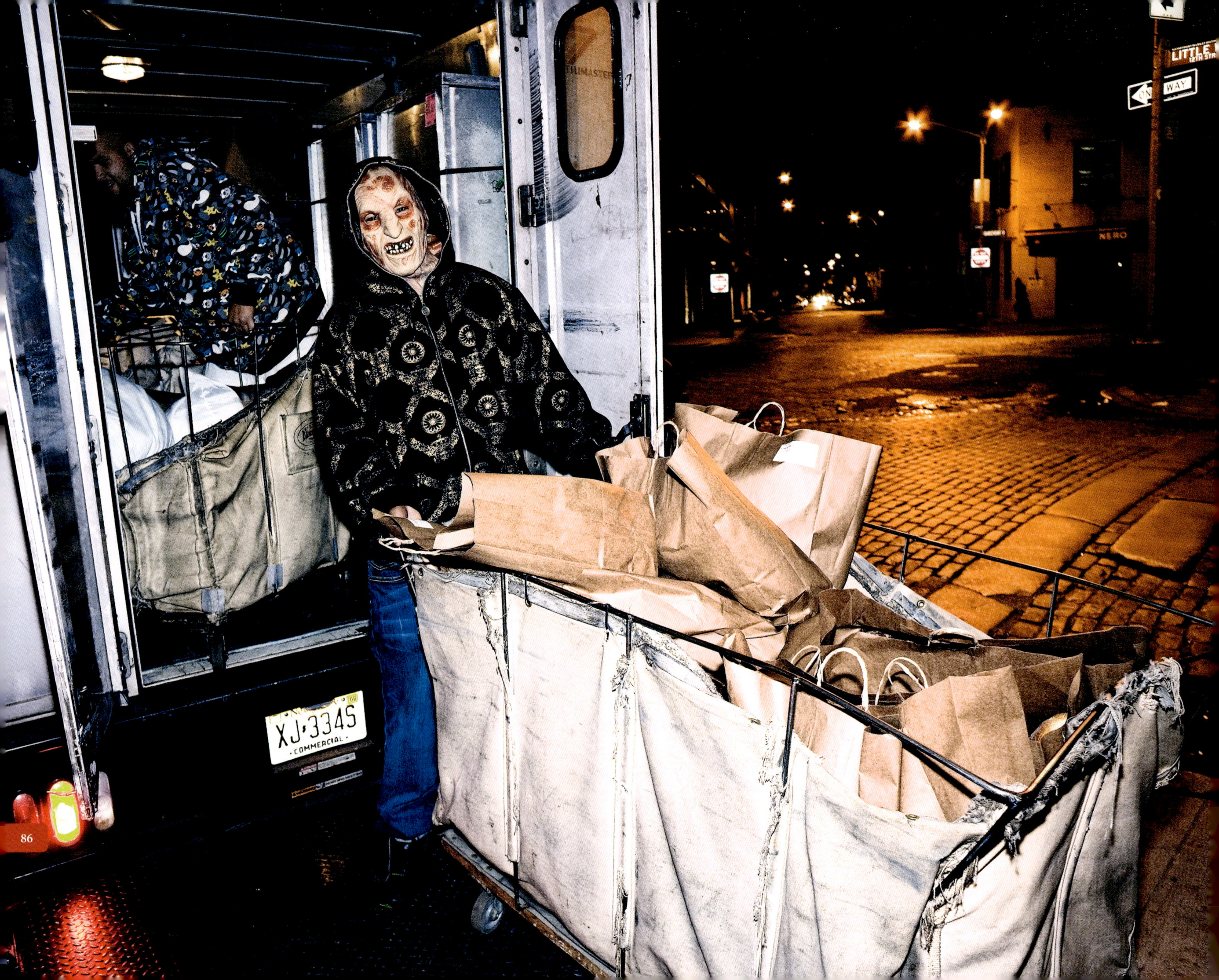
LITTLE
XJ 334S
COMMERCIAL
NERO

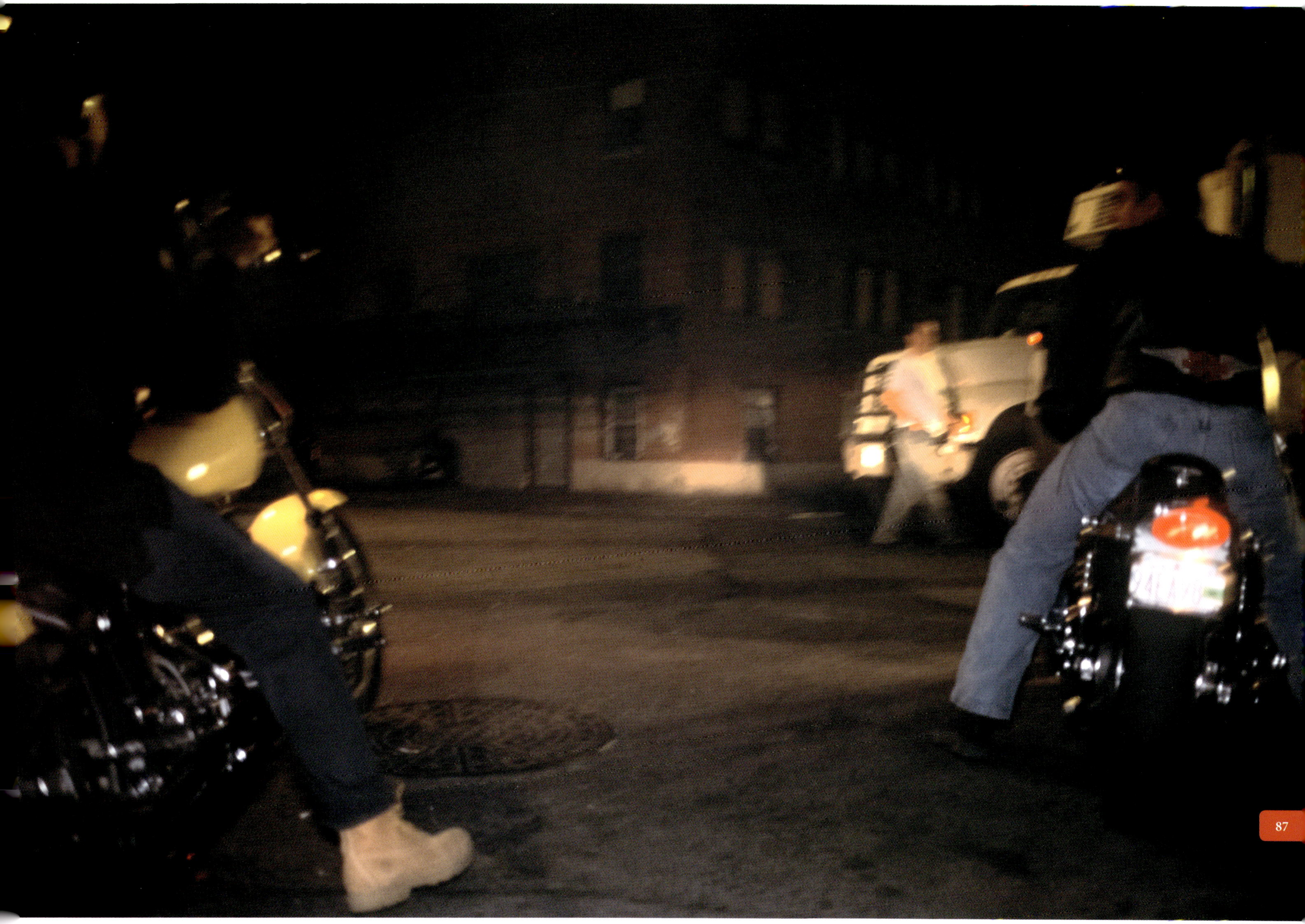

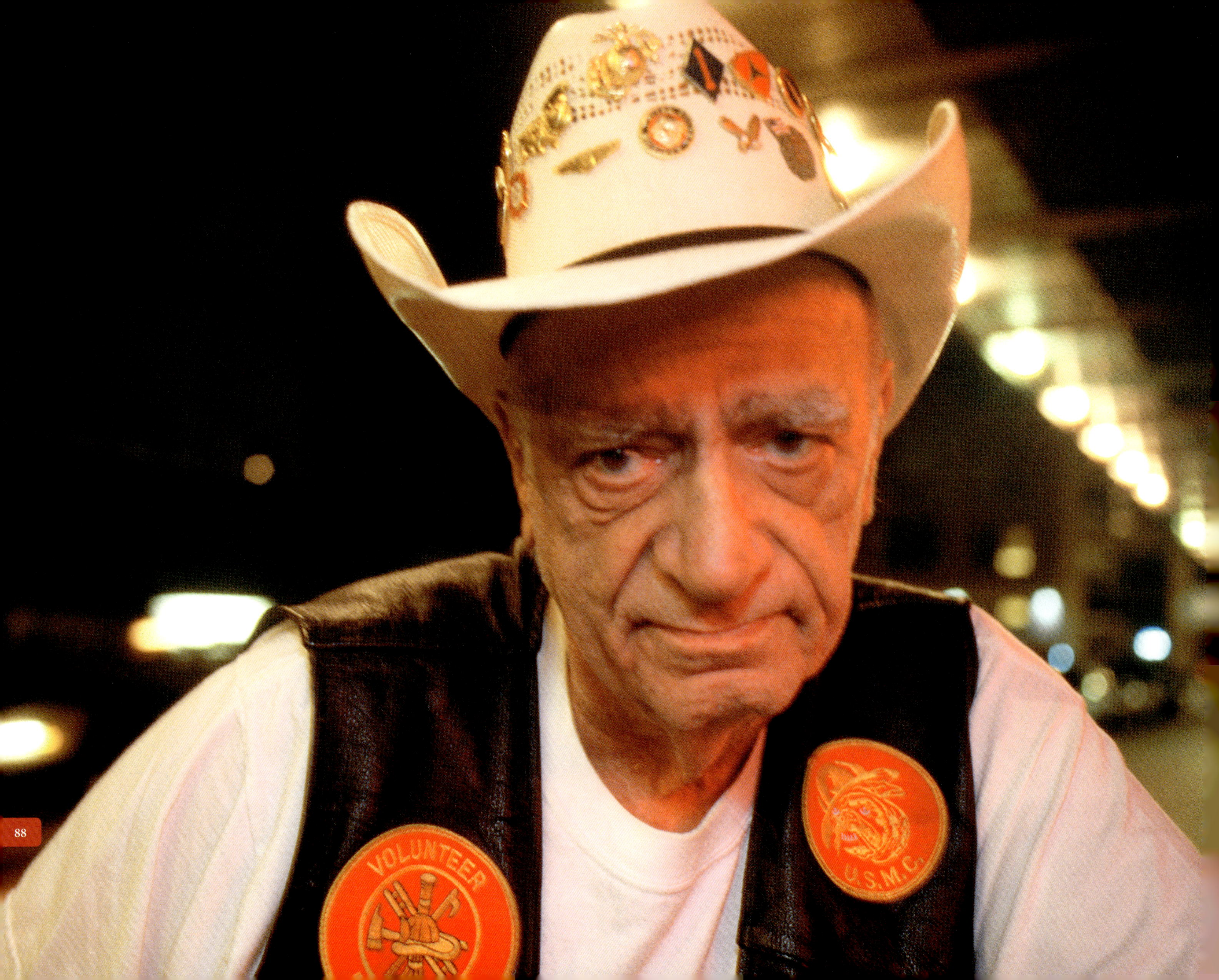
VOLUNTEER
U.S.M.C.

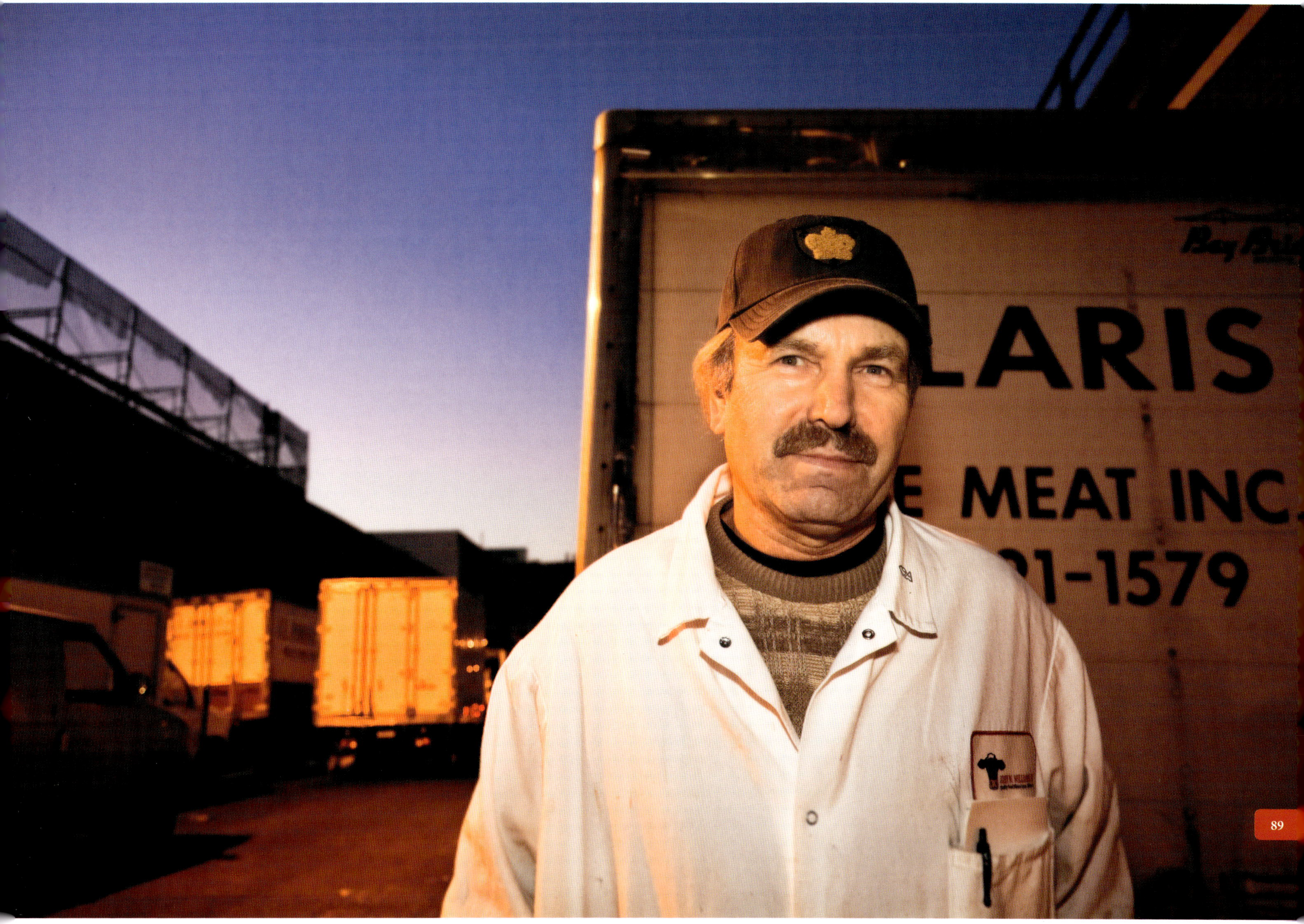
LARIS
E MEAT INC.

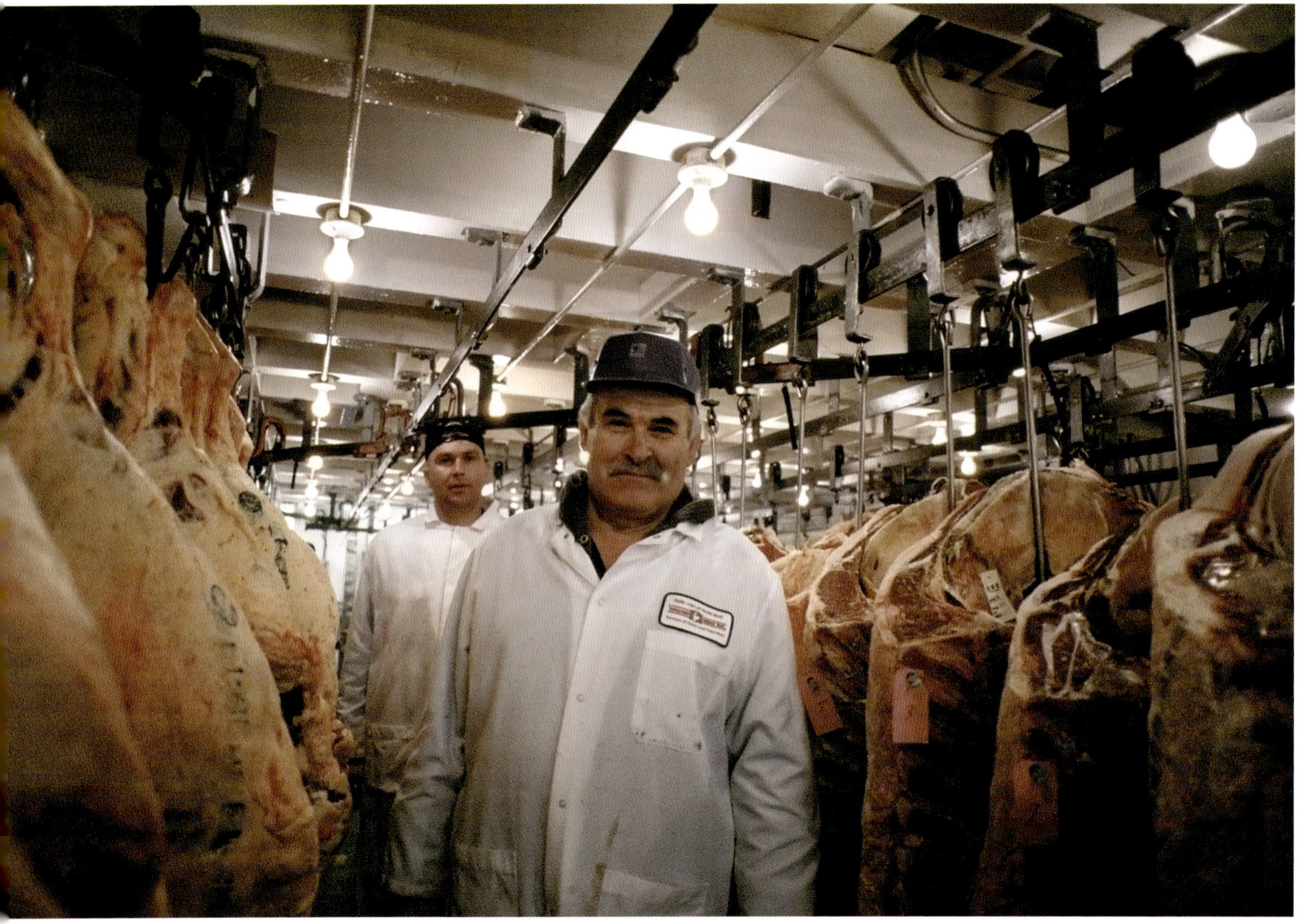

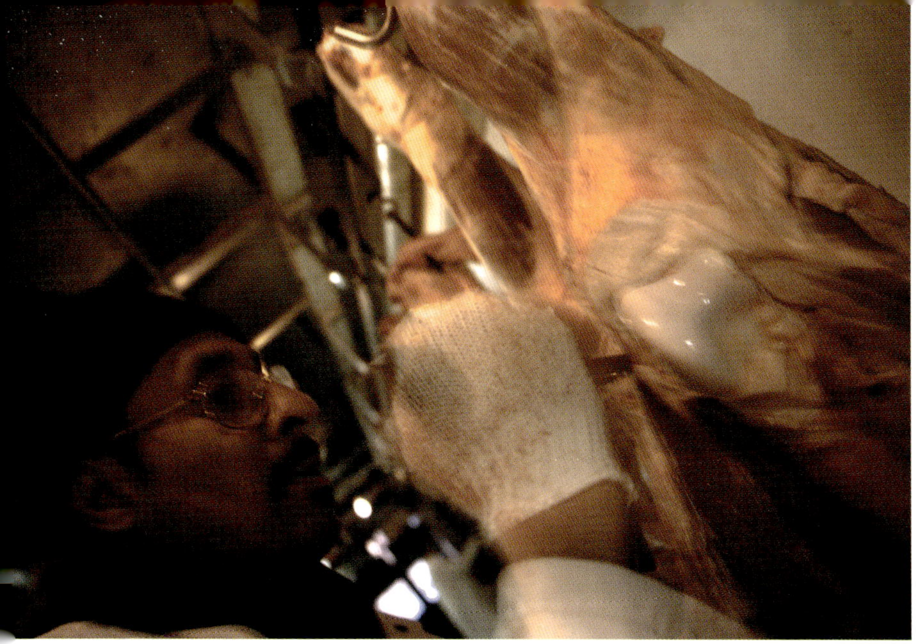

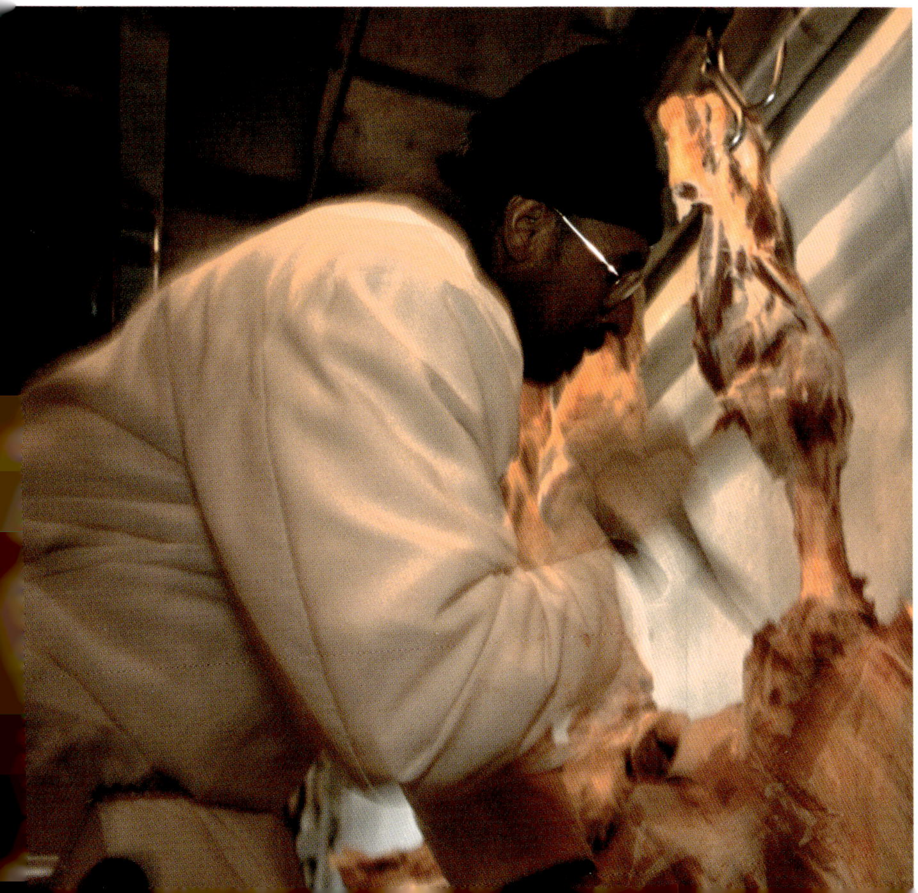

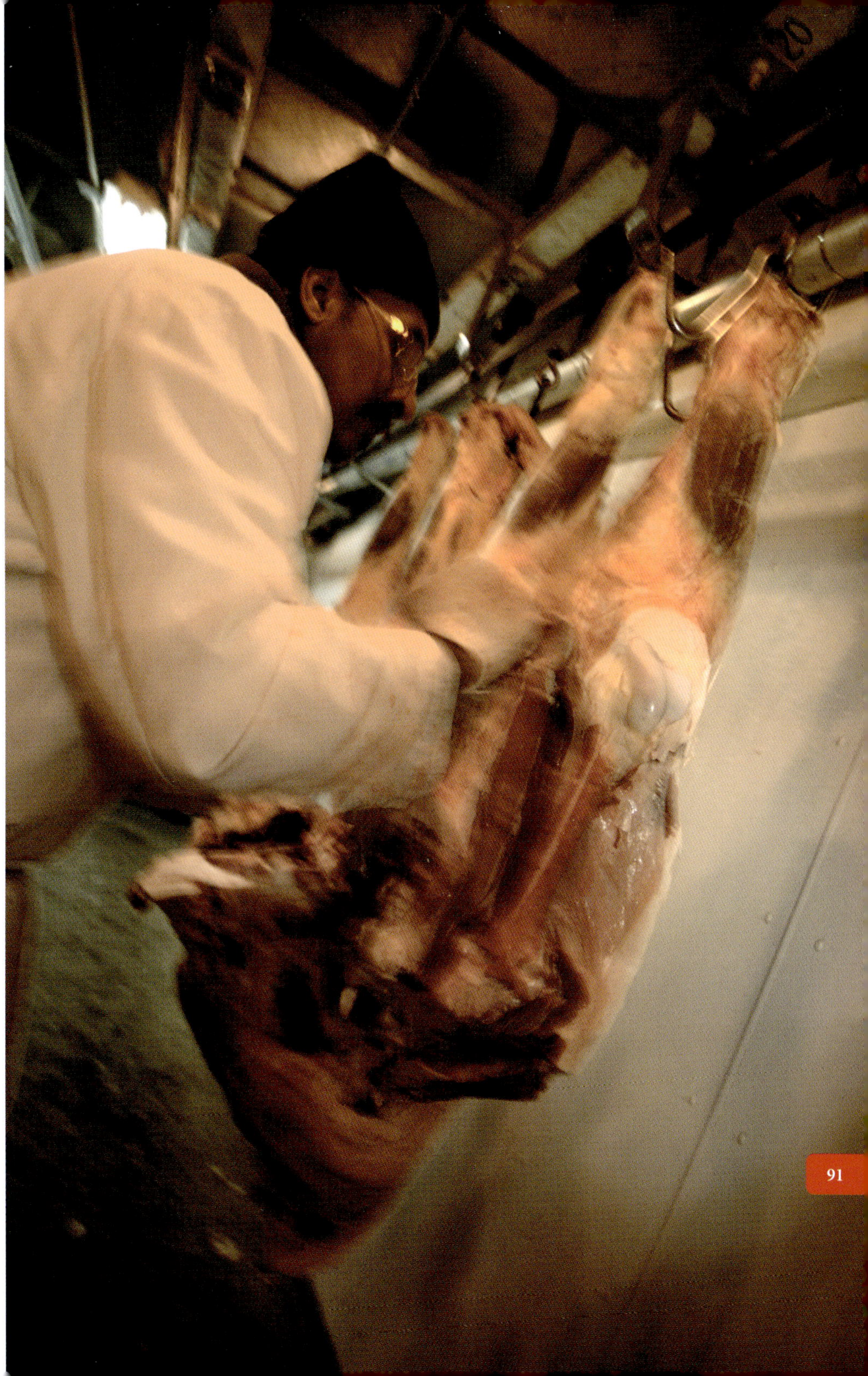

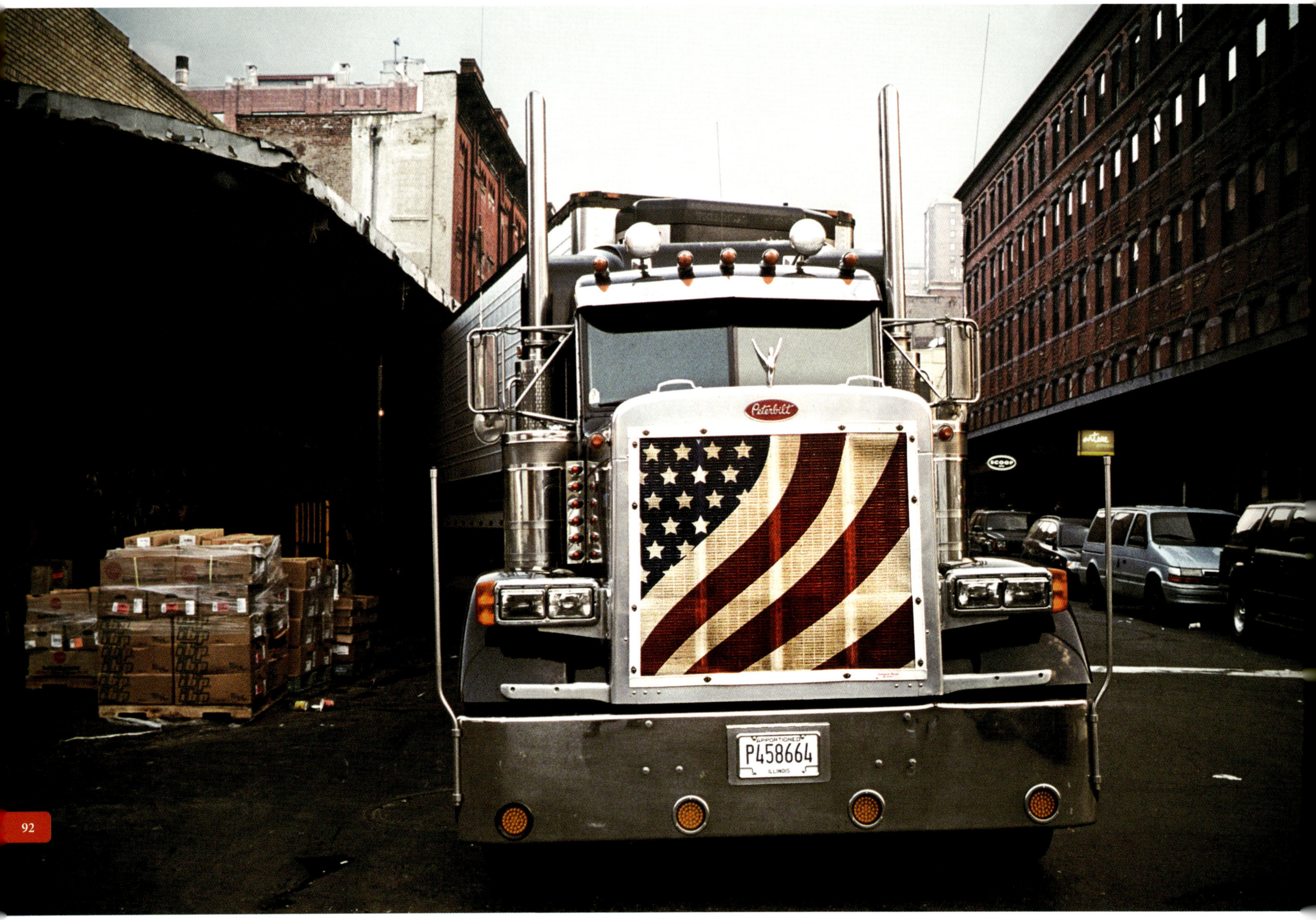
Peterbilt
APPORTIONED
P458664
ILLINOIS
SCOOP

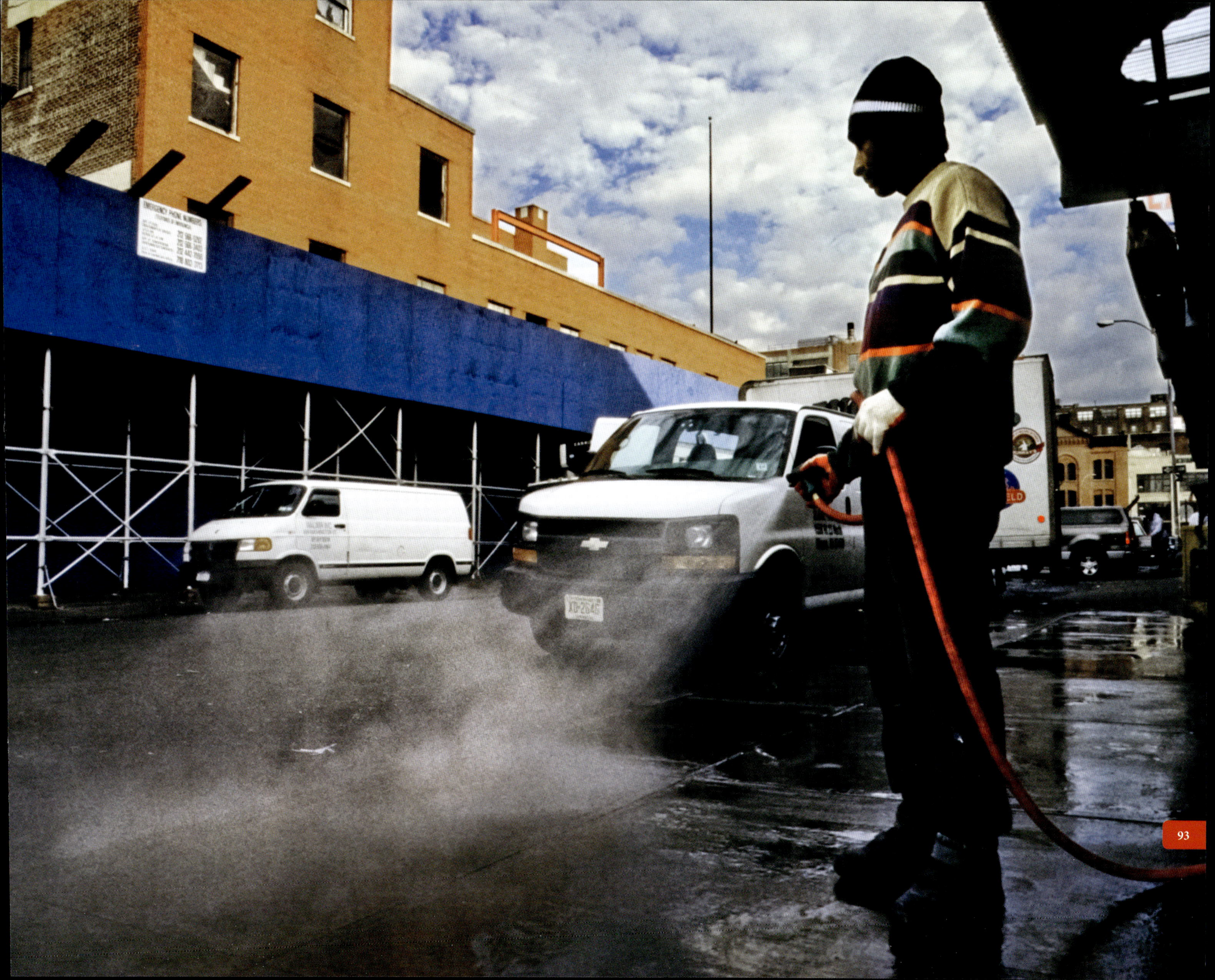

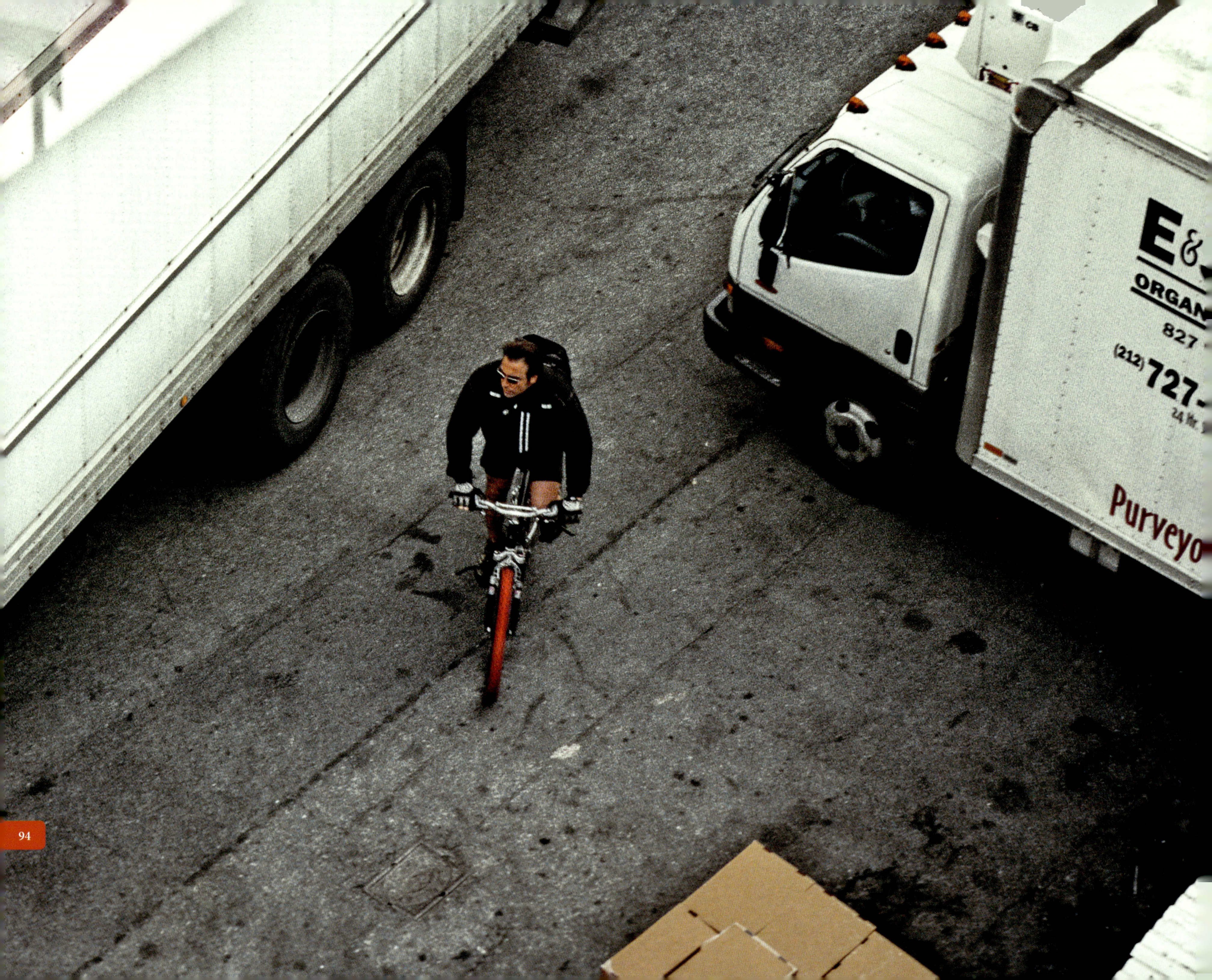
E&
ORGAN
827
(212) 727-
Purveyo

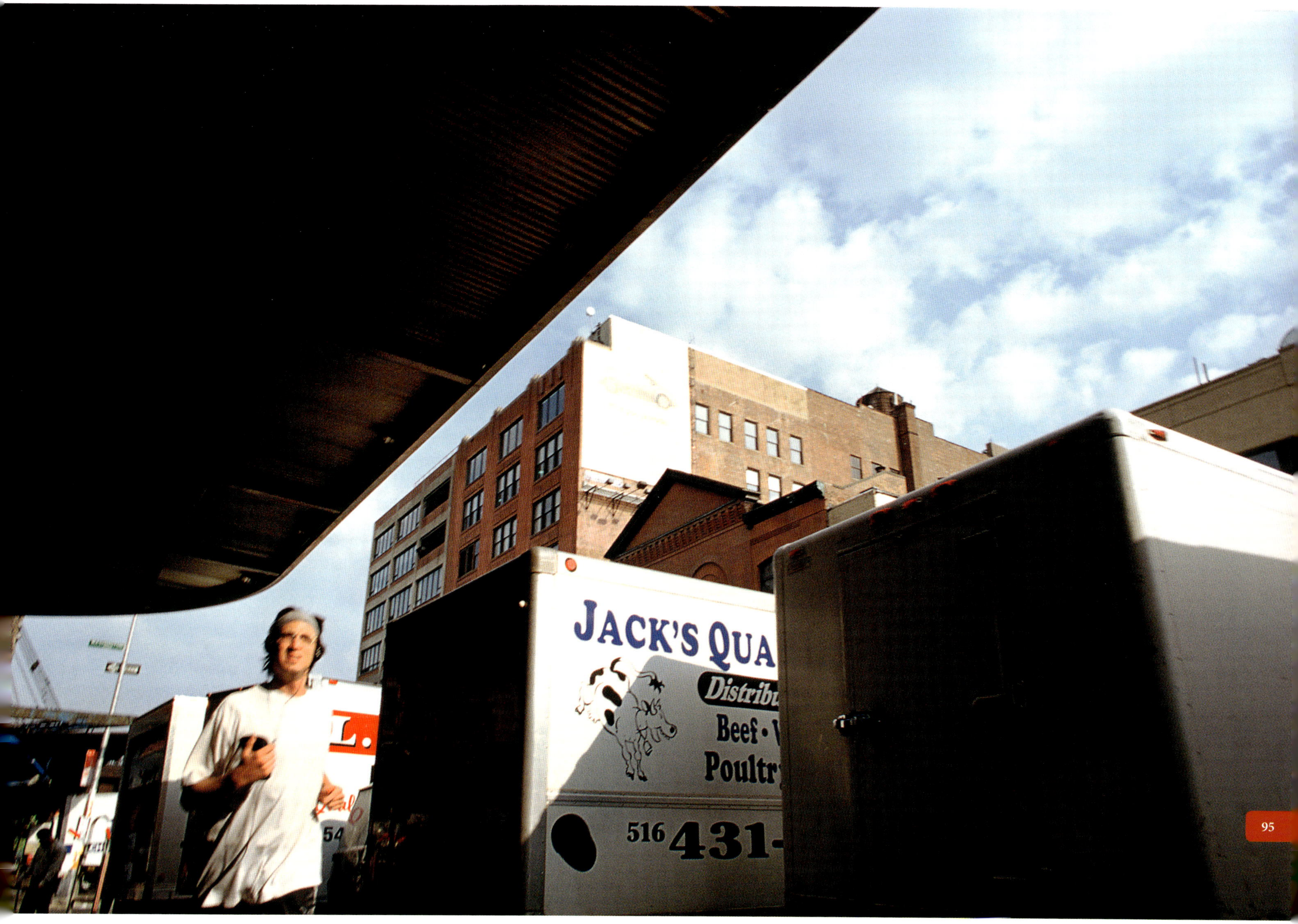
JACK'S QUA
Distribu
Beef •
Poultr
516 431-

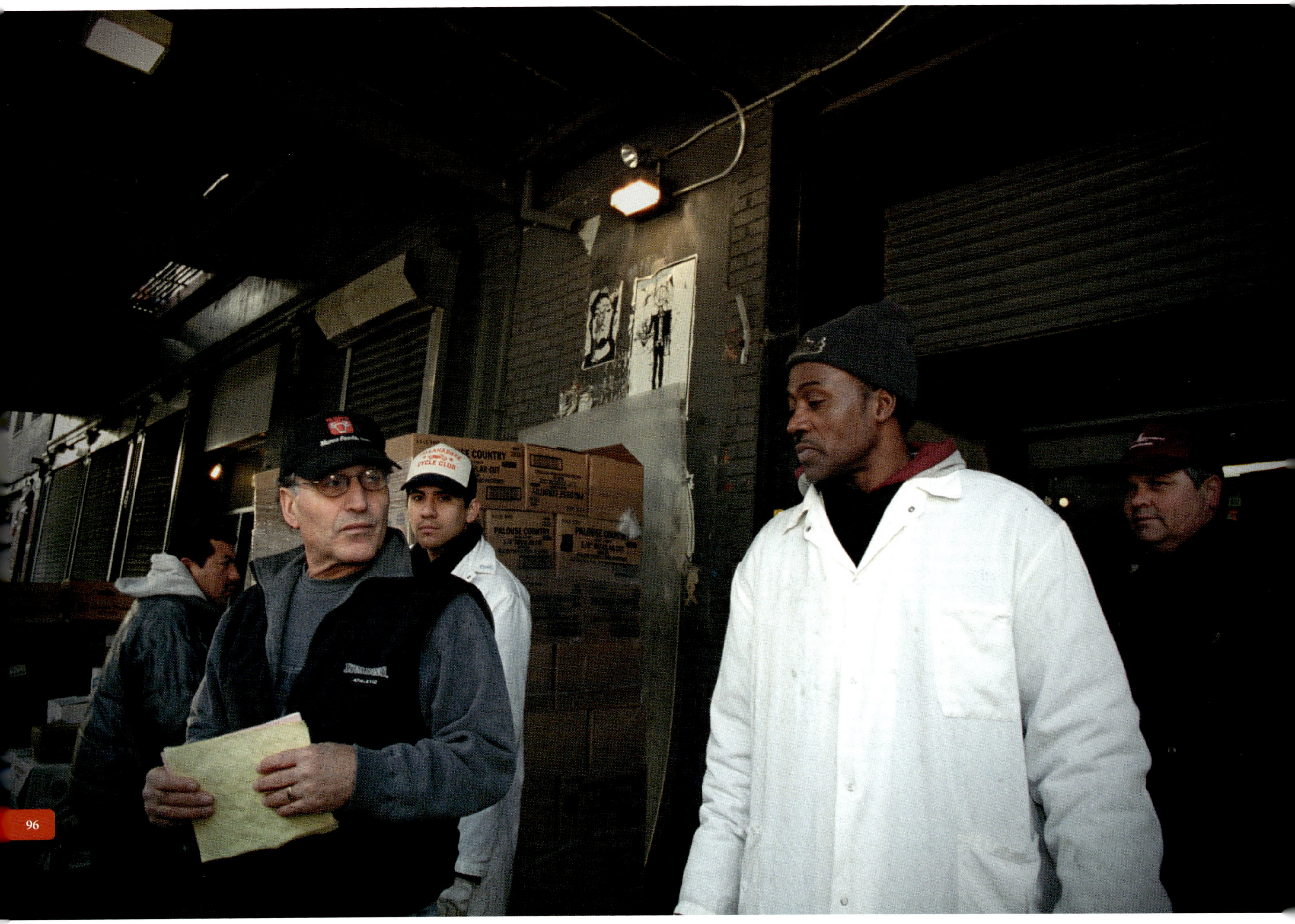
PALOUSE COUNTRY
CYCLE CLUB
PALOUSE COUNTRY
PALOUSE COUNTRY

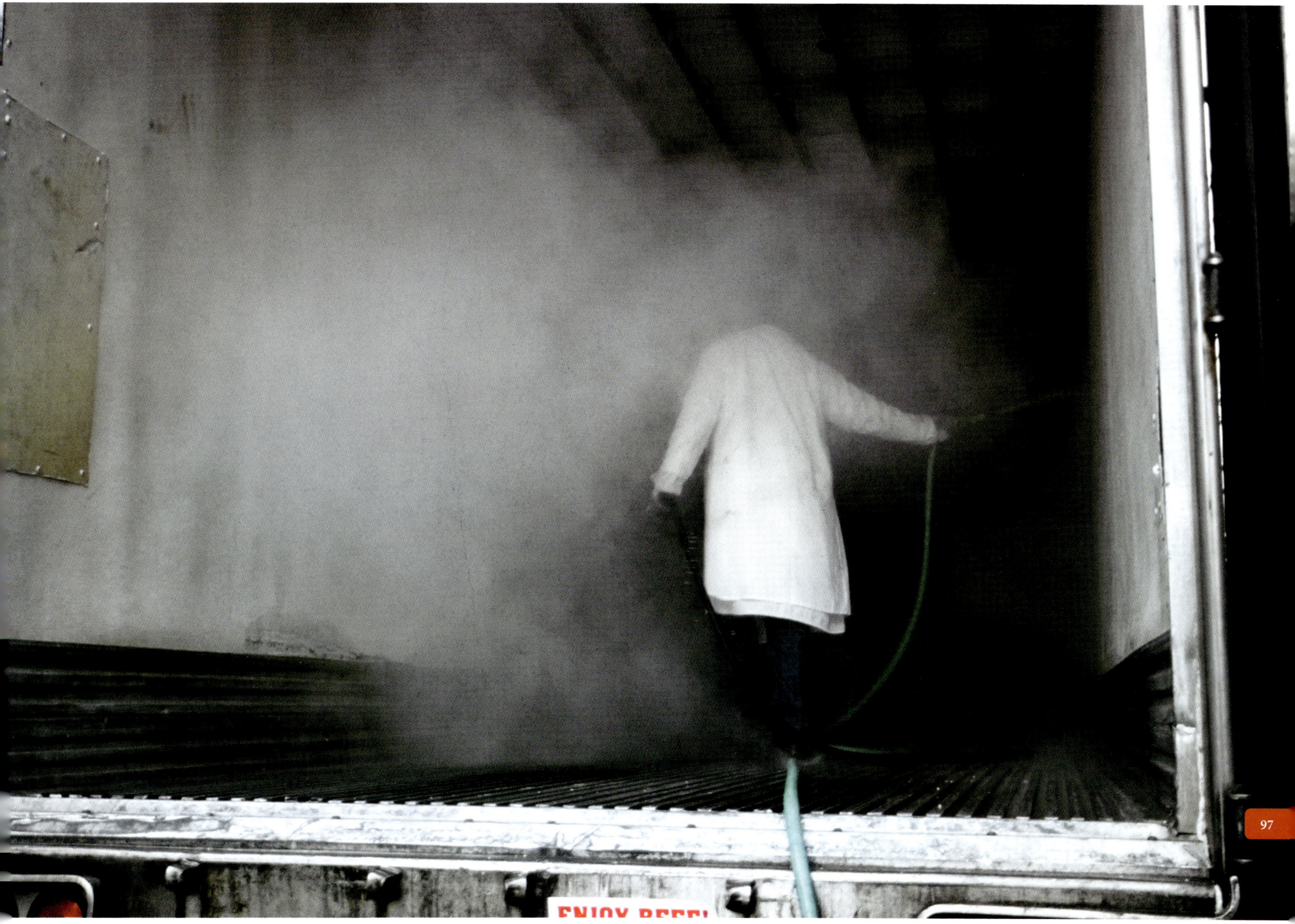

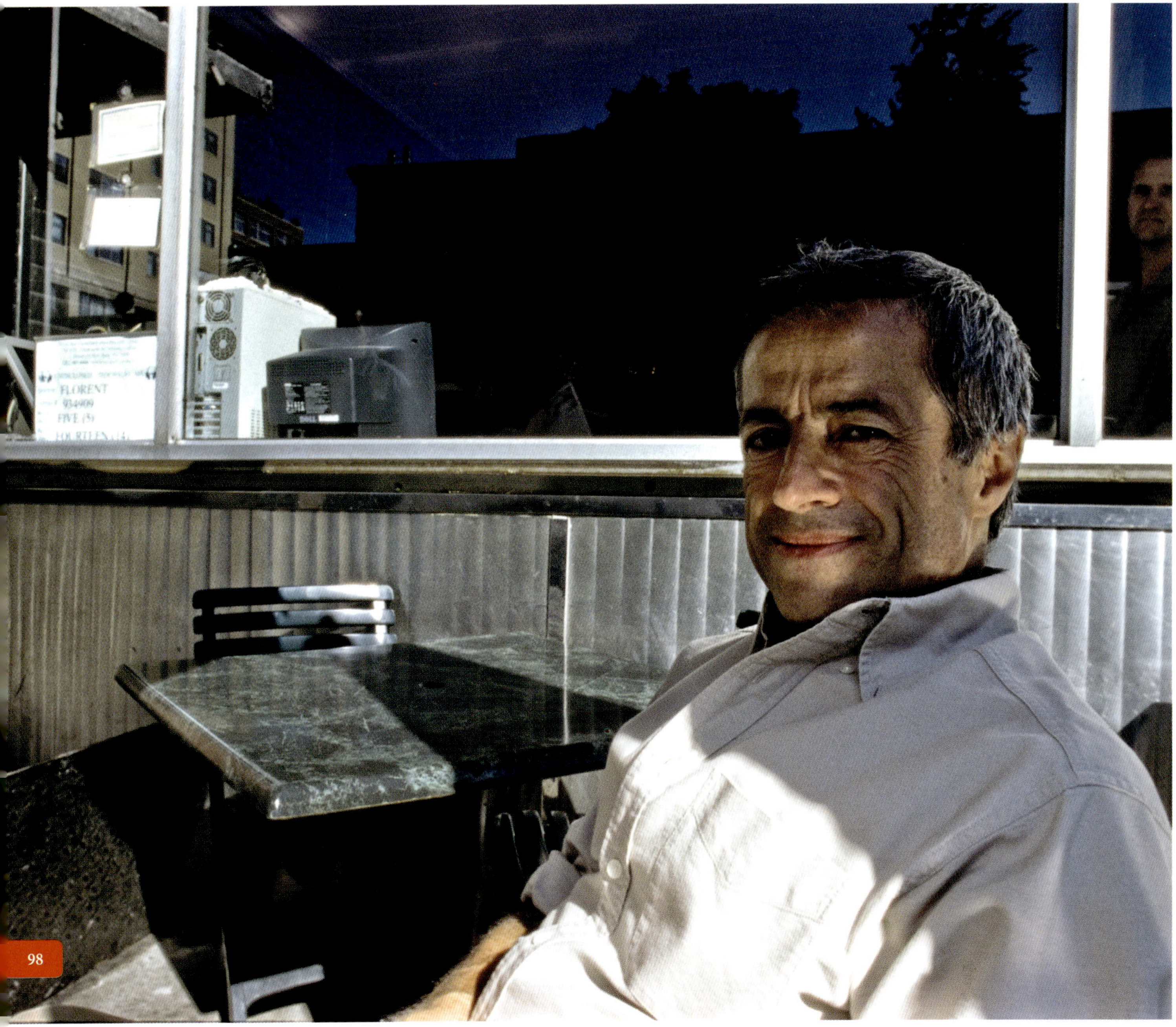
FLORENT
FIVE (5)

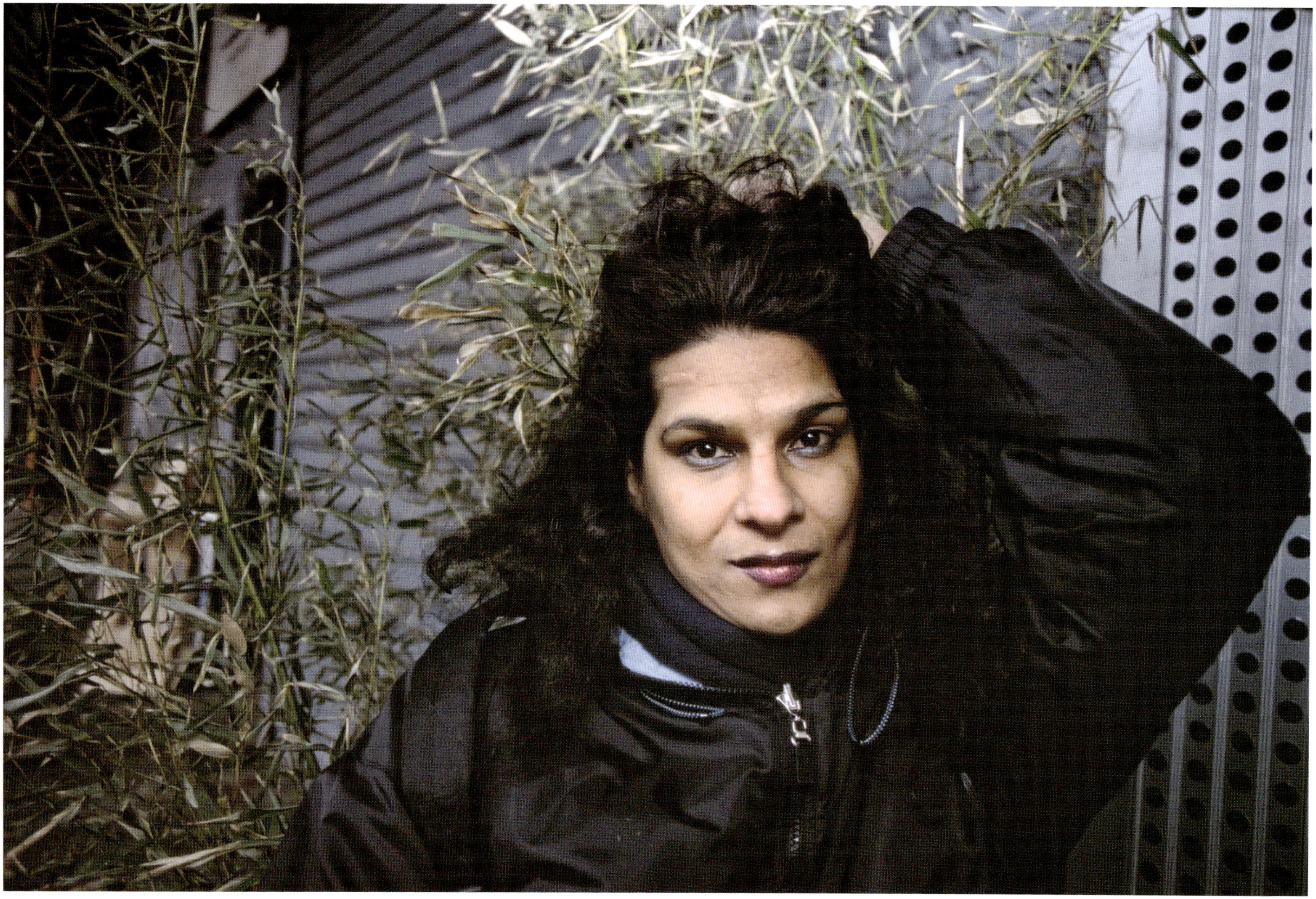

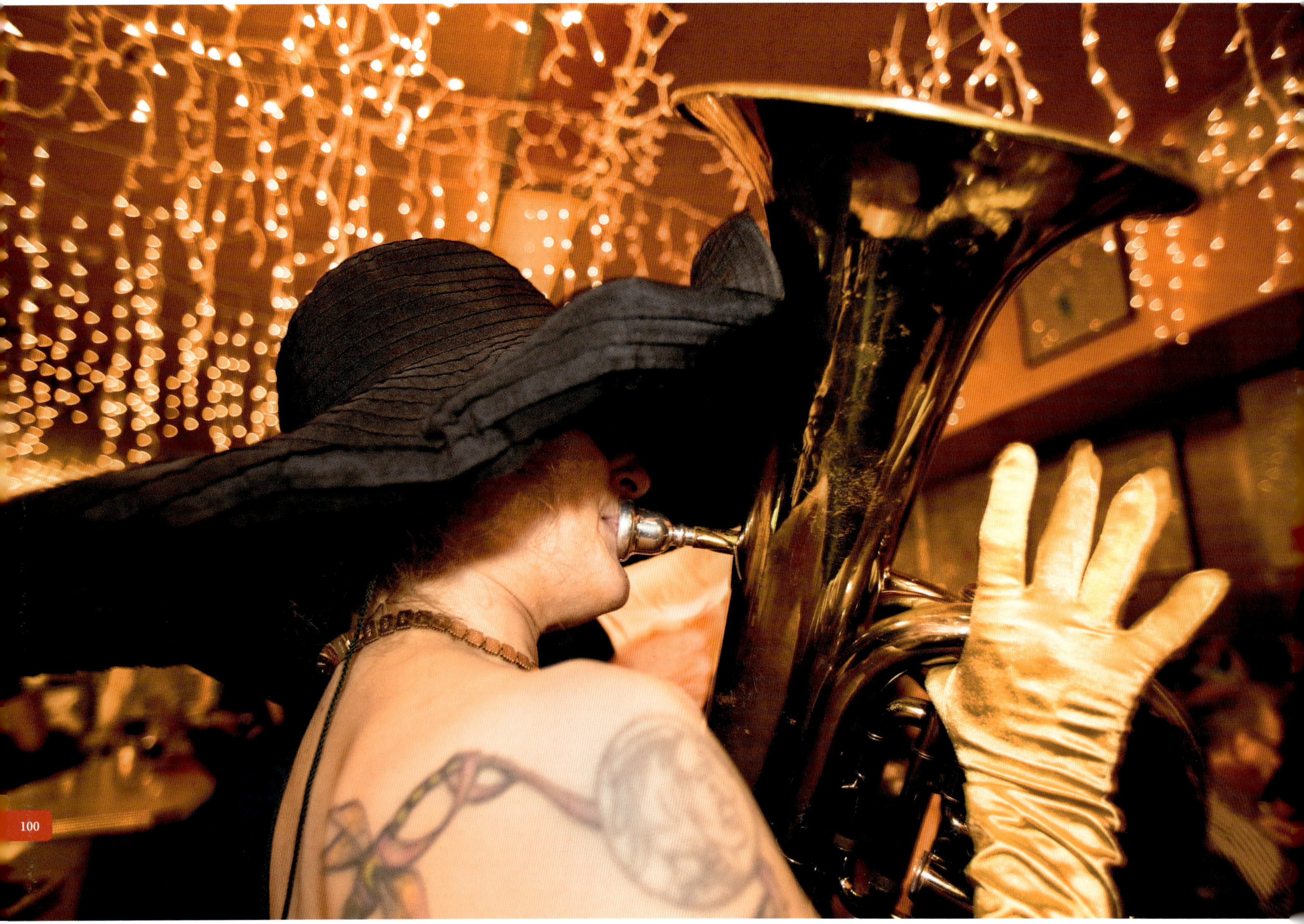

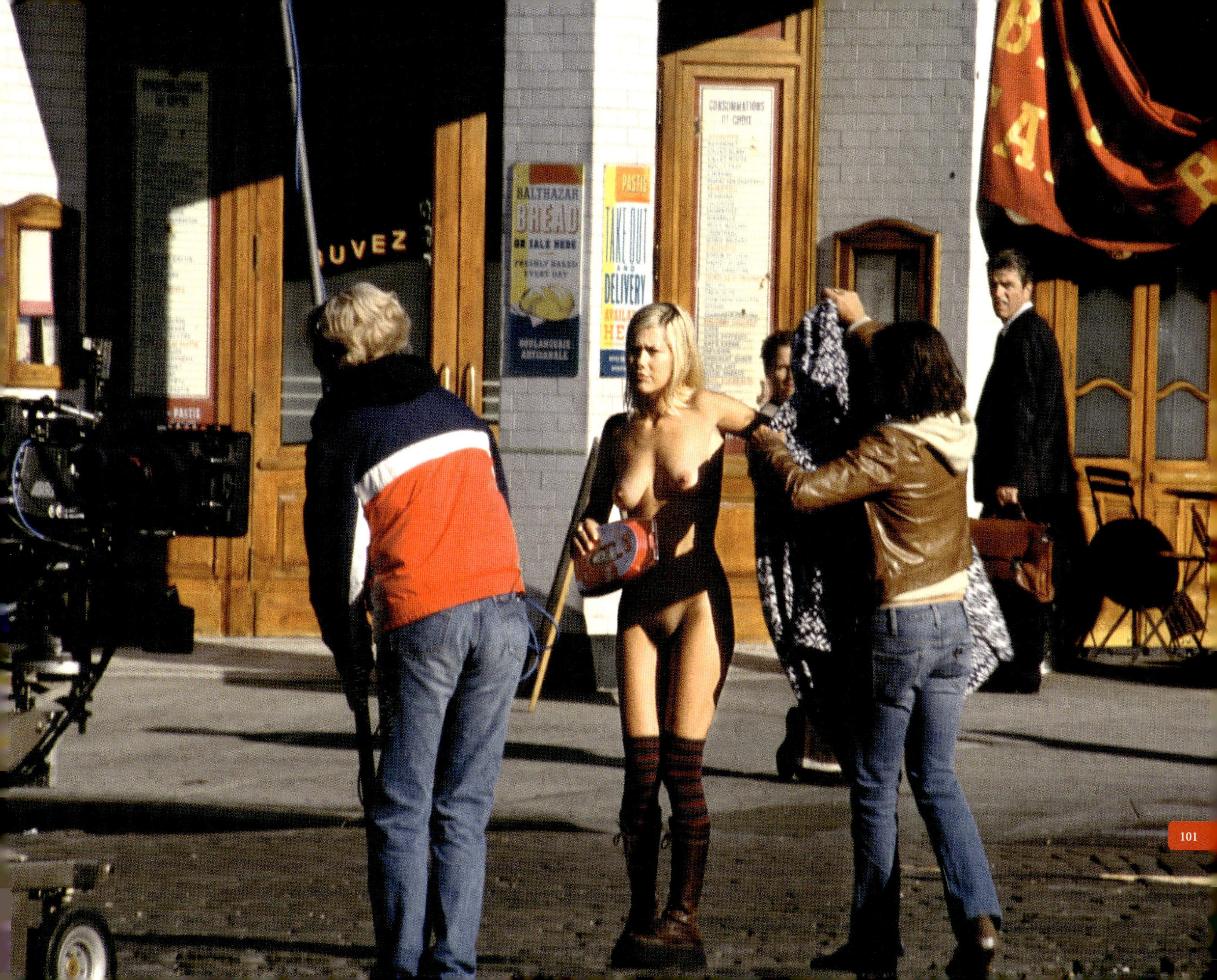
BALTHAZAR
BREAD
ON SALE HERE
FRESHLY BAKED
EVERY DAY
BOULANGERIE
ARTISANALE
PASTIS
TAKE OUT
AND
DELIVERY
CONSOMMATIONS
DE CHOIX
UVEZ

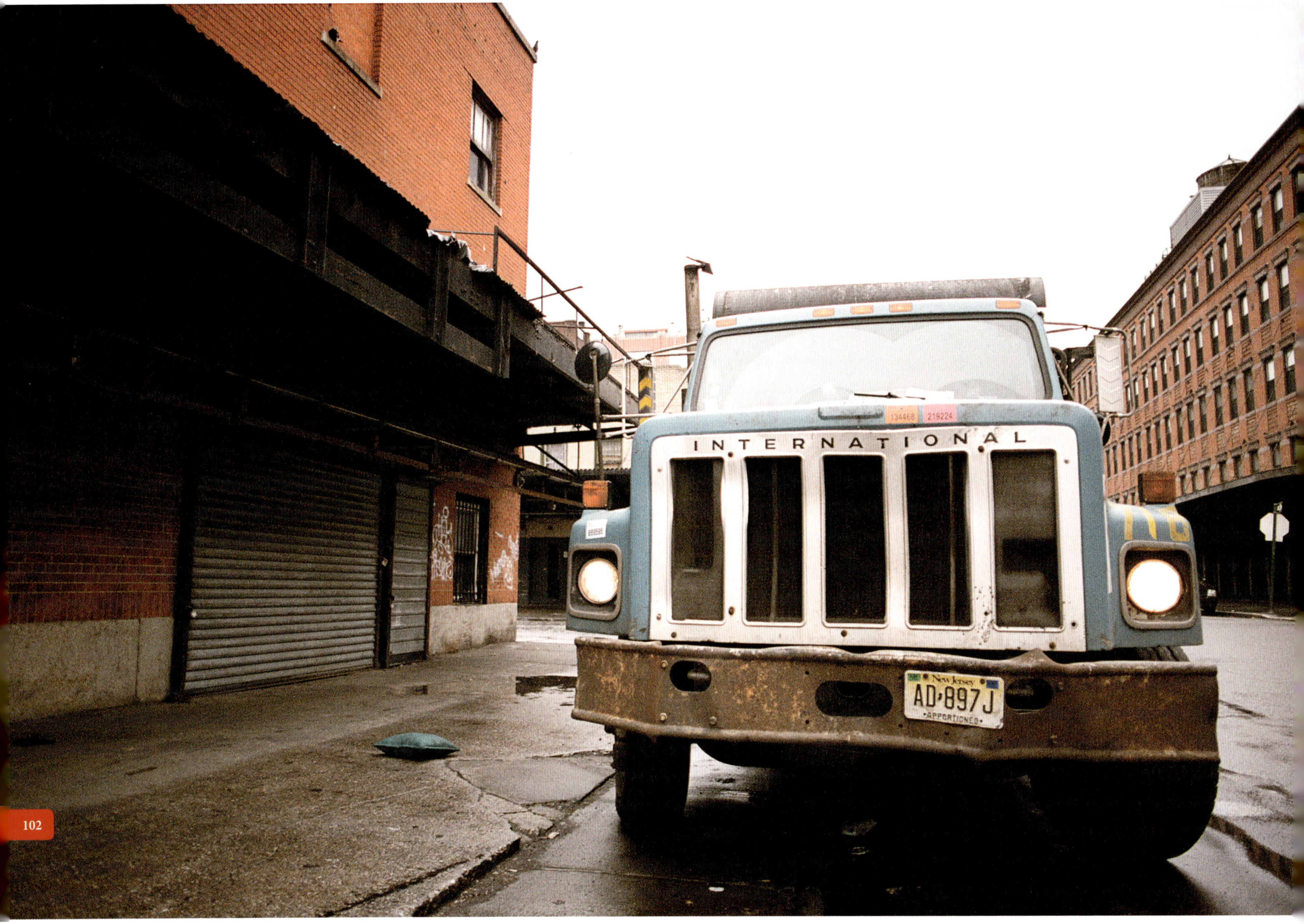
INTERNATIONAL
New Jersey
AD 897J
APPORTIONED

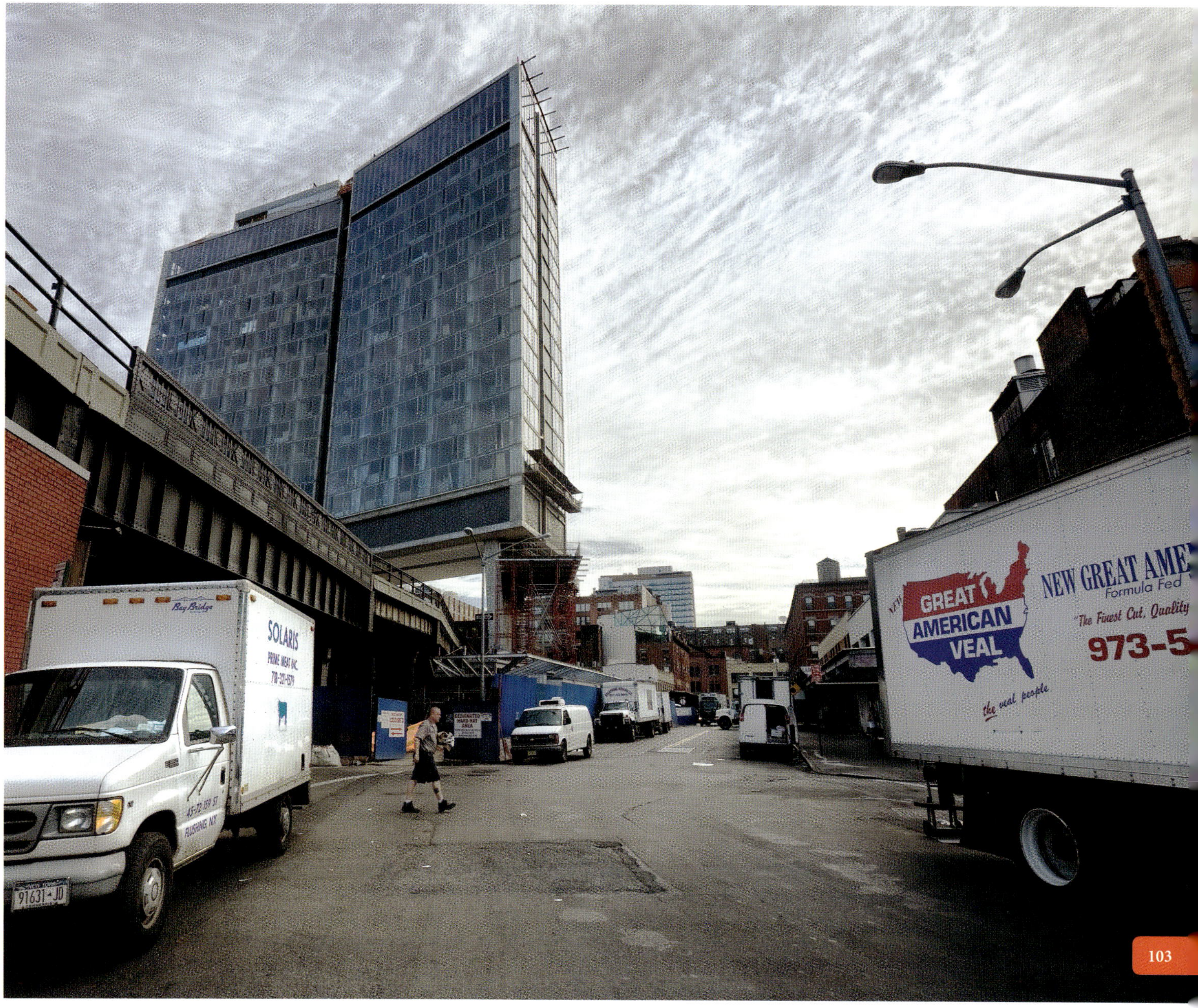
SOLARIS
PRIME MEAT INC.
FLUSHING, NY
GREAT AMERICAN VEAL
Formula Fed
the veal people

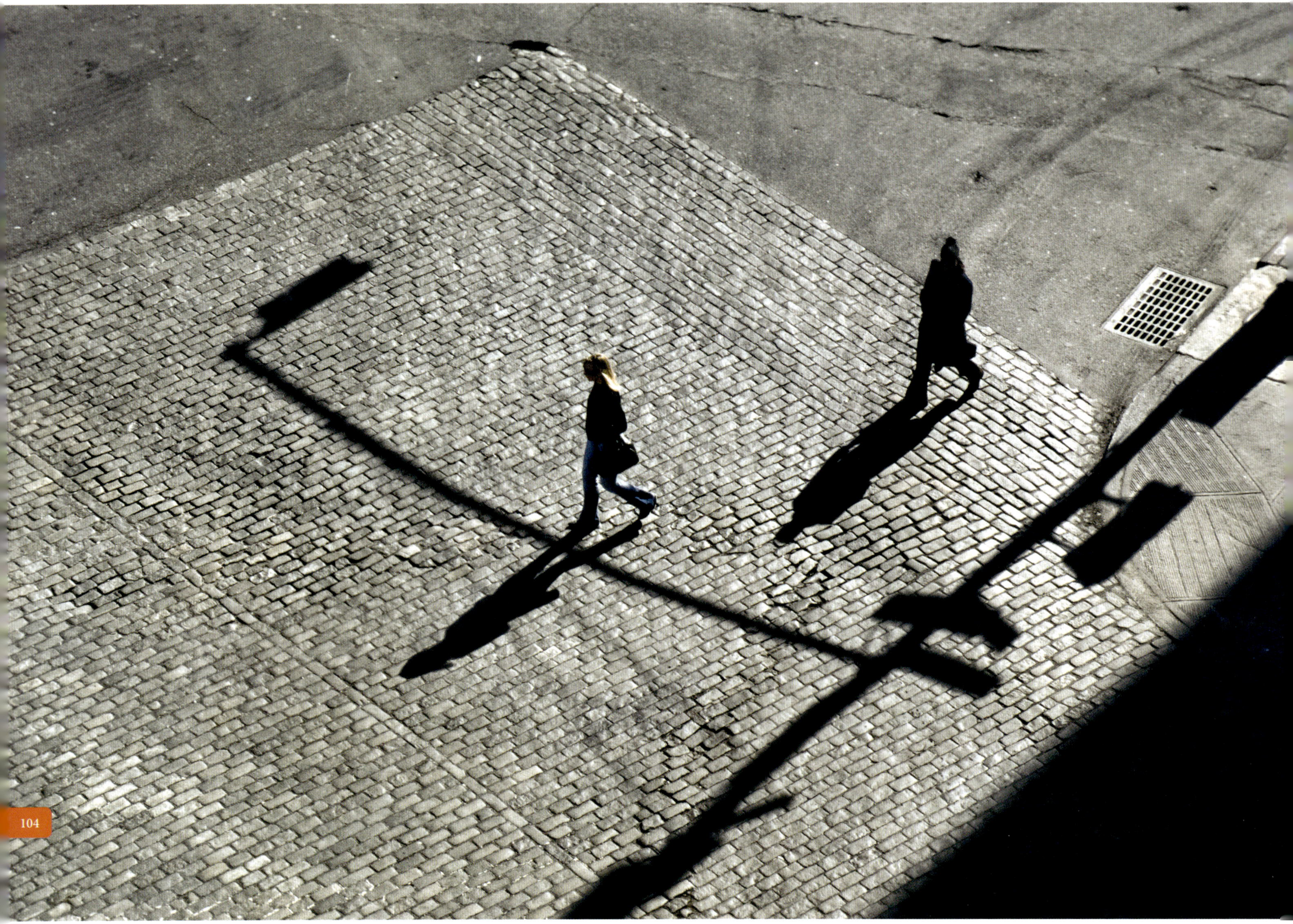

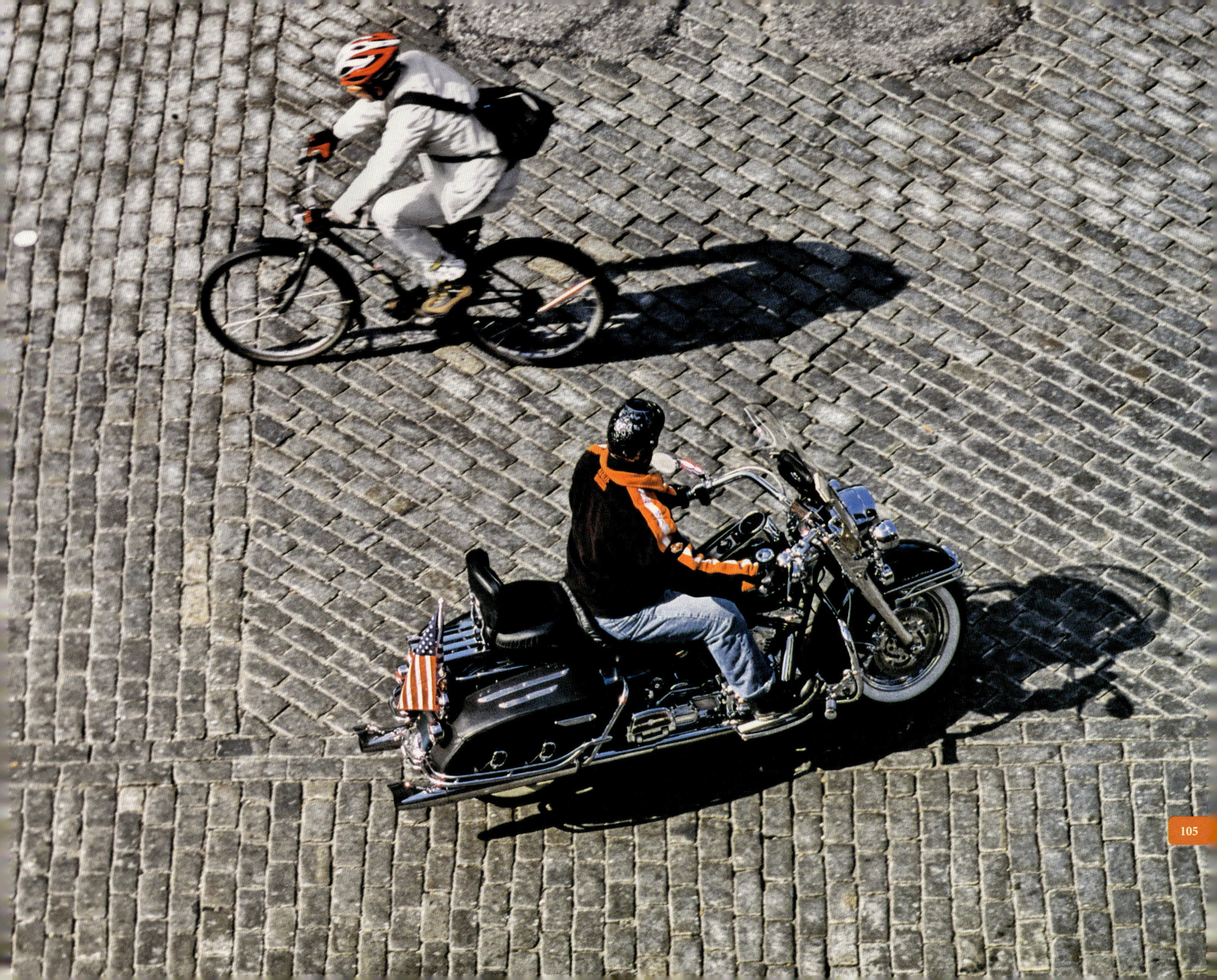

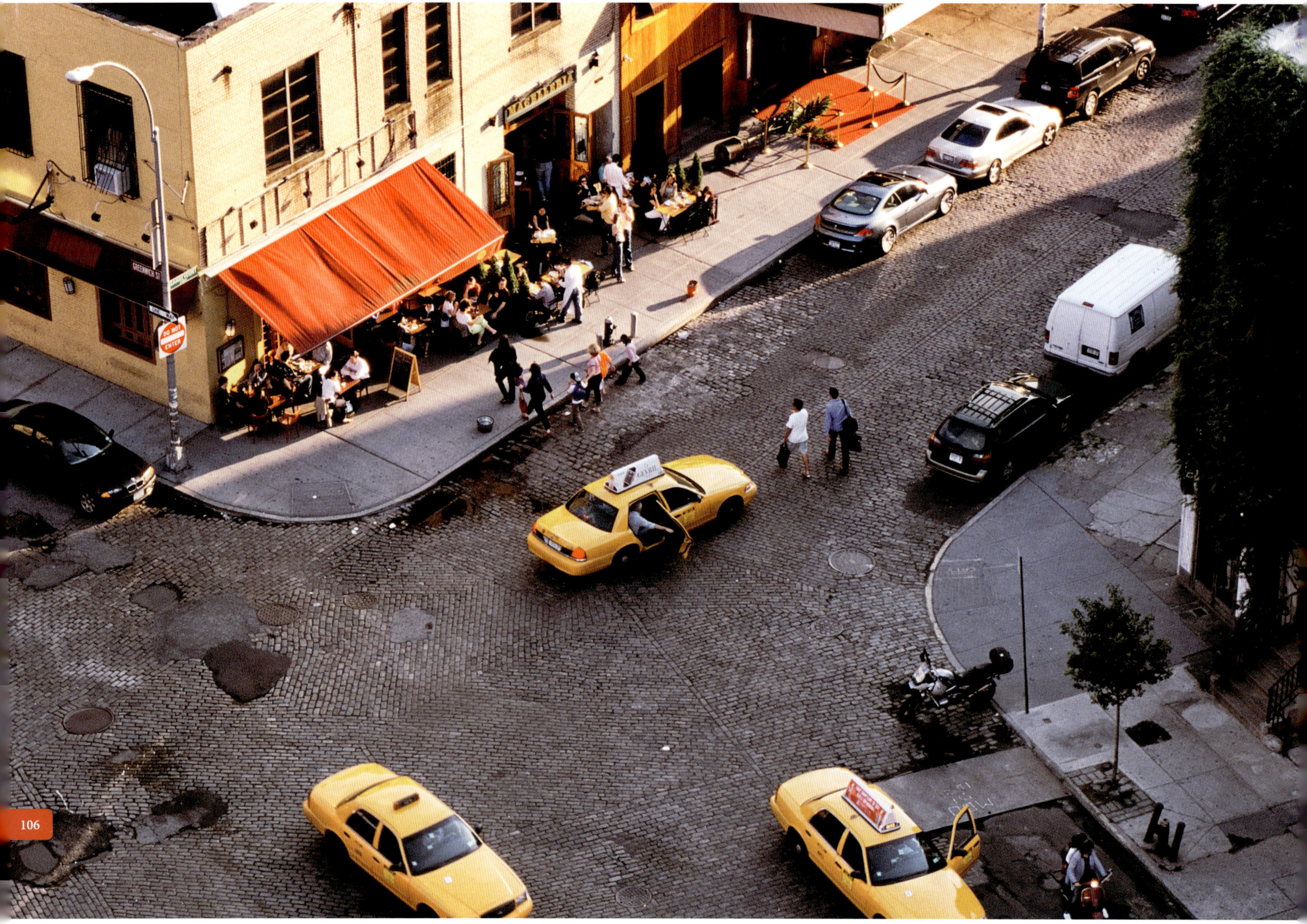
GREENWICH ST
ONE WAY
DO NOT ENTER

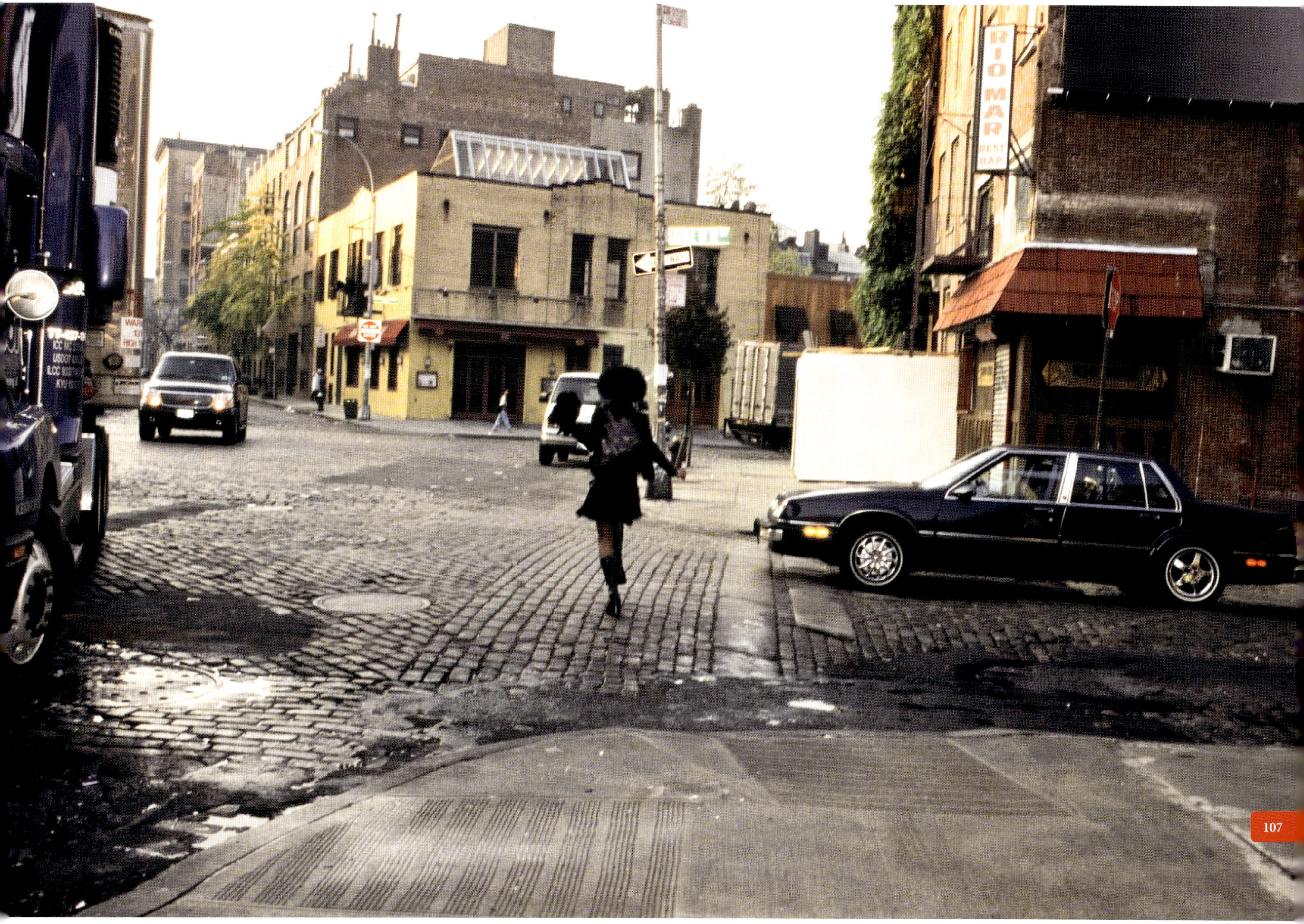
RIO MAR
REST
BAR

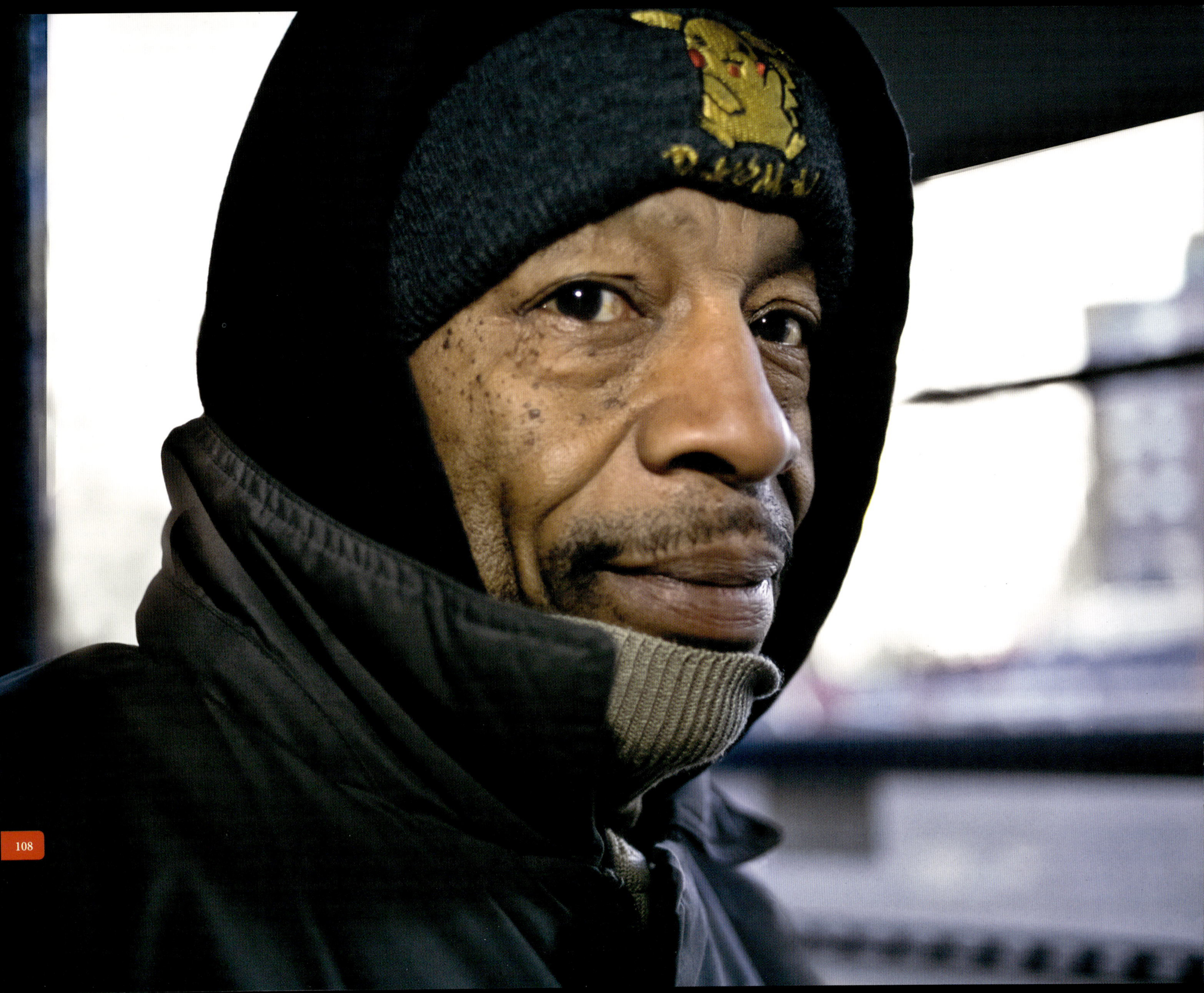

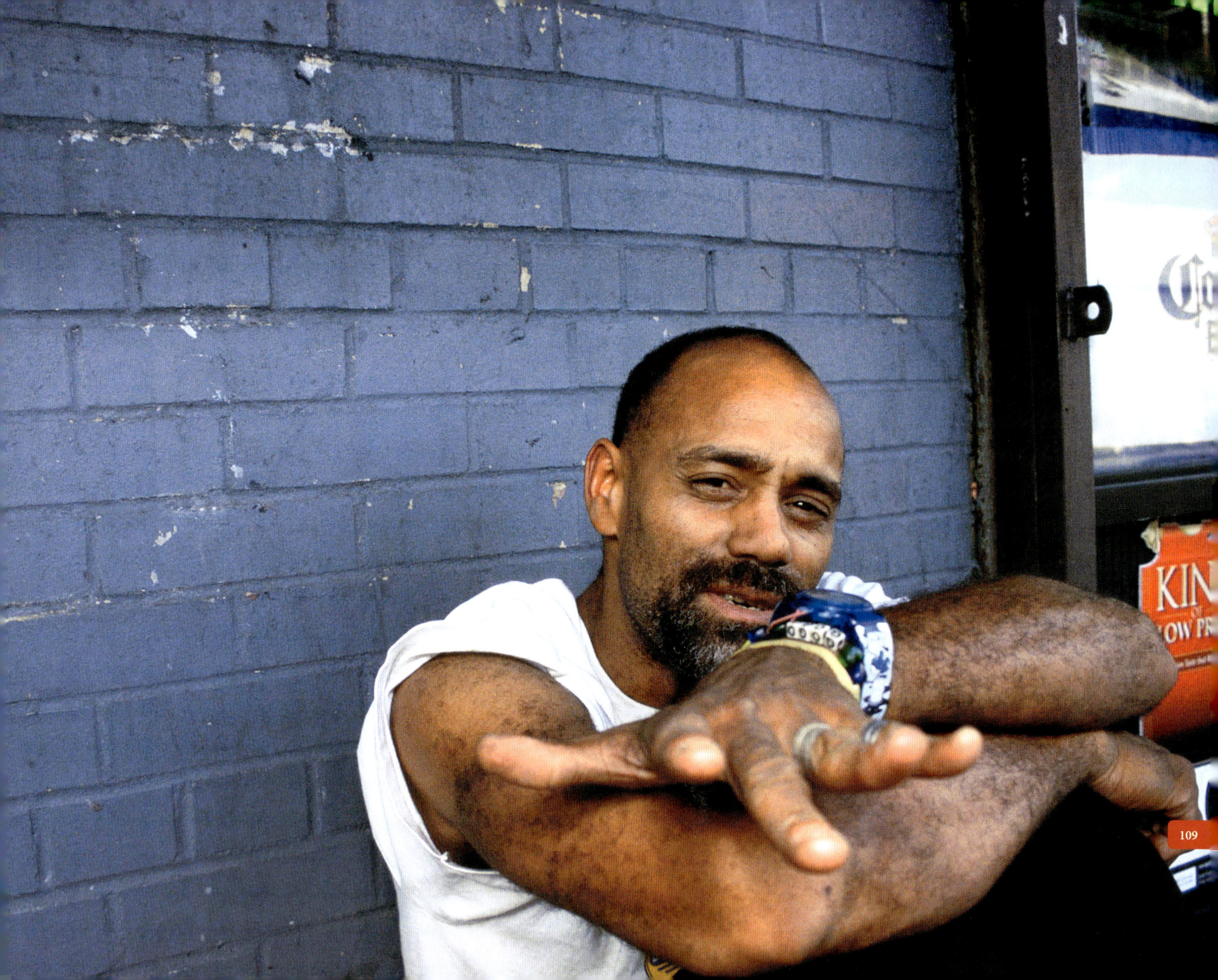

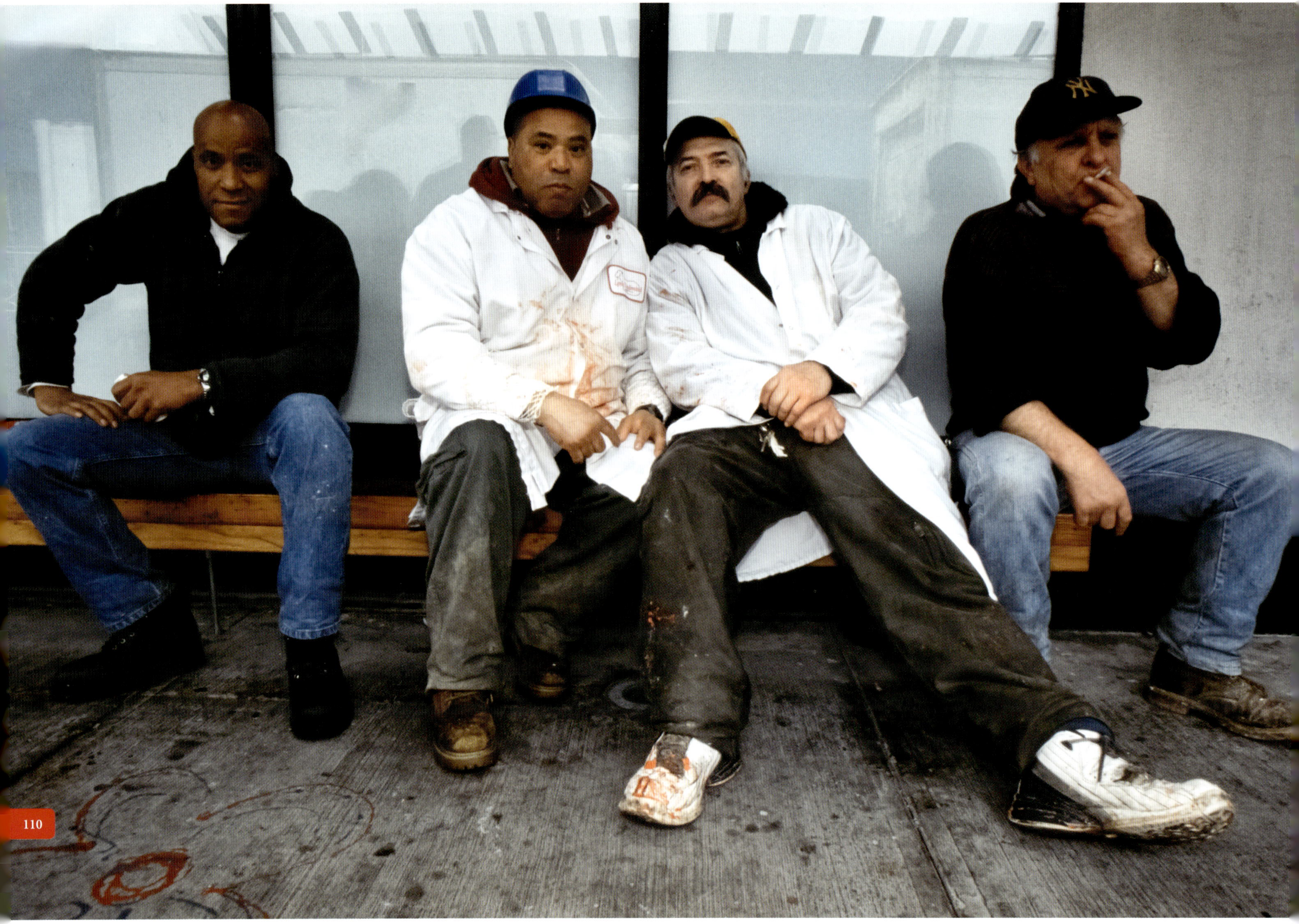

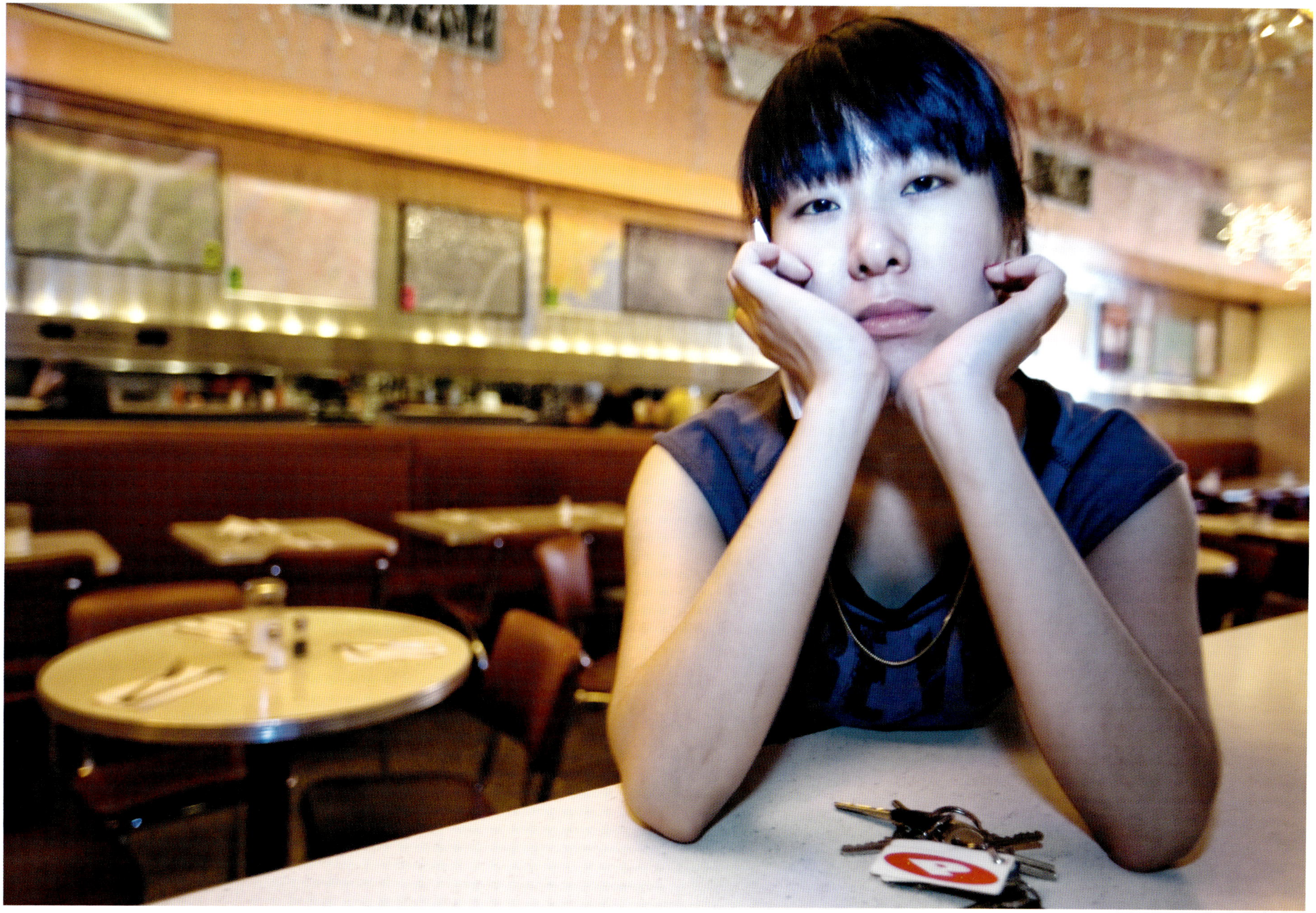

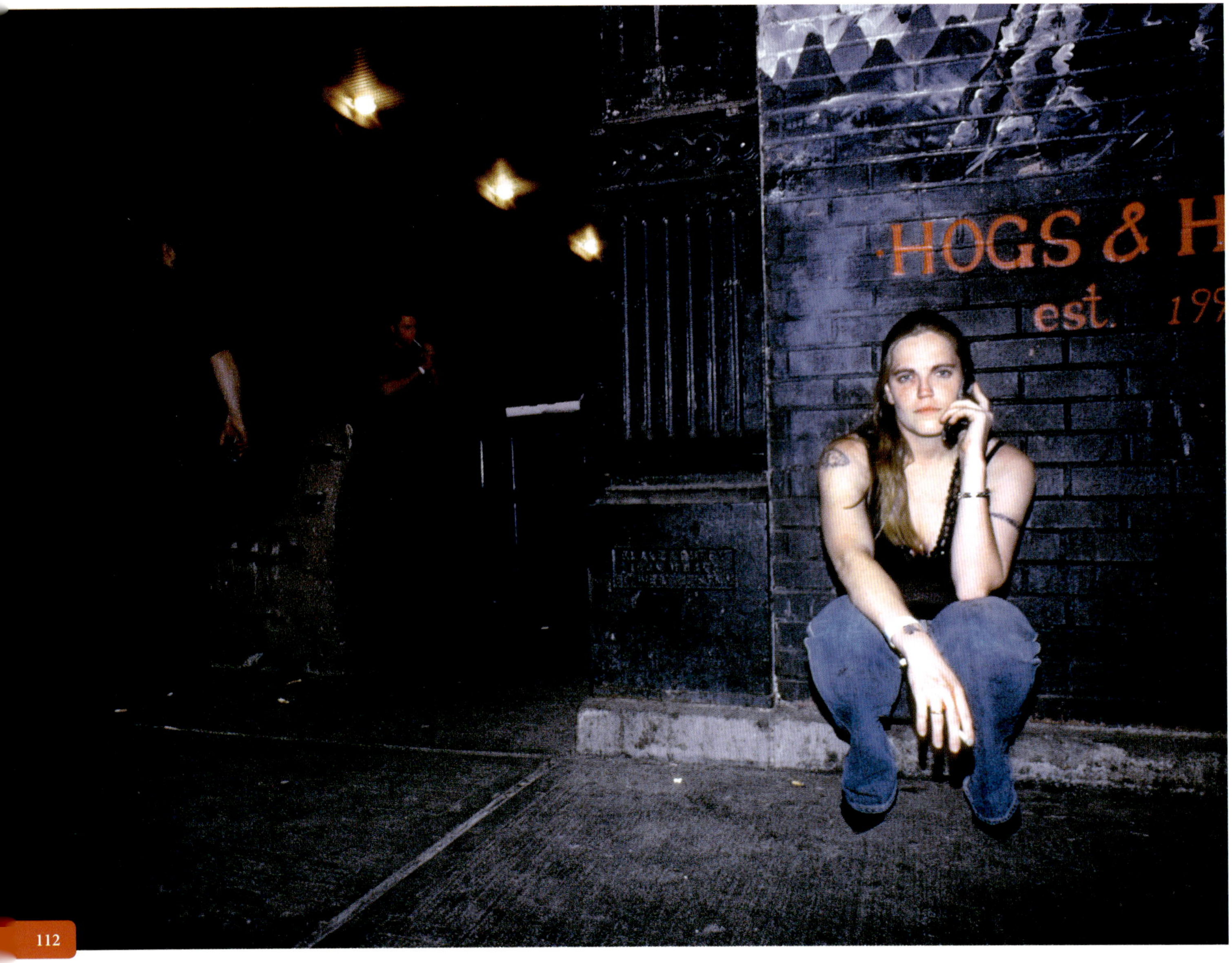
HOGS & H
est. 199

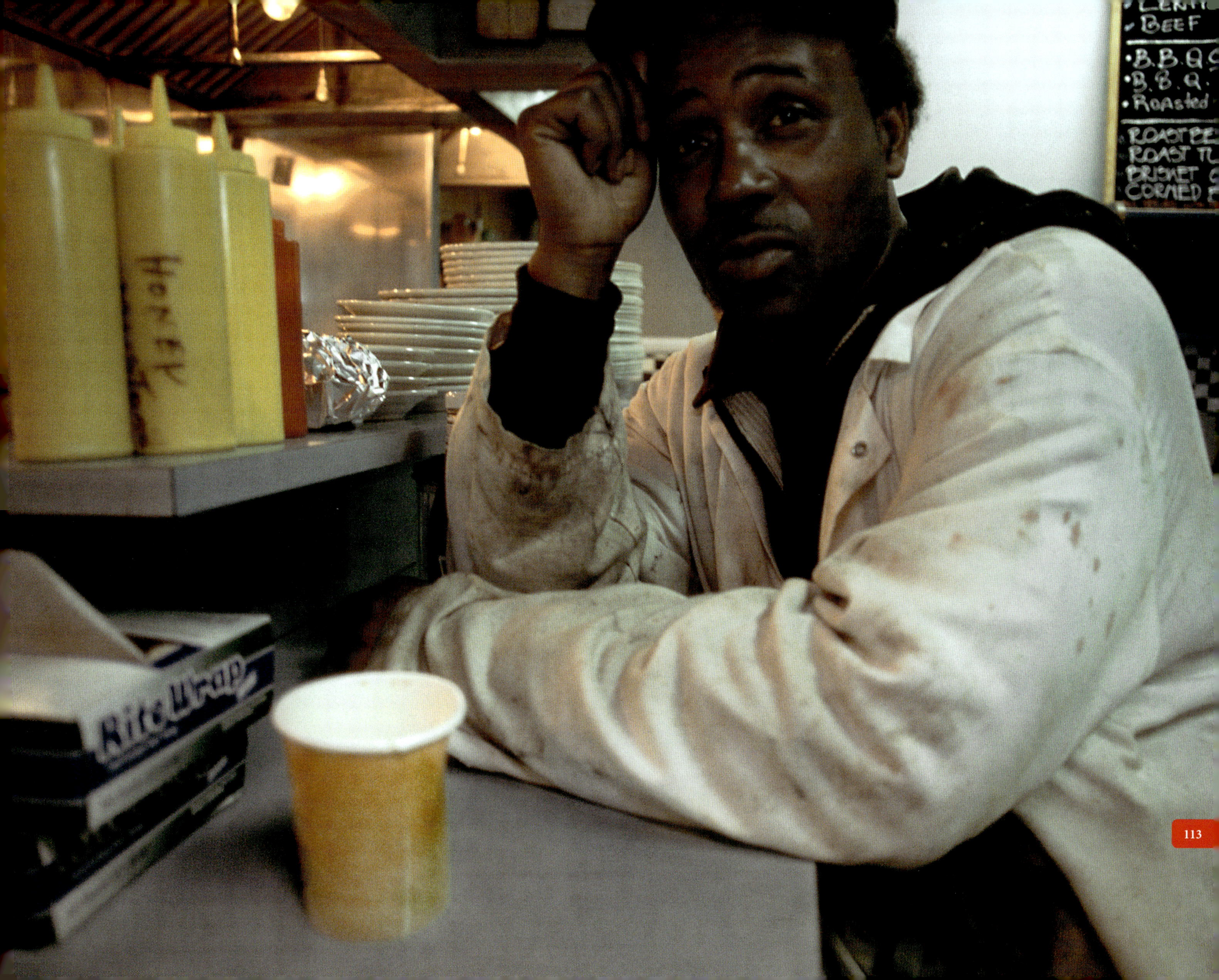
BEEF
Roasted
Rite Wrap

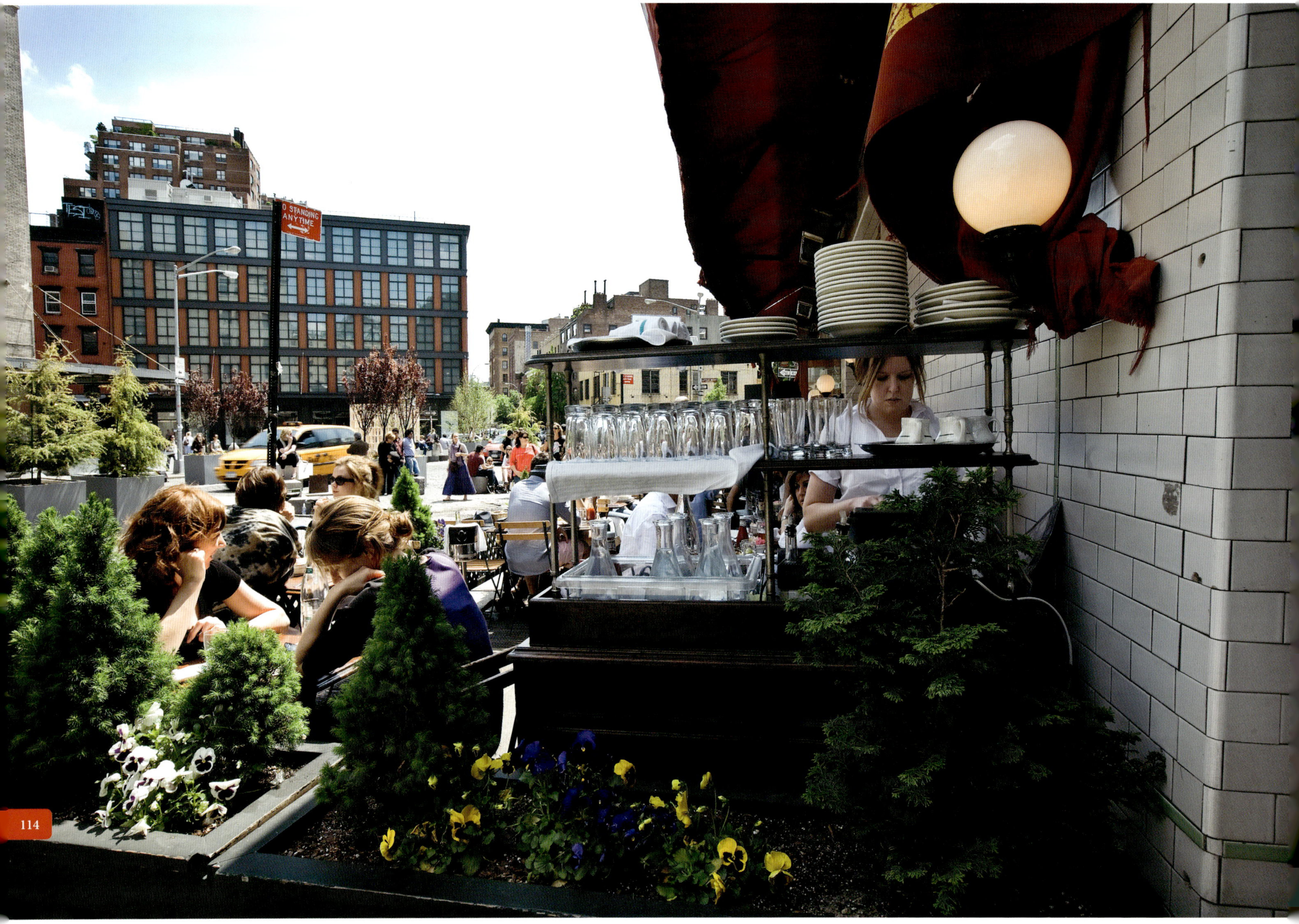
STANDING
ANYTIME

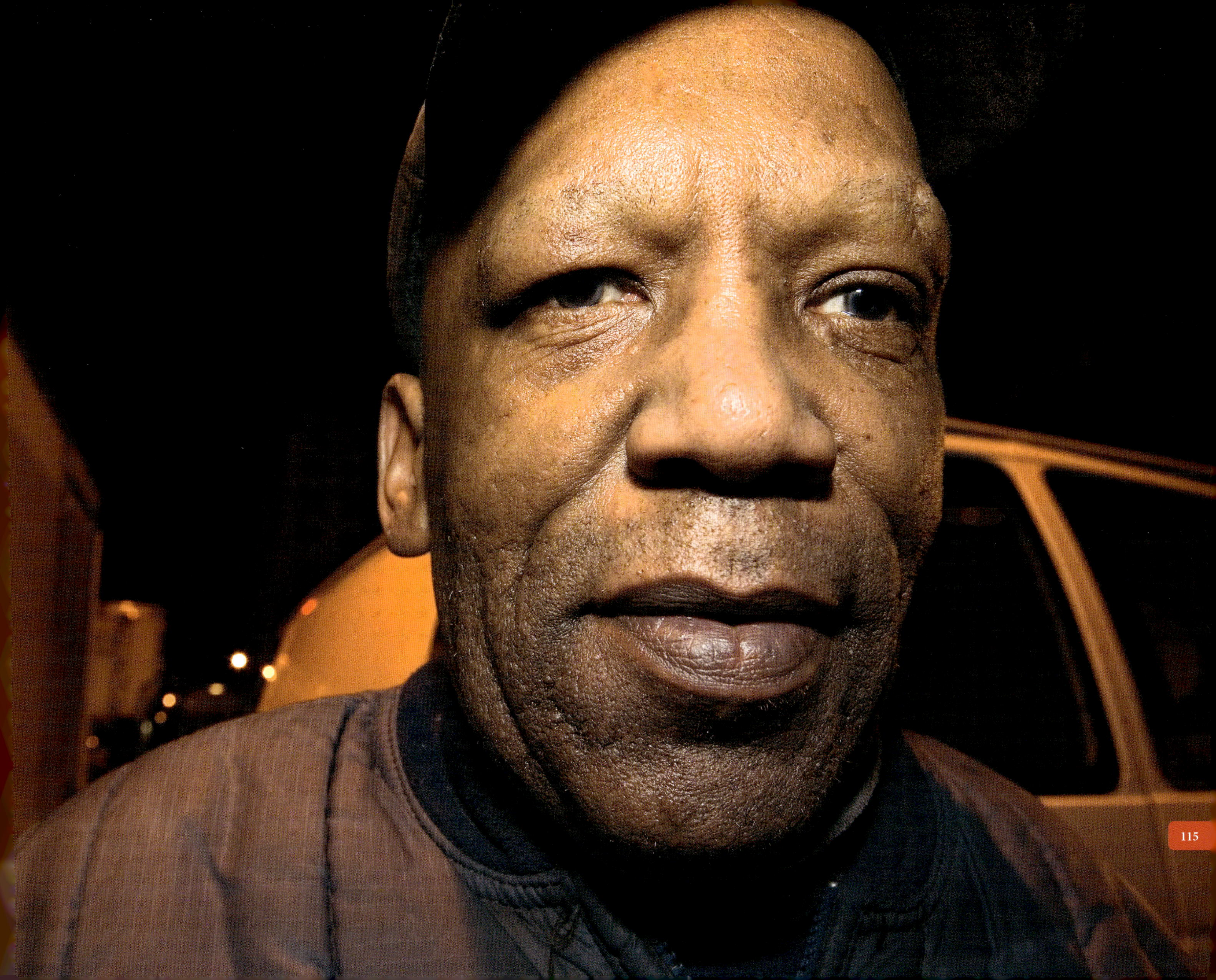

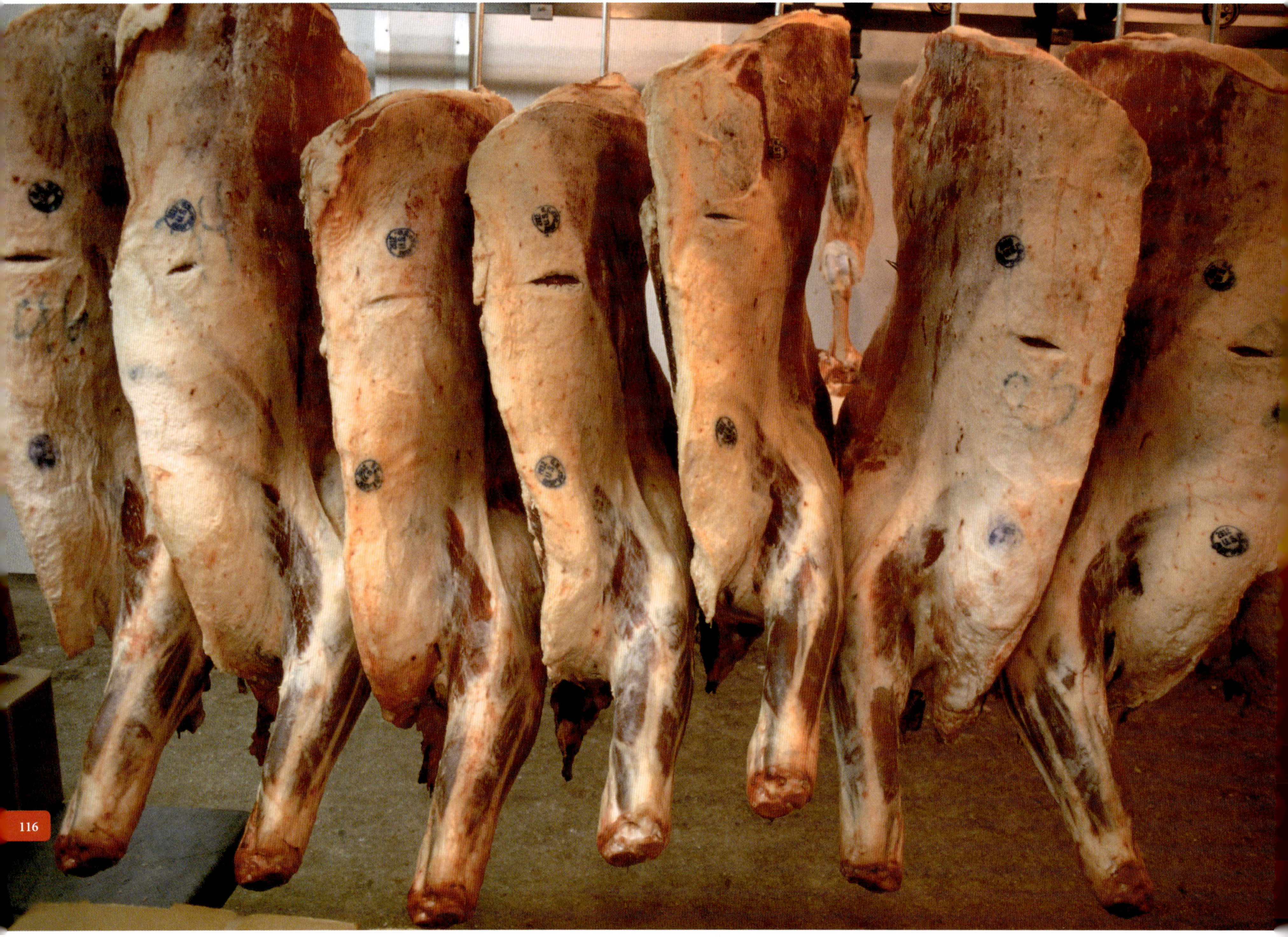

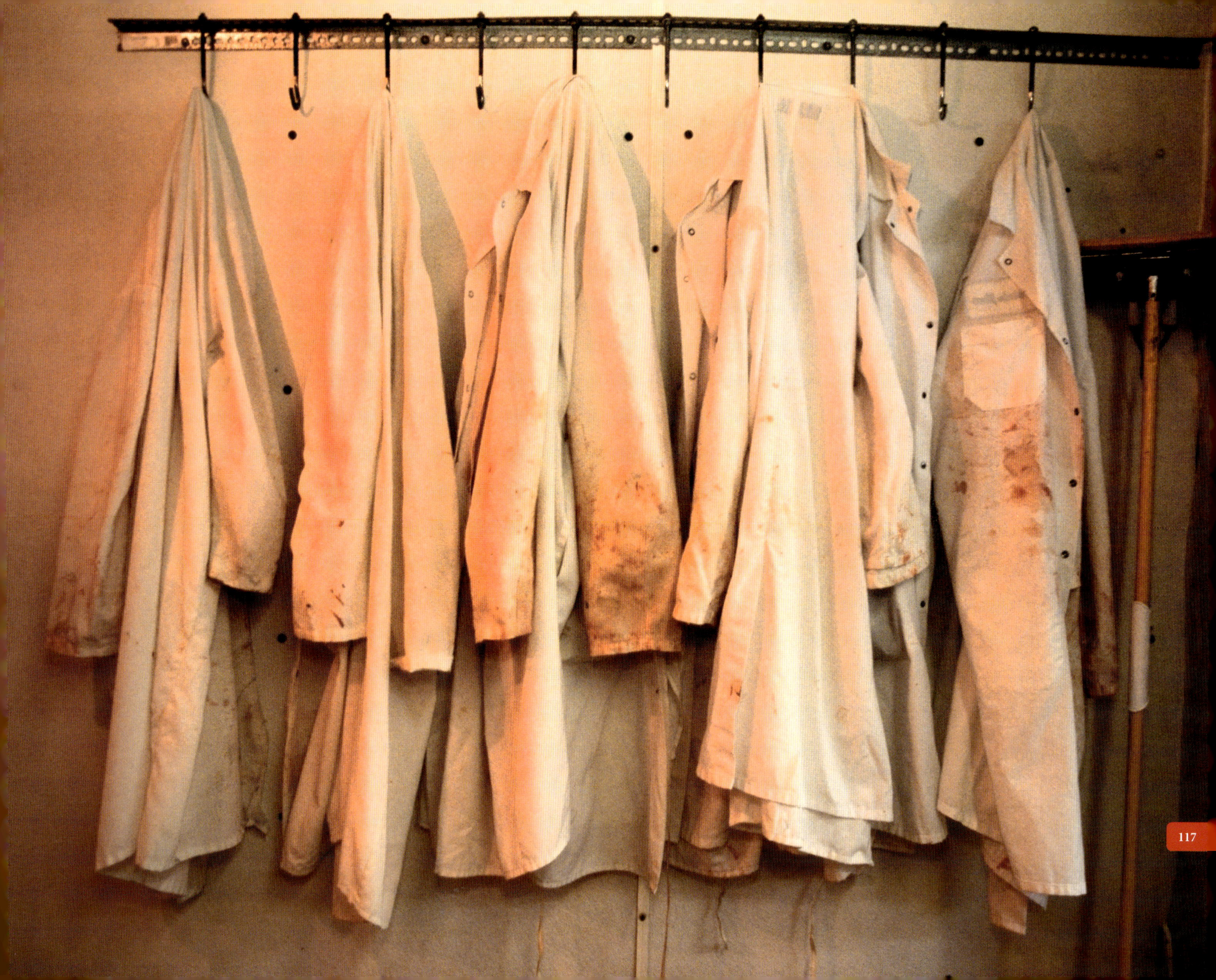

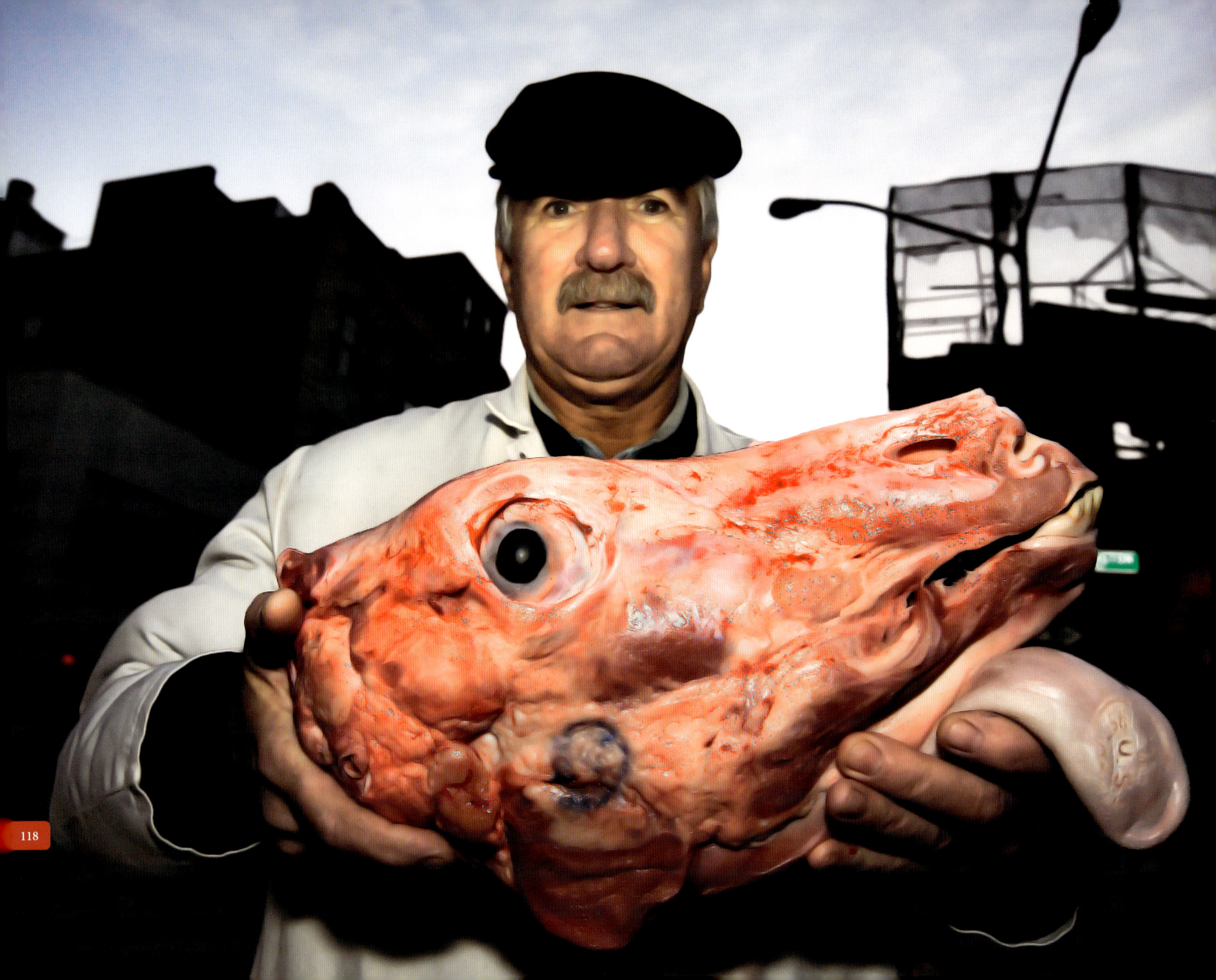

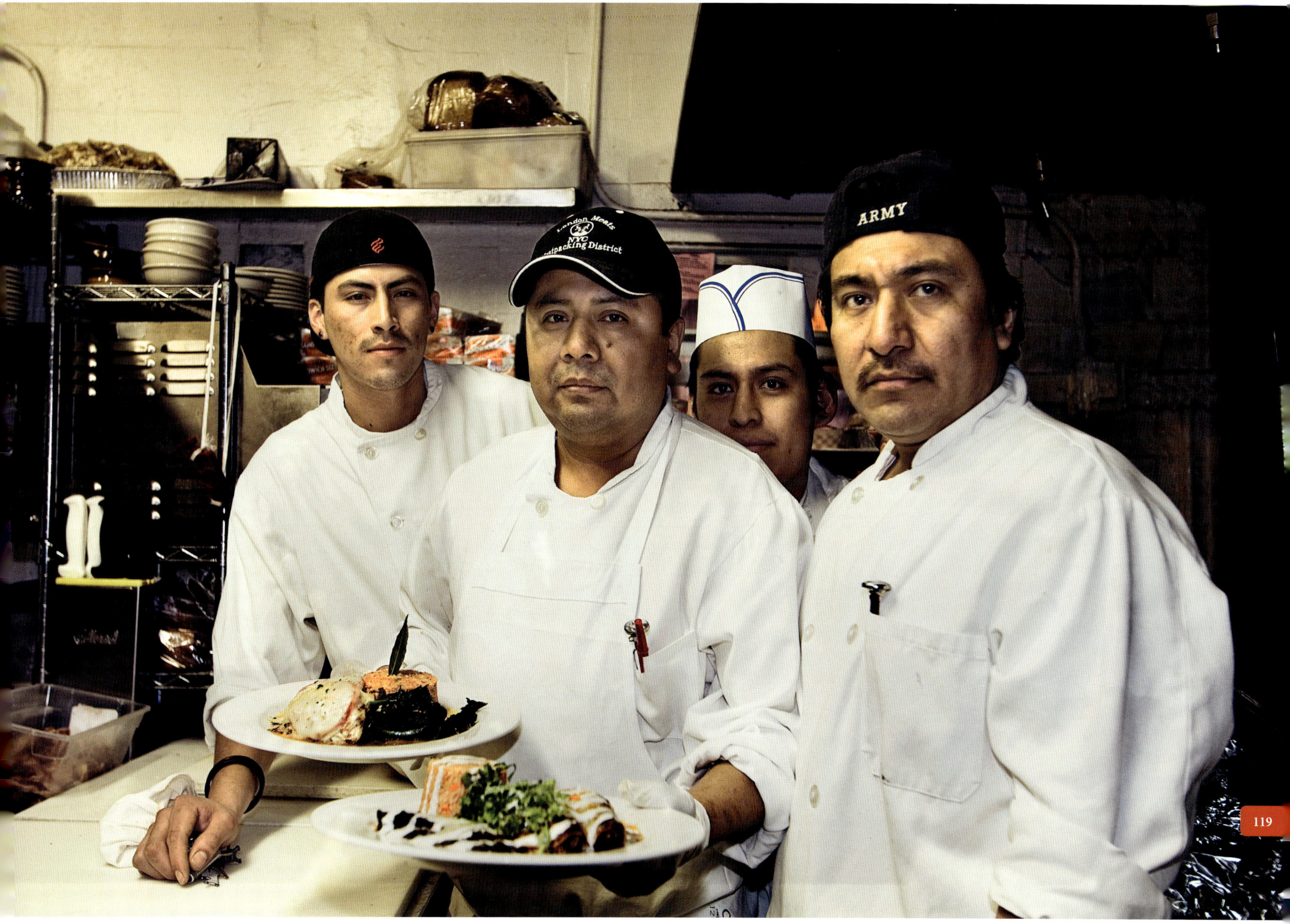
London Meats
NYC
ARMY

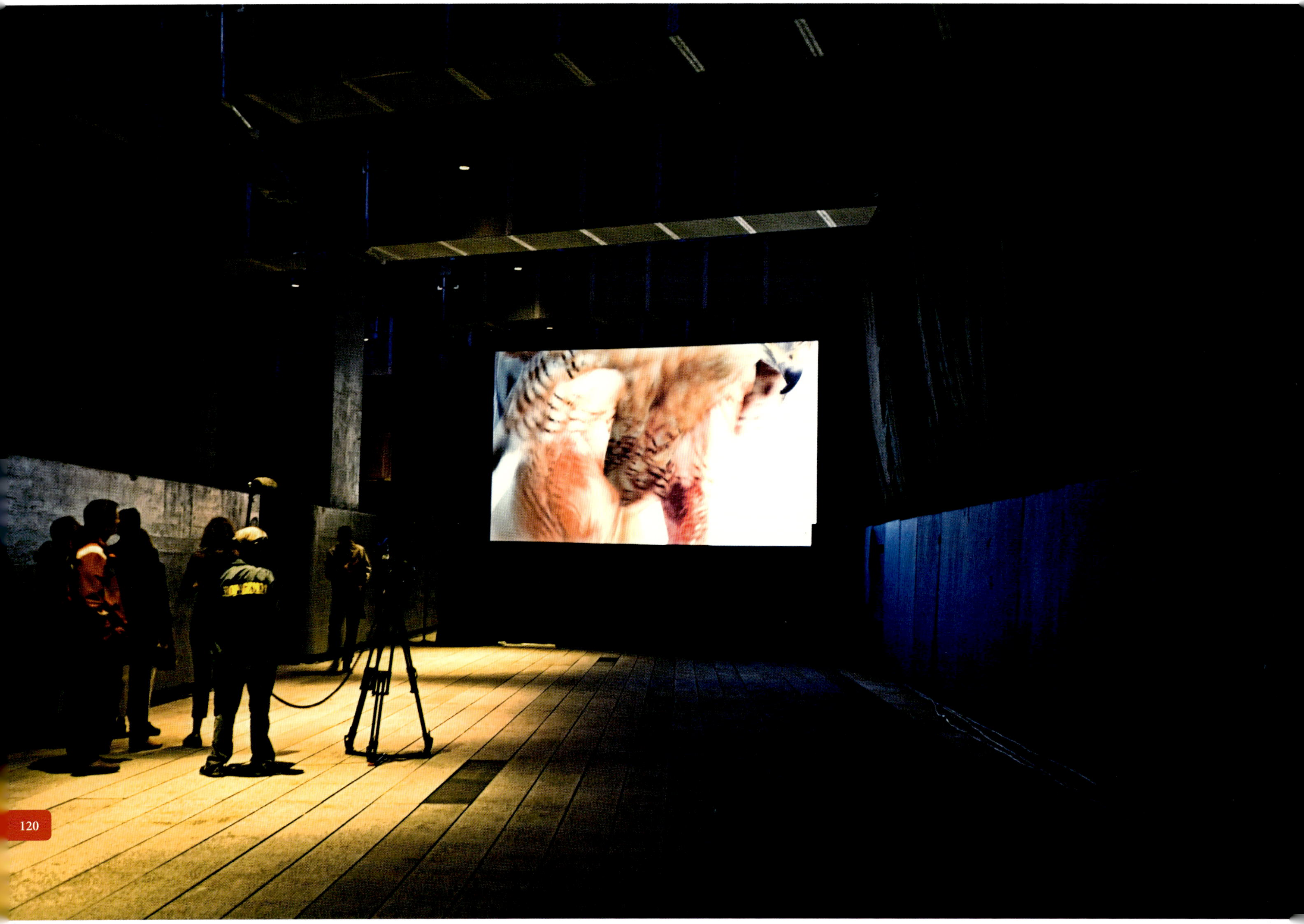

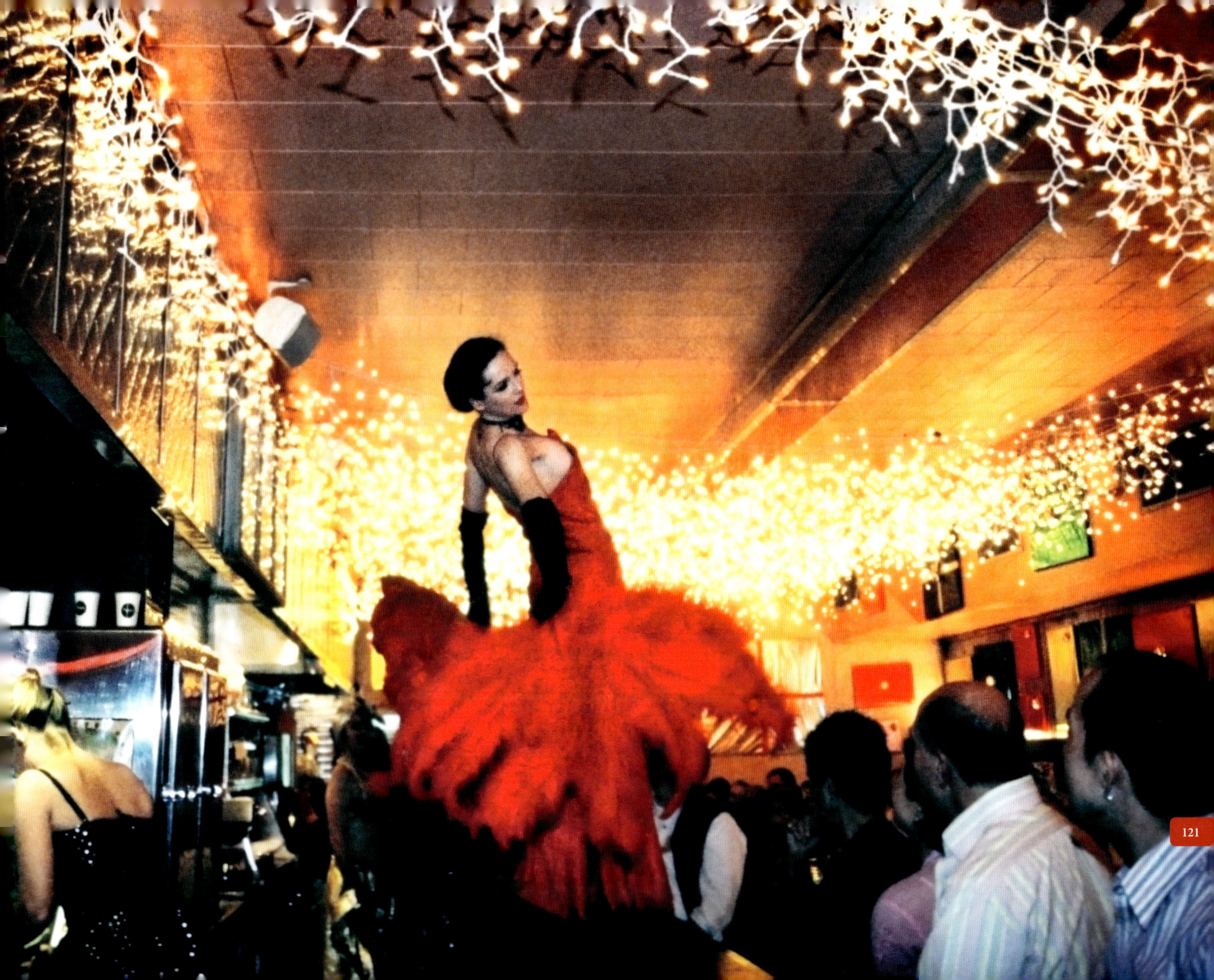

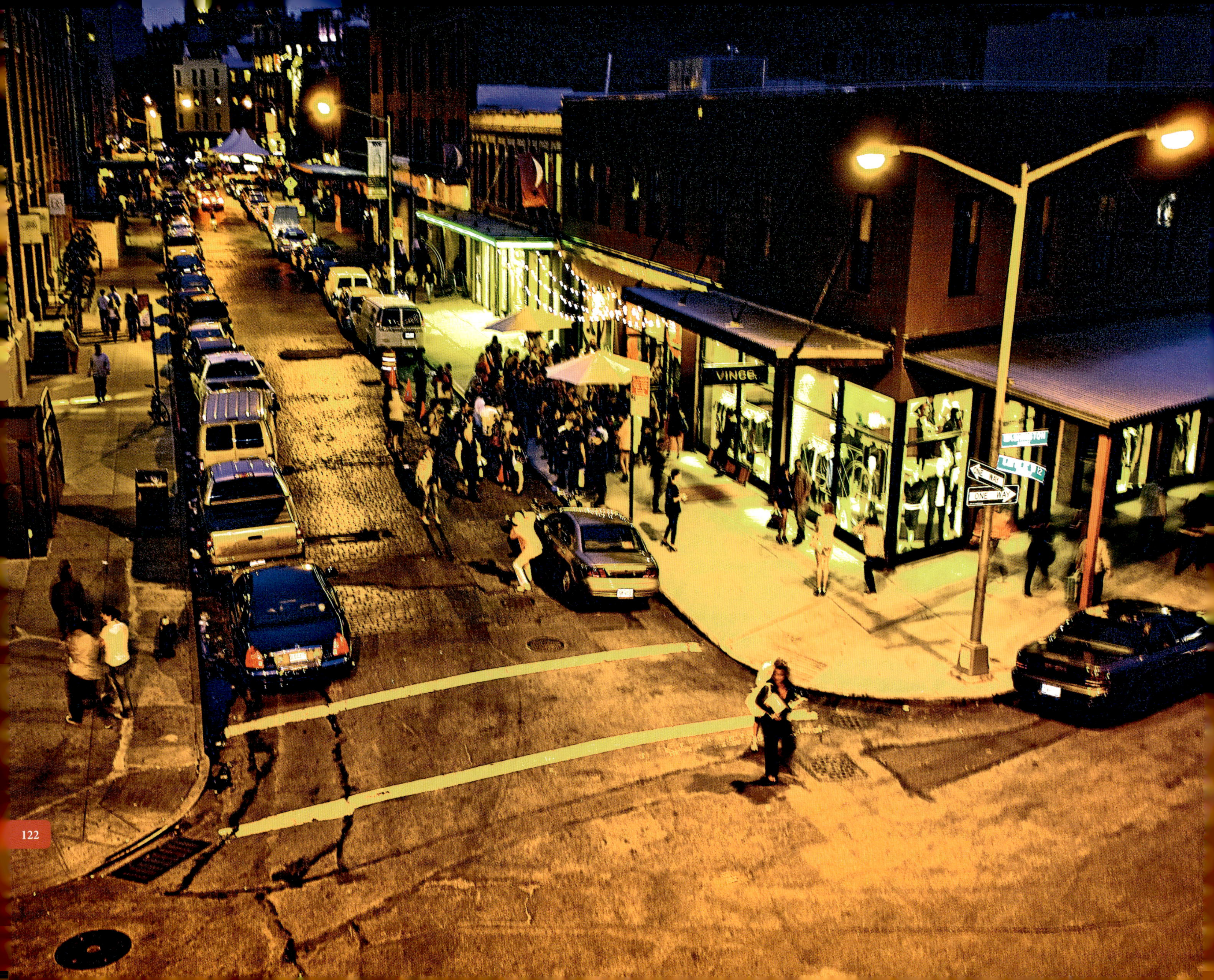
VINCE
ONE WAY
ONE WAY

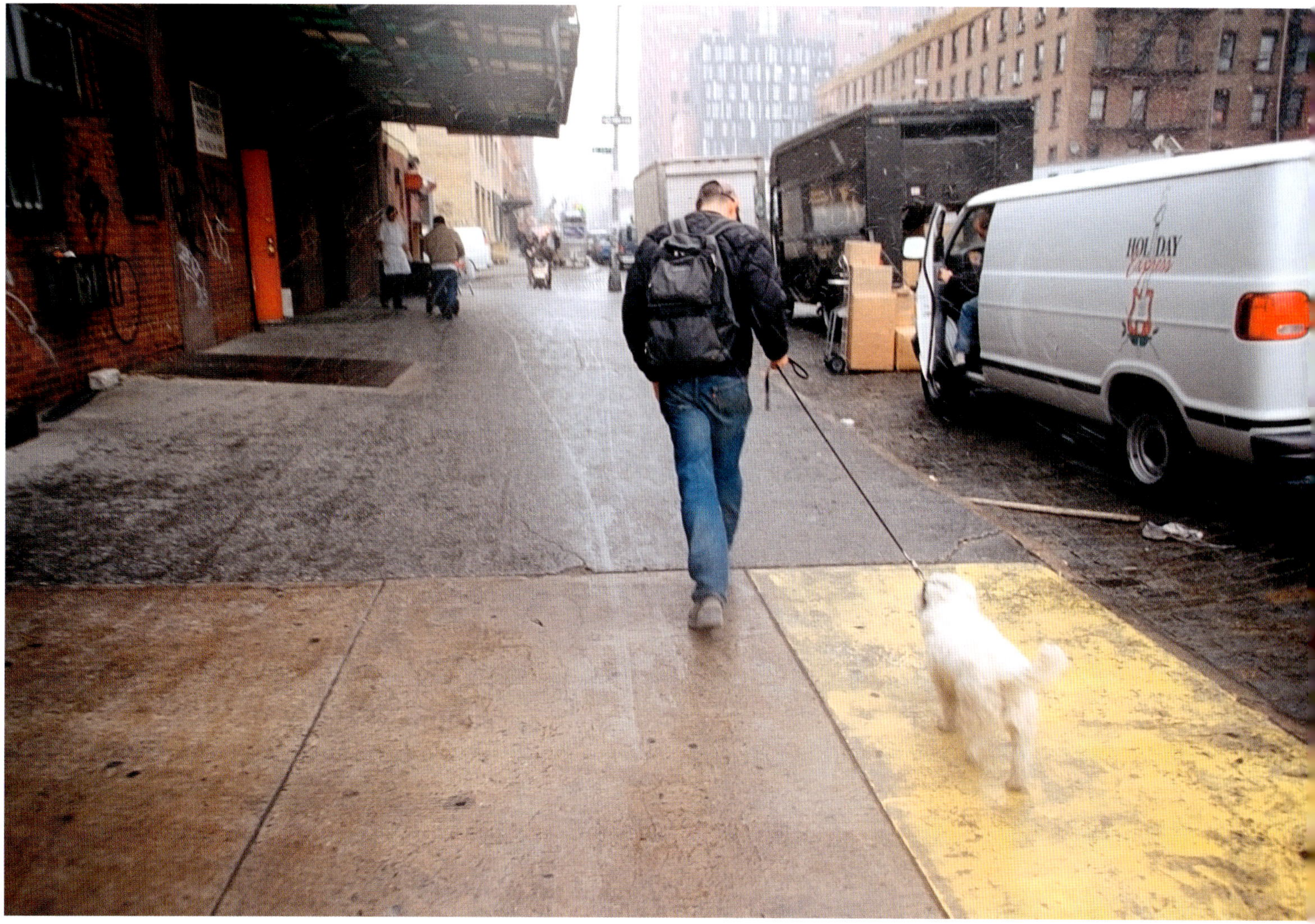
HOLIDAY

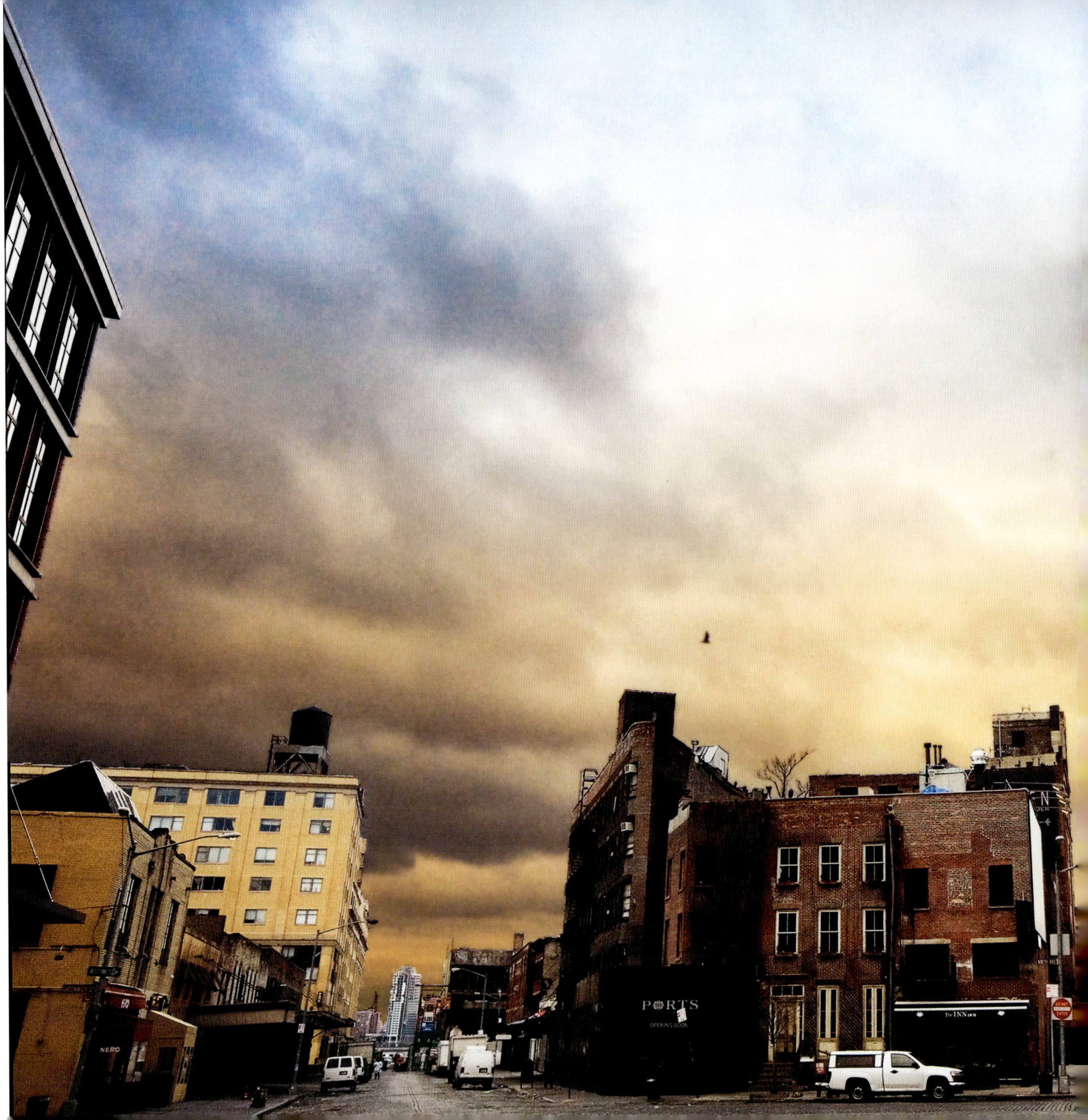
PORTS
NERO

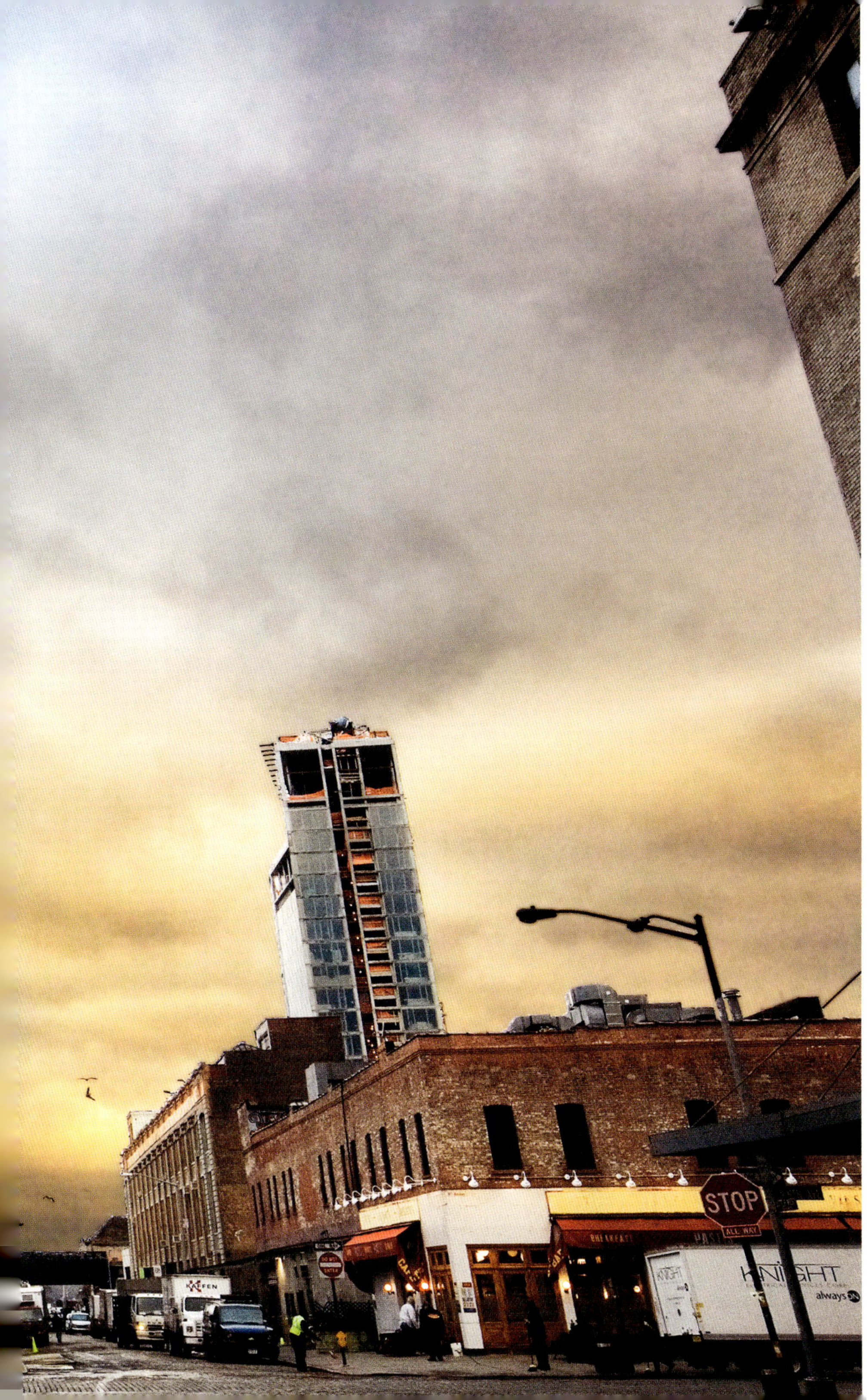
STOP
ALL WAY
KNIGHT
always

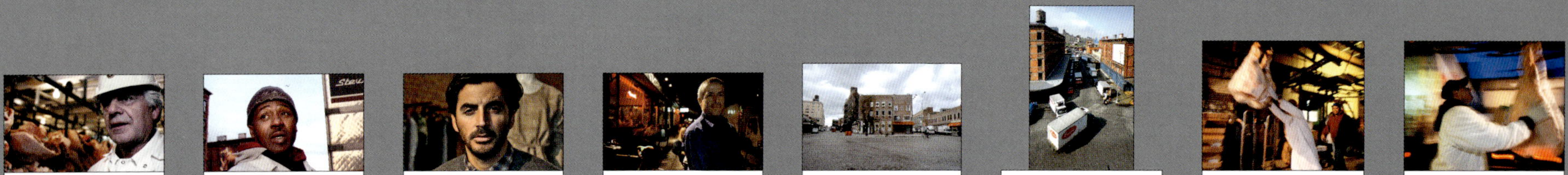

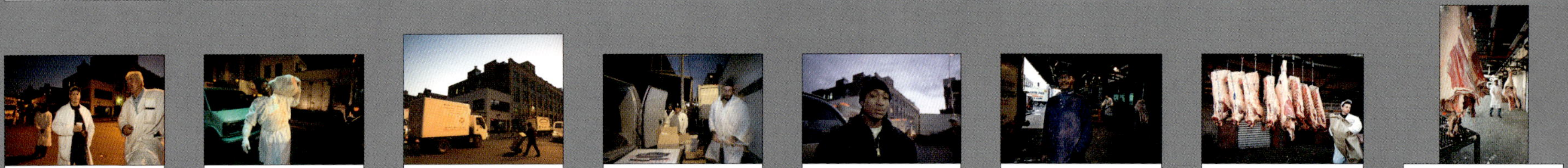

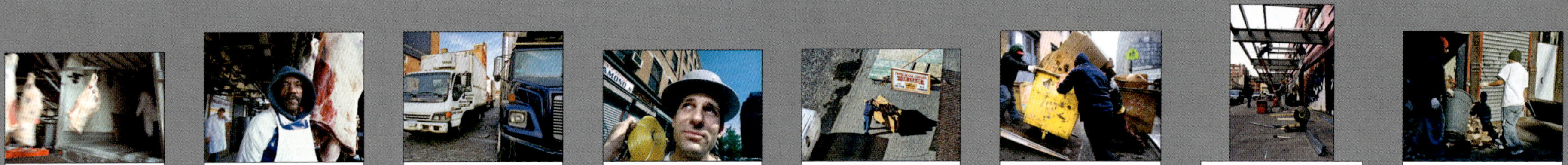

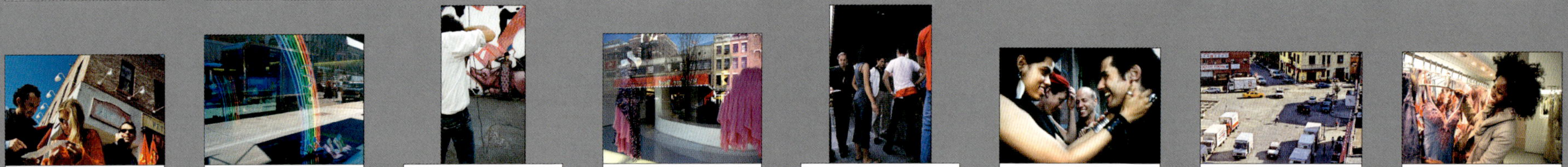

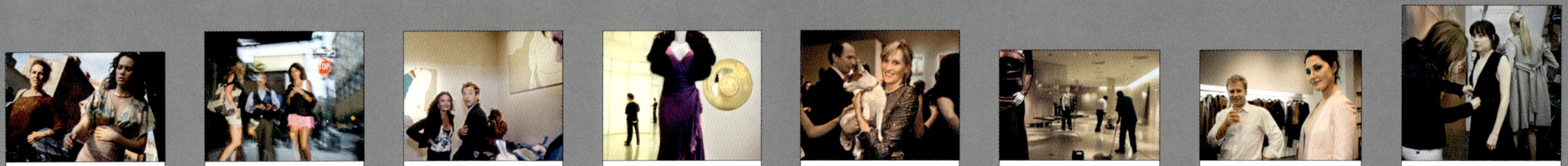

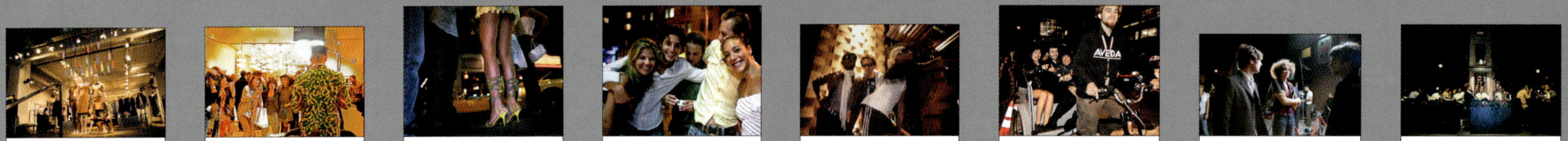

thumbnail index

thumbnail index

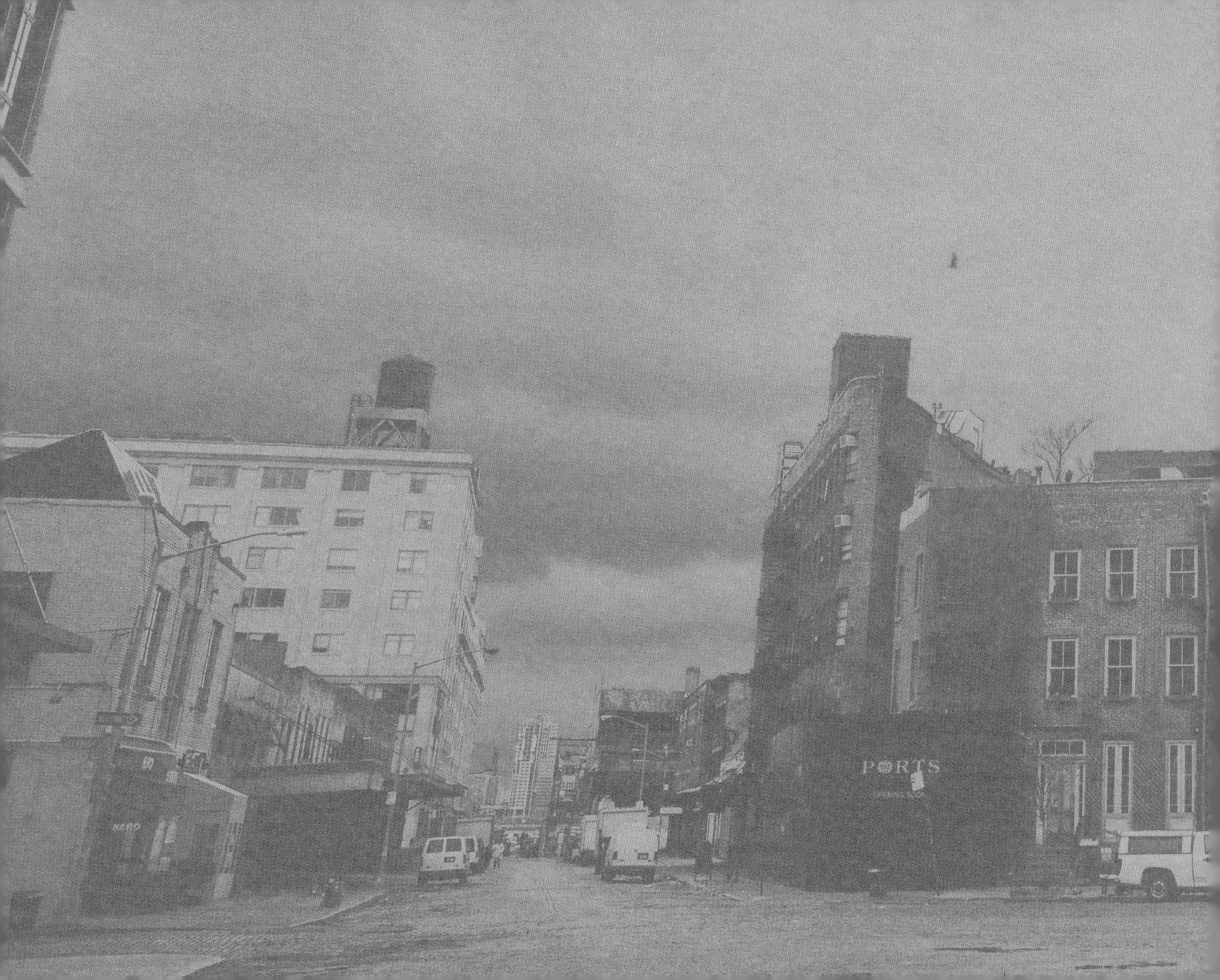
NERO
PORTS